Democracy Administered

How does representative government function when public administration can reshape democracy? The traditional narrative of public administration balances the accountability of managers – a problem of control – with the need for effective administration – a problem of capability. The discretion modern governments give to administrators allows them to make trade-offs among democratic values. This book challenges the traditional view with its argument that the democratic values of administration should complement the democratic values of the representative government within which it operates. Control, capability, and value reinforcement can render public administration into democracy administered. This book offers a novel framework for empirically and normatively understanding how democratic values have, and should be, reinforced by public administration. Bertelli's theoretical framework provides a guide for managers and reformers alike to chart a path toward democracy administered.

ANTHONY MICHAEL BERTELLI is the Sherwin-Whitmore Professor in Liberal Arts, Pennsylvania State University and Professor of Political Science, Bocconi University. Author of five books including *Madison's Managers: Public Administration and the Constitution* (2006), he is a member of the National Academy of Public Administration and winner of the Herbert Simon Award for career contributions to the study of bureaucracy.

Democracy Administered

*How Public Administration Shapes
Representative Government*

ANTHONY MICHAEL BERTELLI
Pennsylvania State University and Bocconi University

CAMBRIDGE
UNIVERSITY PRESS

University Printing House, Cambridge CB2 8BS, United Kingdom

One Liberty Plaza, 20th Floor, New York, NY 10006, USA

477 Williamstown Road, Port Melbourne, VIC 3207, Australia

314–321, 3rd Floor, Plot 3, Splendor Forum, Jasola District Centre,
New Delhi – 110025, India

103 Penang Road, #05–06/07, Visioncrest Commercial, Singapore 238467

Cambridge University Press is part of the University of Cambridge.

It furthers the University's mission by disseminating knowledge in the pursuit of
education, learning, and research at the highest international levels of excellence.

www.cambridge.org
Information on this title: www.cambridge.org/9781107169715
DOI: 10.1017/9781316755167

© Anthony Bertelli 2021

This publication is in copyright. Subject to statutory exception
and to the provisions of relevant collective licensing agreements,
no reproduction of any part may take place without the written
permission of Cambridge University Press.

First published 2021

A catalogue record for this publication is available from the British Library.

ISBN 978-1-107-16971-5 Hardback
ISBN 978-1-316-62109-7 Paperback

Cambridge University Press has no responsibility for the persistence or accuracy
of URLs for external or third-party internet websites referred to in this publication
and does not guarantee that any content on such websites is, or will remain,
accurate or appropriate.

For Larry Lynn

Most citizens encounter government (if they encounter it at all) not through letters to congressmen or by attendance at school board meetings but through their teachers and their children's teachers and through the policeman on the corner or in the patrol car.

Michael Lipsky, *Street-Level Bureaucracy* (1980)

If representatives assume that voters will make up their minds at the next election solely on the basis of the programs put forward at that time, they have complete freedom of action.

Bernard Manin, *The Principles of Representative Government* (1997)

It was assumed that future policies were implicit in the terms of the electoral decision simply because that decision was framed by a predictable universe of choices structured by disciplined organizations with well-defined programs and clearly understood differences. This is no longer the case.

Pierre Rosanvallon, *Democratic Legitimacy* (2011)

Contents

List of figures	*page* xii
List of tables	xiii
Preface	xv
1 Democracy from Public Administration	1
The Values of Representative Government	3
Characters	5
Representatives	5
Policy Workers	6
Managers	6
Champions	7
The Argument in Brief	8
Plan of the Book	12
2 Accountability Values	15
Who Closed the Port of Lampedusa?	18
Theories of Electoral Accountability	23
The Selection View of Electoral Accountability	24
The Sanctioning View of Electoral Accountability	25
Institutions, Parties, and Electoral Accountability	30
Deviations from the Mandate and Conditional Representation	34
Accountability Errors	38
Identifiability Errors	39
Evaluability Errors	42
Citizens' Heuristics for Retrospection	45
Blame Avoidance Strategies	49
Conclusion	52
Appendix: Data, Methods, and Detailed Results	54

Contents

3	Process Values	58
	Pluralism	61
	Epistemic Arguments	63
	Deliberative Arguments	64
	Majoritarianism	66
	Collective Rationality	68
	What Do Citizens Want from Their Democracy?	72
	Conclusion	75
	Appendix: Data, Methods, and Detailed Results	77
4	Governance Structures and Democratic Values	83
	The Champion's Dilemma	84
	The Fundamental Problem of Public Administration	85
	Accountability to Representative Government	86
	Autonomy from Representative Government	90
	Evaluating Governance Structures Democratically	93
	Controlled Agency	95
	The Impossibility of Neutral Controlled Agency	97
	The BAMF-Affäre	99
	Managed Agency	103
	Ingredients of Managerialism	104
	An Escape from Prison Bureaucracy?	106
	Representative Agency	110
	Bringing Citizens Back In	111
	Budgets of the People, by the People, for the People	118
	Independent Agency	124
	Credibility and Independence	125
	The Costs of Independence	127
	Art's Length	131
	Conclusion	135
	Appendix: The Accountability Index	137
5	The Value Reinforcement Hypothesis	139
	Value Reinforcement as a Positive Claim	143
	Accountability and Process Values in New Public Management	144
	Institutional Reinforcement in Britain and the Netherlands	147
	Behavioral Reinforcement among European Managers	152
	A Research Agenda for Value Reinforcement	159
	Theory Development	159
	Empirical Study	160
	Conclusion	164
	Appendix: Data, Methods, and Detailed Results	166

6	The Complementarity Principle	174
	The State and Responsible Policy Work	176
	Legitimating State Power	177
	American Public Administration and the State	179
	Governance Structures and the Representation	183
	The Idea of Responsible Policy Work	186
	Responsible Value Reinforcement	189
	The Complementarity Principle	196
	Conclusion	201
7	Further Problems for Democracy Administered	204
	Bibliography	211
	Index	235

Figures

2.1 Left-leaning and right-leaning references in regional *Movimento Cinque Stelle* manifestos, 2012–15   *page* 40
2.2 Identifiability and evaluability heuristics and voter sanctioning   46
3.1 Agency relationships and collective decision mechanisms in public policymaking   70
3.2 How expectations gaps for democratic values influence citizens' evaluation of their national democracies, Europe, 2016   74
4.1 Governance structures and accountability – Process value trade-offs   94
4.2 Accountability in United Kingdom executive agencies   109
4.3 When ministers should establish a nondepartmental public body in the United Kingdom   132
5.1 Accountability in elections and in governance   157
5.2 Identifiability and structural reliance   158
5.3 Researching value reinforcement mechanisms   161

Tables

2.1	Accountability and the arguments of representatives	page 50
2.2	Voter perceptions of incumbent credibility for reducing immigration and government vote intention, Italian general election, 2018	56
3.1	Process values	72
3.2	Components of expectations gaps, European Social Survey, 2012	78
3.3	Country coverage, European Social Survey, 2012	80
3.4	How expectations gaps for democratic values influence citizens' evaluation of their national democracies, European Social Survey, 2012	81
4.1	Accountability in parliamentary governments	138
5.1	Accountability-enhancing practices	153
5.2	Identifiability enhancing and obviating practices for coordinating policy work	155
5.3	Country coverage and ACI	166
5.4	Accountability in elections and in governance	167
5.5	Identifiability and structural reliance	170

Preface

This book is a synthesis of my own thinking on the problem of maintaining democratic values in contemporary public administration. This problem has been at the core of my scholarly interests for more than two decades, and it flows consistently through my teaching and conversations with colleagues.

The argument of this book originated in one of the most unique academic opportunities I have had in my career. The Jacob Javits Visiting Professorship at New York University, which I held in Spring 2015, gave me the opportunity to develop an argument about democratic public administration for a general audience. In May 2015, I presented my ideas to an engaged group of scholars, practitioners, family and friends of the late Senator Jacob Javits, and the general public at the New York University Law School. My lecture that evening was motivated by a thought exercise: If I were to read the contemporary literature from the perspective of a *citizen*, rather than that of a *scholar* of public administration, what lessons would I draw about democracy? Taking this perspective revealed a challenge for citizenship. Retrospective evaluation may well be a crucial theory behind voting in a representative democracy, but identifying responsible politicians and evaluating their behavior is a very high burden for citizens. Still, all is not lost. There are some criteria for understanding the possibility of democratic evaluation of government performance even when governance is complex. That event, the comments from the audience and the Javits family, as well as some excellent feedback from Peter John, Aram Hur, and Paul Light gave me the resolve to develop a book-length argument. Some of the core ideas in that lecture are present in the pages that follow.

xvi Preface

Kaifeng Yang and Melvin Dubnick, who organized a symposium at the American Society of Public Administration conference in Chicago in April 2015, gave me another stimulating opportunity for the argument in these pages. The paper I wrote for that event, and the generous comments of participants and referees, became an article in the symposium's special issue in *Public Performance & Management Review* (vol. 40, no. 2). My paper in that issue, "Who Are the Policy Workers and What are They Doing? Citizen's Heuristics and Democratic Accountability in Complex Governance," contains ideas that are central to this book, and particularly to Chapter 2. In addition to helping me think about the problem, Gregg Van Ryzin devised a way to test the argument with a survey experiment and the resulting paper appears in *Research & Politics* (vol. 7, no. 3). Those results are discussed in Chapter 2 as well.

As my notes evolved into a sketch of the argument in this book, I took my ideas on the road. Seminar presentations at the University of Leiden, the University of Wisconsin–Madison, the University of Delaware, the German University of Administrative Sciences – Speyer, and Rutgers University – Newark were extremely useful. During these visits, Andrei Poama introduced me to a literature that would focus my argument on representative government as it is practiced. Madalina Busuioc and I developed the idea for a paper, now appearing in *Public Administration Review*, which challenges the epistemic view of bureaucratic reputation from an accountability perspective and makes its way into these pages. Susan Webb-Yackee encouraged me to bring value reinforcement into the traditional narrative of public administration. Donald Moynihan made me see that exemplifying the values and trade-offs was pivotal to the success of the presentation, which shaped Chapters 4 and 5. William Resh, Daniel Smith, and Michael Bauer stimulated me to think about the need for justifying value trade-offs that is now a highlight of my argument. The list of thanks is certainly longer than my notes could possibly reflect.

Working with Christopher Kam on the topic of accountability has made immeasurable contributions to my thinking in the pages that follow. Our paper with Alexander Held that appears in the *American Political Science Review* (vol. 114, no. 3) provides not just data but, rather, a way of thinking about accountability that is crucial to Chapters 2, 4, and 5. My collaboration with Peter John in developing the concept of conditional representation in our book *Public Policy Investment: Priority-Setting and Conditional Representation in British Statecraft* (Oxford University Press) has been indispensable to the pages

Preface xvii

of Chapter 2. George Krause also helped me substantially in my thinking about conditional representation. His efforts resulted, at one point, in a joint working paper entitled "Agenda Construction, Representation, and Presidential Policy Priorities" that was presented at the annual meeting of the European Political Science Association in 2016. Some of the material in Chapter 2 reflects what we learned from writing that paper.

Excellent research assistance was contributed by New York University students Jessica Sederquist, Dahlia Darwiche, Michael Cohn-Geltner, Savanna Fox, Maria Navarro, Nahima Uddin, and Christian Hansen as well as Bocconi University students and researchers Silvia Cannas, Rebecca Kirley, Giulia Leila Travaglini, Eleanor Florence Woodhouse, Federica Lo Polito, Fiona Cece, Nicola Palma, and Benedetta Scotti. I thank students in my Democracy and Public Policymaking and Advanced Public Management seminars at Bocconi University for enduring and helping to clarify the argument. Maria Cucciniello, Valentina Mele, Giulia Cappellaro, Dan Honig, and Jason Anastasopoulos contributed greatly to my thinking about the research agenda in Chapter 6. Helen Ewald and Silvia Cannas served as research assistants without parallel as the book took shape. A special note of thanks goes to Christian Hansen, whose help on this project and on all matters kept me productive while I served as Vice Dean of the Robert F. Wagner Graduate School of Public Service at New York University between 2014 and 2016.

Because my thesis has emerged over many years, I simply cannot thank all of those who made it possible. More recently, I have benefited from the comments and suggestions of Quentin Skinner, Mark Bovens, Thomas Schillemans, Sjors Overman, Stefanie Beyens, Gerhard Hammerschmid, Kai Wegrich, Andrew Whitford, Norma Riccucci, Valentina Mele, Melvin Dubnick, and Sherry Glied. Special thanks are due to Mark Warren, Nadia Urbinati, Andrew Sinclair, Geert Bouckaert, Ryan Pevnick, Norma Riccucci, Sandra Léon, and Stefania Gerevini who each offered more detailed comments and were exceptionally giving of their time. Christopher Ansell, John Bryson, Keith Dowding, Dan Honig, Andrei Poama, and Norma Riccucci read a draft version of the manuscript in the late spring and summer of 2020 and helped to refine the book before you in many ways. I simply can't thank them enough for their generous investment of time and thought. And my wife, Tamaron, endured far too much while this book was being developed and, for her unwavering support, I will always be grateful.

As I completed the manuscript, I was encouraged by the memory of two unforgettable courses with two exemplary teachers who sadly are no xviii *Preface*

longer with us. Mark Perlman's course in the history of economic thought at the University of Pittsburgh, and my many discussions with him, compelled the conclusion that, as a scholar, I should take a chance on big questions, though my efforts might result in "a magnificent failure." That was the title of my last course paper. Mark disagreed, in one way or the other. Bernard Silberman's class at the University of Chicago, for which I read *Economy and Society*, was the first place in which I thought that value reinforcement might not be the same thing as political control. That extraordinary seminar made me understand that academic silos are all of one's own making.

I submitted the first version of the complete manuscript to Cambridge University Press on the very day that I had planned to give a lecture on this subject. I had been chosen as the recipient of the Herbert Simon Award for significant contributions to the scientific study of bureaucracy at the Midwest Political Science Association meetings in Chicago. Instead, my email to Robert Dreesen, whose patience with this book will be responsible for any success it has, was sent from my apartment in Milan on the forty-eighth day of coronavirus lockdown. I am all the more humbled by the award because of the number of previous recipients whose contributions are sprinkled throughout these pages. I am all the more convinced that value reinforcement is essential to public administration because of the government responses to the pandemic that I watched from that isolated vantage.

I dedicate this book to my mentor, collaborator, and friend Larry Lynn. The work that Larry and I did – and the ideas we shared while doing it – influence every page of this book. Larry has long encouraged me to write a book with a big idea. No one may read it, Larry, but you were absolutely right that I should try.

I

Democracy from Public Administration

How does representative government function when public administration has the authority to reshape democracy? Posed in this way, the question may seem contrived, even rather extreme. But the thought exercise, I contend, helps to link public administration to representative government in a way that scholars in the field have not been doing carefully, at least not since the Second World War. This is because the discretion that modern governments give to administrative actors captures not only the means for implementing policies but also democratic values and the authority to make trade-offs among them. Viewed in this way, public administration is not *policy* administered, but *democracy* administered. This book is about these value trade-offs and the challenges they present for representative democracy. It is about the tensions and the harmonies between democratic politics and democracy administered.

To grasp the problem initially, consider the application of Jason Kessler, organizer of the "Unite the Right" rally to public officials in Charlottesville, Virginia, in 2017. On the eve of the event, local officials revoked Kessler's permit to march in a centrally located park but did not do the same for counter-protestors. The location at issue, Emancipation Park (formerly Lee Park), was central to the story, for it was the planned removal of a statue of Confederate General Robert E. Lee that stimulated Kessler's application. Kessler and the American Civil Liberties Union filed suit against the city, and a federal court in Charlottesville held that revoking the permit was a content-based restriction on Kessler's right to free speech. The court did not find the city's argument about public safety convincing.

Democracy from Public Administration

Although the defendants maintain that the decision to revoke Kessler's permit was motivated by the number of people likely to attend the demonstration, the record indicates that their concerns in this regard are purely speculative. ... [T]o the extent the defendants' decision was based on the number of counter-protestors expected to attend Kessler's demonstration, it is undisputed that merely moving Kessler's demonstration to another park *will not avoid a clash of ideologies or prevent confrontation* between the two groups. As both sides acknowledged ... critics of Kessler and his beliefs would likely follow him to Mcintire Park if his rally is relocated there. [...] Moreover, given the timing of the City's decision and the relationship between Kessler's message and Emancipation Park, *supporters of Kessler are likely to still appear at the Park*, even if the location of Kessler's demonstration is moved elsewhere. Thus, a change in the location of the demonstration would not eliminate the need for members of the City's law enforcement, fire, and emergency medical services personnel to appear at Emancipation Park. Instead, it would necessitate having personnel present at two locations in the City. (*Kessler v. City of Charlottesville, Virginia*, No. 3:17CV00056, [W.D.Va. August 11, 2017, p. 4–5, emphasis added)

The argument in this book shifts the insinuations of these facts from a restriction of the content of speech to the influence on democratic values embodied in the choices made by the public administration. My claim is that officials positioned as they were in Charlottesville have been delegated enough authority to reshape democracy, and that the rights discussion, while essential to the legal decision in this case, obscures a more general problem of the structure of the administrative state and its role as democracy administered. In the *Kessler* decision, the court was explicit that the premise for anticipated involvement of emergency services was "a clash of ideologies," a "confrontation" that would be provoked by "supporters of Kessler." The focus of these particular public officials was on competing beliefs, and their choices had implications for what I will call process values in American representative government. The outcome of the "Unite the Right" rally was tragic, reaching its denouement with the death of counterprotester Heather Heyer, killed by a car driven by James Alex Fields, Jr., who was convicted of her murder in December 2018. Because of the complicated facts that emerged after the decision in *Kessler*, and because the nature of public administration as democracy administered is certainly not limited to the United States, perhaps another scenario can provide further illustration.

Consider now, a hypothetical example involving an important Italian official called a *questore*, who plays a coordinating role across police forces to ensure public safety. This official has been given notice that an extreme political group plans to protest in a central public square in his jurisdiction. Article 17 of the Italian Constitution provides that the

The Values of Representative Government

protest is allowable if it is peaceful and if its participants do not carry weapons, while the 1931 *Testo unico delle leggi di pubblica sicurezza* provides that the *questore* may establish a time and place or prohibit the gathering altogether if a substantiated reason leads the *questore* to conclude that the gathering would pose a significant likelihood of danger to conditions of public safety or security. Suppose that the *questore*, in possession of a substantiated basis for restricting the gathering, believes in a basic sense of pluralism as a democratic value that should govern her decisions in such cases, and chooses a time when opposing groups can easily mobilize to bring discordant voices into a discourse with one another. Suppose further that the *questore* ultimately privileges majoritarianism over pluralism, and, consequently, chooses to reject the central square of the town in favor of a site so poorly accessible that no one other than the protestors themselves would be likely to hear the arguments presented. In situations like these, trade-offs among important democratic values are in the hands of those who manage public agencies. My hypothetical *questore* has made those trade-offs, and they may very well be different from those inherent in the Italian constitution, which defines the nation's system of representative government.

In this book, it is not only important *that* officials have the discretion to exchange values in this way. *How* they make these choices, I will contend, should be more prevalent in public administration scholarship than it has been in recent decades. As a consequence, my argument has both positive implications for the study of public administration as well as normative implications for how it can be conceived as democracy administered. This dual purpose is unavoidable in our field of study, and I will argue that the implications of our scholarship for the representative democracies in which it is situated must be confronted directly. The subject of this book is not political theory or political science, per se. It is a book about public administration. Yet in order to understand how public administration can achieve its promise as democracy administered, I must draw deeply from literatures about the nature of politics and government and ultimately contribute to them. In particular, those literatures must guide me to a useful framework for understanding representative government.

THE VALUES OF REPRESENTATIVE GOVERNMENT

Democratic values – principles or standards about how representative government ought to operate to maintain rule by the people – will be situated at the heart of every paragraph in this book. What are those values? Can they all be achieved at once? How does the structure of public administration influence which ones are privileged? What are the implications of value choices as the structures of governance become more complex? How does the structure of public administration shape the beliefs officials hold about democracy? How do those belief systems relate to values embedded in the representative governments that these officials serve? How do those who design and implement structures of public administration think about value trade-offs? How should they? I address these questions in the chapters that follow.

My focus on representative government places an essential scope condition on the argument in this book. My intent is not to compare democracy to autocracy. My argument does not facilitate comparisons among different economic systems, such as capitalism or socialism. Its comparative potential is among the representative democracies of the world. The implications of my arguments are intended to compare systems with more or less accountability, majoritarianism or pluralism in relation to others. This book also has no ambition to be a critique of representative democracy, of which there are many important examples. Instead, it is a reflection about public administration in the systems of government prevailing in most of the nations of the world. According to the Polity project, in 2017, 96 of 167 nations with populations of 500,000 or more had some form of representative government and were considered democracies (Desilver 2019). While the examples and empirical contexts in this book are drawn from a selection of countries – and a selection based on the availability of data and the appropriateness of illustration – the scope of the argument I advance is much broader.

When thinking about representative government, the authority for public administration to reshape democracy should not surprise us. In his *Notes on the State of Virginia*, Thomas Jefferson warned that "[a]n elective despotism was not the government we fought for," preferring, instead, one "in which the powers of government should be so divided and balanced among several bodies of the *magistracy* as that no one could transcend their legal limits" (Jefferson 1975 [1801], 164, emphasis added). This reflected the enlightenment idea that the rule of law legitimized public administration, and a scheme of incentives worthy of the organizational theorist and manager Chester Barnard (1938) could help it to do that. By contrast, I will argue from the view that elections can allow citizens to articulate the basic aims toward which government should orient its policies and which are the relative priorities among them. The means of constructing policies that serve these aims are appropriately in the hands of those with varying degrees of expertise, be it in the technology of policymaking or in the technologies that dominate policy domains from the environment to public health to national security.

Public administration has always played a pivotal role in translating aims and priorities into concrete programs that serve them. What is more, institutional arrangements protect value compromises in the widest variety of contexts. In *What Money Can't Buy*, the political theorist Michael Sandel (2012) argues that the incentives of markets are not value neutral: changing the incentives for providing a good or service changes the *meaning* of that good or service (see also Milanovic 2019; Satz 2010; Walzer 2008). In this book, I contend that institutions, and in particular, public administration, can reorient democratic values. Changing the rules and incentives for providing a public good or service changes its *democratic* meaning. This is the essence of what translates public administration into the output of democracy administered.

CHARACTERS

The questions that motivate this book can be addressed by understanding the interacting perspectives, roles, and preferences of four principal characters. Each character represents a large group of individuals, and each group exists across a range of national and substantive contexts. The reader should see each character in the same way that a game theorist sees a player, that is, as an abstract construct that shares just enough characteristics with an individual or organization of theoretical interest to make the analysis evocative of the interaction under study.

I will make consistent reference to these characters – representatives, policy workers, managers, and champions – throughout. My hope is that doing so will streamline my arguments for the reader. It should also provide a measure of clarity as the ideas in the book become more complex. Each character is described here, and all take up their parts immediately thereafter.

Representatives

The politicians in my argument are elected representatives of the people. They are directly chosen by voters in elections that are more or less competitive. Their primary role is the enactment of laws that set forth the goals of policymaking and they can serve at national or subnational levels of government. They are legislators, cabinet ministers, presidents,

6 *Democracy from Public Administration*

mayors, and city councilors. Whether they serve in parliaments, are chosen to take ministerial responsibility for departments, or are directly elected to executive positions, it is the electoral connection with the people they represent that defines their character in the pages that follow.

Policy Workers

The individuals who perform the tasks required for implementing the laws representatives make are called policy workers in this book. They do work – policy work – that implements the goals established in laws by representatives, and they are subject to the rule of law, either in their formal roles within, or in their contractual commitments to government. Laws enacted by representatives both empower and restrain their behavior, and they shape policy workers' interests and beliefs about their role in representative government.

The class of policy workers is very large. It includes a vast number of individuals whose effect on my argument and on public policy is not particularly significant. The manager of a building in which government offices are located is a policy worker. Her role may become crucial over time, or, rather, at a single crucial point in time, as when the policy workers in the building must continue to serve the public during a pandemic. Policy workers are government bureaucrats protected by civil service laws, and independent contractors whose relationship with the government does not exceed the four corners of an agreement to provide a good or service. They work for nonprofit and international organizations, both within and outside the boundaries of the countries in which they have citizenship.

What binds policy workers together as a construct is their efforts to implement the laws enacted by representatives and, whether small or large, their *discretionary authority* to do so. Discretion gives policy workers the rights to make choices about the means of achieving the aims of these laws, and the policies they encapsulate, and to act on those choices. The formal sources of those rights are in statutes, contracts and the like, and these rights are mediated by informal norms of administrative practice.

Managers

Many of the arguments in this and other books about public administration are oriented primarily toward one particular type of policy

Characters 7

worker. Managers are policy workers whose discretionary rights extend to trade-offs about resources and, crucially for my argument, among democratic values. The Charlottesville officials responsible for denying the demonstration permit to Jason Kessler and my hypothetical *questore* are managers. Laws often directly mention such individuals or their supervisors, identifying them with categories of decisions and granting them the discretion to make them. Managers can be appointed to their positions by representatives, serve in established civil service career structures that provide some insulation from political influence, or have the power to make resource and value trade-offs by virtue of contracts with other managers within government. For these reasons, managers can, formally speaking, work both within and outside of government. They serve at various levels in organizations and governments, exercising a wide variety of duties in their organizations. The common bond of this group of policy workers is their discretion legitimized by law and adherence to it, not an electoral connection. Their pivotal role in this book concerns the implications for representative government of the ways that they use their discretion.

Champions

The final character in this book advocates proposals for a particular way of performing policy work. In this sense, they are champions of a cause, which may be great or small. In *Reinventing Government,* David Osborne and Ted Gaebler (1992) were champions for contracting and private sector provision of many public services, and Gaebler was also a champion for these ideas while serving as the city manager, an appointed post, of Rancho Cordova, California. Champions can be representatives, managers, other policy workers, and interested stakeholders. Scholars are often champions, and such is my role in this book because I argue that public administration ought to be democracy administered. The defining feature champions share is their advocacy of a proposal about the way that policy work is done. This makes them different from what the political scientist John Kingdon called policy entrepreneurs, whose "defining characteristic" requires self-interest, namely, a "willingness to invest their resources – time, energy, reputation, and sometimes money – in the hope of a future return" from policy work (Kingdon 1995 [1984], 122). The champion may, but need not be, driven by a discernable self-interest in future benefit.

THE ARGUMENT IN BRIEF

In the traditional narrative of public administration, democratic values are confined to the relationship between representatives and managers through a variety of *governance structures*, that is to say, the configurations of rules that govern public administration. In this way, governance structures enable and constrain managers whose decisions guide the process of policy implementation and affect its outcomes (e.g., Lynn, Heinrich, and Hill 2001). This relationship has been theorized in various ways with a focus on grants of powers by representatives, who hold them legitimately, to managers in government bureaucracies, who in turn exercise some of those powers through legal delegations. Laws are an imperfect tool and managers' discretion is an inevitable consequence of this imperfection, but discretion is also a tool for representatives to make "good" policy. Discretion allows for expertise to be deployed and can even incentivize policy workers to develop a greater capacity for meeting the aims of the public.

The traditional narrative balances the accountability of managers to representatives, a problem of *control*, with the need for policy workers to do policy work effectively, a problem of *capability*. Champions of governance structures provide various ways to balance the control and capability problems. When those mechanisms are put in place, they shape policy work.

My inquiry in this book concerns an additional problem beyond those of control and capability. When the *questore* has the discretion to privilege pluralism over majoritarianism in my hypothetical case, the problem is neither one of control nor capability, but, rather, it concerns her beliefs about her place in the Italian system of representative government. Latent in the traditional narrative of public administration is the problem of how governance structures influence managers' *democratic belief systems*, or, arrangements of democratic values and attitudes. When champions design governance structures, they constrain democratic belief systems in that a change in one value or attitude would require a corresponding change in another (Converse 2006 [1964]). That is, governance structures compel trade-offs among democratic values.

Does the *questore* privilege pluralism because the mixed proportional representation of the Italian electoral formula is less majoritarian than its first-past-the-post counterpart in the United Kingdom? Or does the governance structure that enables and constrains her policy work shift her democratic belief system to a more pluralistic one? And if a similarly

The Argument in Brief

situated public safety official in the United Kingdom makes the same trade-off, has the governance structure created tension with the country's idea of representative government? Ought a governance structure to do this? These positive and normative questions of *value reinforcement* are implicit in the traditional narrative, but left largely unexplored. In this book, I offer a framework for understanding and legitimating the actions of the policy workers that feature in each question. Value reinforcement is an essential ingredient of the informal means through which policy work finds harmony with representative government.

Control, capability, and value reinforcement must jointly render public administration into democracy administered. This means that champions play a starring role. For this essential reason, champions must both consider and make plain the impact of governance structures on the democratic belief systems of policy workers, and most of all, on managers, who have the discretion to reshape representative government.

My argument considers trade-offs among two types of values in representative government. While contemporary political theory considers a distinction between substantive and procedural values, I think that the more appropriate distinction for public administration considers the object to which the value relates. Actor-relative values apply to representatives and policy workers. Process-relative values concern the procedures by which democratic influence over policy work can be achieved, such as those governing decision-making. To be sure, traditionally procedural values can be found in either category. What is more, the values at the heart of my argument are not a comprehensive list of those relevant to policy work (see, e.g., Lever and Poama 2018). I contend that designing governance structures requires trade-offs among values that regulate policy workers and the procedures of policy work that influence the ability for public administration to approach the goal of democracy administered.

Accountability values are actor-relative and relate to the identifiability, evaluability, and probability of sanctioning representatives, managers, and policy workers. *Process* values are process-relative because they live in the contrivances through which citizens shape the policy work that is done for them. When the policy aims of citizens are collectively revealed, as when we vote in elections, the interests of majorities or pluralistic expressions of competing interests can shape policy work. Which of these happens depends on the values built into representative governments *and* into governance structures. Moreover, the extent to which citizens can collectively address all, rather than just some, of the problems facing the polity is crucial to understand. No governance structure can embody all of these process values at one time. Champions face a dilemma because no structure is neutral to democratic values; each one enhances some values while compromising others.

Confronting this *champion's dilemma* is necessary, but it elides the central puzzle in the traditional narrative. This normative problem is not solved completely when representatives do a good job of structuring delegation in the laws they enact. The *fundamental problem of public administration* is faced by policy workers, and most acutely by managers. How can policy workers use their discretion to fulfill the aims of the public as expressed through the institutions of representative government, and how can they do this through policy work that is effective given their capabilities? The extent to which managers embrace this problem depends on their democratic belief systems, which are shaped, to an important extent, by governance structures. This fundamental problem is one of managerial *responsibility*, and I contend that it transcends the problems of control and capability in the traditional narrative of the field (see Bertelli and Lynn 2003).

Accountability and process values are shaped and reshaped by governance structures, and I offer a framework for categorizing the trade-offs required by the champion's dilemma. *Accountability-enhancing* structures enrich the connection between managers' behavior and representatives' policy goals. *Process-enhancing structures* create a means of addressing process values that revises or extends their expression in representative government. *Accountability-obviating* structures rely on deliberation by groups of citizens, not elections, to realize the policy aims of citizens, or to detach policy work – more or less – from representative government. *Process-obviating* structures replace institutional means for respecting process values with managerial decision-making. Strengthening or weakening these values are the trade-offs intrinsic to the champion's dilemma.

These choices about values result in four basic types of governance structures, each of which shapes democracy in a particular way. *Controlled agency* enhances accountability by connecting policy work to the representatives to the people, retaining the same trade-offs among process values as the system of representative government in which the structure is positioned. *Managed agency* eases the process values of representative government, but maintains accountability to representatives for outputs or outcomes, not for the procedures of policy work. *Representative agency* obviates a direct accountability of policy workers

The Argument in Brief

to representatives in favor of a process that allows citizens some direct input into policy work, and with regard to both its aims and means. In *independent agency* structures, representatives restrain themselves from interfering in policy work and with its outcomes, but without requiring a form of citizen involvement to lend legitimacy to the process values in policy workers' democratic belief systems. This relaxes both categories of values. Variations of these basic structures capture the way in which champions design contemporary public administration, and how they mean to shape the democratic belief systems of policy workers.

The fundamental problem of public administration, once again, is responsibility, which is a problem for policy workers. I hypothesize that governance structures reinforce the values of the representative governments they serve by shaping managers' beliefs about those values. That is, if a political system embraces stronger process values, its governance structures will enhance beliefs in those process values, and if the system is strong on accountability, its governance structures will also emphasize it. This *value reinforcement hypothesis* has empirical implications that I demonstrate through the comparative literature on New Public Management reforms and in a novel statistical analysis of survey data in European parliamentary governments. The *reinforcement mechanisms* that oblige this hypothesis are both institutional, due to the formal roles of representatives and policy workers, and behavioral, resulting from the democratic belief systems of policy workers, and most of all, of managers.

The value reinforcement hypothesis is not a prediction of positive theory, but, rather, plays a normative role in legitimating a state conceived as powerful and separate from citizens. Representation means, in essence, that policy work is done on behalf of citizens. Representation gives birth both to the state and to the need for public administration to be cast as democracy administered, and it can be the subject of accountability. Policy work is legitimated through representation and the rule of law, and policy workers must reinforce the democratic values of representative government unless what they would need to do is unlawful. Champions, for their part, must design governance structures with this mandate in mind. They must adhere to a *complementarity principle*: the democratic values of policy work ought to complement the democratic values of the representative government for which it is done. Both policy work and governance structures, in this way, address the fundamental problem of public administration. And with control and capability, value reinforcement serves to resolve it.

12   *Democracy from Public Administration*

The framework in this book is, then, a guide to resolving the champion's dilemma to practice policy work responsibly in a way that ameliorates the fundamental problem. It is a guide for champions, policy workers, and theorists, but also for empirical researchers who can assess the performance of governance structures in democratic terms. If we take up such an agenda, public administration will begin to reclaim the normative project, that of democracy administered, it has been sidestepping in recent decades.

PLAN OF THE BOOK

In the next two chapters, I discuss the democratic values that are shaped by governance structures. Chapter 2 considers accountability and its requirements or its values, of identifiability, evaluability, and the probability of sanction. I distinguish the sanctioning theory of accountability, which my argument acknowledges, from a competing claim in which citizens prospectively select representatives on the belief that their aims and the way in which they might make trade-offs are similar. Building on some of my own recent work, I describe how the system of political parties and the electoral formula interact to strengthen or weaken electoral accountability. From the perspective of representatives, I mark out how they can prioritize the aims of the public not just on their expression by the public, but also through the expertise representatives have in understanding how the state of the world shapes those aims and the trade-offs citizens make among them. From the perspective of citizens, I consider heuristics that citizens can use to allocate responsibility to representatives or policy workers, the types of accountability errors they can make when doing so, and the strategies of avoiding blame that representatives and policy workers can adopt when policy work goes wrong (Bertelli 2016).

Chapter 3 examines three process values in representative government: majoritarianism, pluralism, and collective rationality. I draw on social choice theory to show why these three values cannot all be respected by a rule meant to collectively reflect the preferences of citizens. Because trade-offs are inevitable, I discuss the implications of relaxing each of these process values. The chapter concludes with some empirical evidence about the process values that Europeans think their systems of representative government ought to embrace.

In Chapters 2 and 3, the main characters are representatives and managers. Champions move to the foreground in Chapter 4. But what

Plan of the Book 13

emerges is the champion's dilemma and its relationship to the fundamental problem of public administration, that of responsibility. I introduce a framework in which the trade-offs among accountability and process values confronted in the champion's dilemma can be understood. Four basic governance structures result from these trade-offs – controlled, managed, representative, and independent agency – and each is detailed and considered in the context of an extended example.

The value reinforcement hypothesis comes in Chapter 5. To illustrate its positive implications, I analytically review a literature on the implementation of New Public Management reforms in countries having representative governments with more or less electoral accountability. Then, I examine extensive cross-national survey data to evince a correlation between electoral accountability and the ways in which managers undertake policy work. This correlation is consistent with value reinforcement, and it illustrates the need for research into the mechanisms behind it. I close the chapter by sketching what a positive research program that can uncover the institutional and behavioral mechanisms of value reinforcement might look like. That program has qualitative and quantitative, observational and experimental, and also theoretical elements.

Chapter 6 turns to the normative basis for value reinforcement and what it means for the program of public administration. Understanding that policy workers must reinforce the democratic values of their specific representative governments without acting beyond their legal discretion begins with a concept of the state. This state has two important characteristics: it is powerful, but also separate from citizens. In it, policy work is done on behalf of citizens. This is representation, which both brings forth the state and makes it crucial for policy work to become democracy administered. When policy work is responsible and when it adheres to the rule of law, it addresses the fundamental problem of public administration. I conduct a thought experiment to reveal that each of the basic governance structures discussed in Chapter 4 can produce responsible value reinforcement. What responsibility requires of policy workers is fundamental to champions: they ought not to design structures that motivate policy workers to actions that are irresponsible, actions which do not reinforce values, or exceed their legal discretion. When governance structures internalize a complementarity principle – governance values should complement political values – the champion's dilemma is resolved in a way that addresses the fundamental problem of public administration.

The conclusion begins with a reflective summary of my argument. I then offer some comments on the promise and challenges of hybrid governance structures for value reinforcement, the pathologies that can arise when the fundamental problem of public administration is not addressed, and the urgency that today's many arguments for "unpolitical democracy" create for realizing democracy administered.

2

Accountability Values

What are the essential democratic values that policy workers must try to sort out when doing their jobs? I believe that addressing this question requires a structured look at the quiddity of representative government, and in doing this, I take a *practice-based* approach (e.g., James 2017, 2013; Sangiovanni 2016). This means that I consider the institutions of representative democracy as they are, rather than as they ought to be, when constructing the argument that follows.

To understand how the values of representative government correspond to those in governance structures, I do not accept on their face the values that a particular champion believes ought to be important. Instead, I reason back to the values of representative democracy that may be strengthened or relaxed by a governance structure. To do this, I will in Chapter 4 begin by describing governance structures "at first in relatively uncontroversial terms," then "work up a general characterization of the practice, in light of its distinctive organizing structure and generally assumed purposes" (James 2013, 45) and, finally, reason through the implications of governance structures for the values of representative government discussed in this and the following chapter. This strategy of inquiry is important, I think, because it is a method for discovering which values of representative government are strengthened or relaxed by the institutional arguments of champions. More importantly, this approach allows me to construct a framework for analyzing value trade-offs in governance structures more generally that, I think, has both positive and normative worth for scholars of public administration.

To be sure, I do not argue categorically that specific values should not be strengthened or relaxed in the service of "better" governance structures. In Chapter 3, I explain that such trade-offs are necessary when it comes to process values, so I could not make such an argument. What I do argue is that we must have a good analytic framework for understanding what must be given up if champions' claims are to win the day. And when those trade-offs undercut any of the values of existing representative government, champions must carefully advocate *why* their regimes are capable of producing democracy administered. In Chapter 6, I will argue that this is a normative requirement of champions as policy workers must act in ways that complement the values of the representative governments in which they serve.

Specifically, then, the argument in this book is formed through what Sangiovanni (2016, 15) calls a method of mediated deduction. This, in essence, means that I take the values of representative government that are described in this chapter and in Chapter 3 as values to which societies with representative governments have made a commitment at the constitutional level. What I intend to understand is how these values might operate at a "middle-level," which, for present purposes, is the governance structure. Sangiovanni likens this to "the relation of a genus to a species, rather than the relation of a means to an end" (2016, 15). For the matter at hand, the genus is the way in which an accountability or process value is specified in a form of representative government and the species is the specification of that value in some governance structure envisioned by a champion. This reflects the possibility that there can be different specifications of the same value.

I hasten to add that this approach does not, in any way, assume that representative democracy does everything well. Perish the thought. Malapportionment in single-member district electoral systems has created vast inequities in representation (Samuels and Snyder 2001). Pressure from special interests creates a tenuous link between the interests and priorities of citizens and the agendas and policies established by representatives (Kollman 1998). Nonetheless, I contend that champions cannot ignore the values of the genus of representative government when making their arguments about the species of governance structure they would like to have in place. What is more, managers and other policy workers must understand very well that structural trade-offs against the values of representative government have consequences for them. Whether one believes that the representative government in his or her country is not performing in terms of accountability or process values *empirically* – as a citizen of both the United States and Italy, I certainly agree that "my" systems are not ideal at the moment – it is still true that "our"

Accountability Values

representative governments embody values that our empirical assessments suggest are being compromised.

Through the method I have just described, I aim to provide an analytic strategy to challenge champions, managers, and policy workers to understand when their efforts compromise the values of representative government. What results, I hope, is a helpful guide for understanding how public administration – by treating seriously the problems of control, capability, and value reinforcement – can approach democracy administered. Two categories of values are central: actor-relative *accountability* values are the subject of the present chapter and procedure-relative *process* values are presented in detail in Chapter 3.

My focus on accountability does not have the broad scope of the framework offered by public administration scholars Barbara Romzek and Melvin Dubnick, for whom accountability "involves the means by which public agencies and their workers manage the diverse expectations generated within and without the organization (Romzek and Dubnick 1987, 228)." Their distinctions among "bureaucratic," "legal," "professional," and "political" accountabilities are more about control than value reinforcement in my reading (228–29). Moreover, their most relevant "political" accountability moves too far from representative government: it is about whom the policy worker can be said to "represent" from "the general public, elected officials, agency heads, agency clientele, other special interest groups, and future generations" (229). Representation features prominently in my normative justification for value reinforcement in Chapter 6, but it grounds that idea of representation more securely in the nature of the modern state.

What is more, I am not addressing the problem of accountability as a general concern, of individual versus collective conceptions of answerability and responsibility, and so forth (e.g., Bovens 1998, 2007; Tadros 2020). To exemplify how my argument is distinct, consider the work of the public policy scholar Ioannis Papadopoulos (2010), which draws on the work of the legal and public administration scholar Mark Bovens on the accountability deficit in policy networks. We share a focus on what I call identifiability – the difficulty in determining who is responsible for decisions because "network pluralism favors representation but inhibit[s] accountability" (Bovens 1998, 1034). Yet he sees policy networks as "uncoupled and remote from representative government" because the long "chain of delegation combined with the magnitude of administrative discretion" as well as representatives "lack of time and expertise" for oversight over expert policy workers deeply weakens the relationship to

Accountability Values

electoral accountability, which is at the heart of this chapter (Bovens 1998, 1035). Moving beyond democratic accountability, Papadopoulos identifies limitations of peer accountability among policy workers that works through the enrichment of expertise and learning rooted in mutual professional scrutiny (2010, 1039–40). Ultimately, he concludes that policy networks can display a more general form of accountability because it is accompanied by "a multiplication of control mechanisms, composite as well as diffuse, leading to a more diversified and pluralistic set of accountability relationships" (Papadopoulos 2010, 1041). My focus will be on the accountability of policy workers to representatives and citizens with an explicit grounding in the theory of representative government.

To clarify my purposes and approach, I think it will be helpful to begin the discussion of accountability by considering an incident that received substantial media attention in Europe and beyond.

WHO CLOSED THE PORT OF LAMPEDUSA?

In June 2019, a vessel called the *Sea-Watch 3*, which was operated by a humanitarian group, rescued migrants from an inflatable boat in the Mediterranean Sea. The crew sought entry into an Italian port but were denied. Seeking to suspend an Italian order that prevented the vessel from landing in Lampedusa – an island 70 miles from the Tunisian coast that is part of the Sicilian region of Agrigento – the crew of the *Sea-Watch 3* initiated a legal and administrative process involving a variety of official actors and ultimately ending with the arrest of the ship's captain by Italian authorities. Many international journalists depicted the process as a simple accountability relationship, as did this *Deutsche Welle* account: "The Sea-Watch 3 rescued more than 50 migrants drifting in an inflatable dinghy off the coast of Libya on Wednesday, but *Italy's populist government did not allow the ship to enter an Italian port*" (*Deutsche Welle* 2019, emphasis added). The highlighted statement reveals a great deal about two important conditions for accountability in representative government. *Who* was involved in refusing entry to the vessel and *what* did they do?

On June 15, while the *Sea-Watch 3* remained in international waters, a Security Decree came into force, which gave the Italian Ministry of the Interior the authority to adopt measures aimed at prohibiting or limiting the entry of boats into territorial waters for purposes of combating unusual levels of asylum seeking (AGI Cronaca 2019; Ferrari 2019). On the same day, Interior Minister Matteo Salvini signed the Security Decree, and at that point only ten migrants – minors, pregnant women, and men suffering from illness – were authorized to disembark for reasons of health and vulnerability (*Deutsche Welle* 2019).

Relations between the European Commission and individual member states with regard to asylum and migration are governed by the "Dublin Regulation," officially, Regulation (EU) No 604/2013, that establishes the criteria for determining which member state has competent jurisdiction to examine an asylum or protection request. Article 3, Section 2 of the Dublin Regulation states that "[w]here no Member State responsible can be designated on the basis of the criteria listed in this Regulation, the *first* Member State in which the application for international protection was lodged shall be responsible for examining it" (emphasis added). The Dublin Regulation further provides that where "proof or circumstantial evidence" establishes "that an applicant has irregularly crossed the border into a Member State by land, sea, or air having come from a third country, the Member State thus entered shall be responsible for examining the application for international protection. That responsibility shall cease 12 months after the date on which the irregular border crossing took place" (Article 13, Section 1).

The implication of these provisions is that if the passengers of the *Sea-Watch 3* who had been rescued by the crew were, in fact, allowed to disembark on Lampedusa, they could make an asylum application in Italy, which, as the first member state in which an application was made, would have to handle it. Mr. Salvini, whose *Lega* party had campaigned on a staunch program of reducing immigration of this "irregular" sort, sought a way around these regulations once the Security Decree was in place. He asked his Dutch counterpart as well as the European Commission to take charge of the migrants, arguing that the country whose flag the boat was flying – the Netherlands, although Sea-Watch is a German nongovernmental organization – is responsible for who is on board before landing (*La Repubblica* 2019b).

The authority of the European Commission to intervene is derived from its function of exercising coordination with the member states for the transfer of migrants once they arrive in a member state, which was not the case when Mr. Salvini made his request (*Il Sole 24 Ore* 2019). What is more, the European Commission has no competence to determine the safe place or port for landing following a sea rescue operation. In fact, EU law allocates the responsibility for identifying a safe port to the member state or states in which the rescue operation is carried out (Zirulia 2019b).

After identifying the dinghy off the coast of Libya, the crew of the *Sea-Watch 3* called the operations room of the Italian coast guard to ask for directions on how to reach the first safe port. The coast guard then alerted the prefecture, which represents the Ministry of the Interior among other national agencies in the province of Agrigento. The prefect sent the *Guardia di Finanza*, an agency of the Ministry of Defense with authority over smuggling, to the border of Italian territorial waters to assess the situation. After this, the Security Decree was applied in the port of Lampedusa when the Ministers of the Interior, Defense and Transport signed an order to prohibit "entry, transit and stop" to bar disembarkations from the *Sea-Watch 3* (Zirulia 2019b).

Seeking a temporary suspension of the Security Decree that prevented landing on Lampedusa (Zinti 2019), the *Sea-Watch 3* crew first appealed to a Regional Administrative Court (Tribunale Amministrativo Regionale, TAR) arguing that the application of the administrative decree will harm a legitimate interest (StudiLegali 2015). If the TAR were to agree that the Security Decree was illegitimate, it could modify, revoke, or annul it. In the most serious cases, the TAR can grant "precautionary protection" (like an injunction by a common law court), that is, suspend the Security Decree to avoid serious and irreparable damage to the appellants. The TAR rejected the appeal of *Sea-Watch 3* on June 19 on the grounds that everyone in danger had disembarked, and the ship remained in international waters (Zirulia and Cancellaro 2019).

The crew then turned to the European Court of Human Rights (ECHR) with another appeal (Attianese 2019). Appeals to the ECHR alleging state violations of rights and guarantees under the European Convention on Human Rights can be made by any person, nongovernmental organization, or group of individuals. The *Sea-Watch 3* appeal was made by the individuals present on board and referred to Article 2 (Right to Life) and Article 3 (Prohibition of Inhuman and Degrading Treatment) of the Convention. Their claim was that the Security Decree, which forced a prolonged stay of passengers on an overcrowded ship unsuitable to house them for such an extended period of time, violated these provisions (Zirulia and Cancellaro 2019). The crew asked the ECHR to order the immediate disembarkation of the migrants by issuing an interim emergency provision. The court also has the authority to request that Italy adopt what the Council of Europe defines as "urgent measures" necessary to "prevent serious and irreparable violations of human rights" (*La Repubblica* 2019a). The judges in Strasbourg, after questioning both the appellants and Italian officials about the situation on

Who Closed the Port of Lampedusa?

board, nevertheless decided *not* to make an order that would have allowed the passengers to disembark in Italy. They did, however, ask the Italian authorities to continue to provide humanitarian assistance to the passengers on the *Sea-Watch 3* (Zirulia and Cancellaro 2019).

The situation then dramatically escalated when the captain of the *Sea-Watch 3*, Carola Rackete, chose to breach a blockade and to enter Italian territorial waters. In doing so, the ship rammed – or bumped, depending on the account – a far smaller boat operated by the *Guardia di Finanza* that was positioned to block the forward progress of the Sea-Watch 3 into the harbor. At the port of Lampedusa, Captain Rackete was arrested by the *Guardia di Finanza* for striking the boat and violating the blockade. Swiftly, the Agrigento prosecutor's office, which has jurisdiction on Lampedusa, opened a criminal investigation of Captain Rackete for aiding illegal immigration and violating the navigation code (Zirulia 2019a).

So, who is accountable for the policy work that kept the *Sea-Watch 3* from landing on Lampedusa until Captain Rackete forced her way to a landing? The answer is certainly more complicated than the journalistic statement with which I began: "*Italy's populist government* did not allow the ship to enter an Italian port" (*Deutsche Welle* 2019, emphasis added). To locate accountability with "the government" requires citizens to disjoin accountability from a variety of policy workers and managers. There was Mr. Salvini, in his role as representative, as well as his counterparts Elisabetta Trenta in the Ministry of Defense and Danilo Toninelli in the Ministry of Transport, all of whom signed the Security Decree. There were managers at the Agrigento prefecture as well as the *Guardia di Finanza*, and it was policy workers from the latter who were on the front lines, in the boat that Captain Rackete rammed, and who placed her under arrest. There were the judges of the TAR and the ECHR who denied the crew's appeal of the order, and managers at the European Commission, including Commission President Jean-Claude Junker, as well as representatives and managers in the Dutch government who did not intervene.

What did those policy workers and managers do? How can citizens evaluate it? Did they act appropriately? Who did and who did not? If a policy worker or manager acted inappropriately, did they act *so* inappropriately that they should be sanctioned? What is more, several actions could be evaluated in the discussion above. The signing of the Security Decree could be assessed for its appropriateness. The legality of the Security Decree might be a stretch for the average citizen, though this was what the TAR and ECHR did address. Was their determination appropriate and sufficient? The managers and policy workers on board the coast guard vessel who made the call to the prefecture, and the managers and policy workers in that office who referred the matter to the *Guardia di Finanza* seemed to be acting pursuant to legally conferred discretion. How might citizens evaluate that use of discretion, however restricted it might have been by statutory law enacted by their representatives? The discretion of the prosecutor in Agrigento, a manager, precluded inaction, but did allow this official to prioritize a criminal investigation and the development of a plan by which the investigation could be carried out; both the priority and the plan might also be evaluable by citizens, though it would certainly require legal information that is quite technical. The decision of managers in the European Commission not to intervene is also potentially evaluable, but like that of the managers and representatives in the Dutch government, it mixes many legal and political considerations.

Overall, the case of the *Sea-Watch 3* leaves Italian citizens with a significant tripartite challenge of identifying one or more managers or policy workers, evaluating what they did when playing their parts in this difficult situation, and determining whether these managers and policy workers or representatives should be sanctioned for what happened. Such questions, I argue in the remainder of this chapter, are crucial to understanding accountability in representative governments with complex governance arrangements like these.

The argument I will make in this chapter differs from the current literature in two important ways. First, while a growing literature in public administration (e.g., James et al. 2016; Mortensen 2013) and political science (e.g., Gasper and Reeves 2011) addresses the ability of citizens to sanction representatives for the quality of policy work, it does not confront the value trade-offs that are being made by managers and policy workers when, for instance, public services are delivered. Second, one influential argument would have us give up on the possibility that electoral accountability can be retrospective in the way that the sanctioning theory of accountability requires. Political scientists Christopher Achen and Larry Bartels (2017) contend that as an empirical matter, voters do not vote retrospectively, but, rather, just stay with party loyalties most of the time. Citizens only deviate from voting their party when bad things happen that need not be within the control of representatives. To provide evidence of this, Achen and Bartels (2017) study shark attacks along the New Jersey coast in 1916. The relationship has also been shown in relation to poor football team performance (Busby, Druckman, and Fredendall 2016; Healy, Malhotra, and Mo 2010). Such evidence leads Achen and Bartels (2017, 116–45) to argue that the incursion of such random reasons enters into citizens' logic for sanctioning incumbent representatives for bad outcomes. This, in turn, leads the incumbents to reduce the effort they expend for improving citizens' welfare because they will be blamed no matter what role they played in causing a bad outcome, what Achen and Bartels call "blind retrospection." While I take no position on whether the limitations of retrospective voting must lead us to abandon the kind of accountability I have described in favor of a group-based identity politics as Achen and Bartels do (2017, 297–328), I do believe that monitoring policy work can remain in the interests of representatives if their retrospection is just a little less "blind," and I offer a different theory later in this chapter.

THEORIES OF ELECTORAL ACCOUNTABILITY

The relationships between policy workers and managers, between managers and representatives, and between representatives and citizens, are the province of accountability. Structures of accountability in these relationships are, as a classic text in the field makes plain, "methods, procedures, and forces that determine what *values* will be reflected in administrative decisions" (Simon, Smithburg, and Thompson 1950, 222, emphasis added). Note the centrality of values in this statement. Accountability is not simply mechanical, it is not some Weberian sense of answerability of a subordinate to a superordinate. Instead, accountability is a democratic value *itself*, one which recognizes the necessity of discretion in the hands of managers and policy workers. The economist and public management scholar Laurence Lynn and I have argued that "[a]ccountability is not an ideal for regimes or governments so much as it is an ideal for the *individuals* who serve in official capacities" (Bertelli and Lynn 2006, 147, emphasis added). This conception remains consequential for my present argument. Representative governments demand adherence to the democratic value of accountability from their managers and policy workers. It is the central value for defining responsible policy work (Bertelli and Lynn 2006). I certainly agree with the political theorist Jeremy Waldron that "[t]oo often, accountability is simply identified with elections or with 'catching out' those who are charged with public responsibilities, without any sense of what exactly it contributes to our understanding of democracy" (Waldron 2014, 1). Without understanding what accountability means in the representative governments *for* which policy work is done, one has no hope, I contend, of understanding the responsibility of managers and policy workers. This is because it is the citizens who give representative government its authority, and policy work is done in the service of the people.

Whether governments, in fact, succeed in obtaining the adherence to the value of accountability they demand is the crucial question for positive theorists and empiricists. A large literature has concerned itself with it (see generally Epstein and O'Halloran 1999; Gailmard 2009; Huber and McCarty 2004; Huber and Shipan 2002; McCubbins, Noll, and Weingast 1989; McCubbins and Schwartz 1984; Volden 2002). However, the normative importance of accountability to representative government is my present focus, and I will return in Chapter 3 to that positive literature. At the heart of my argument in this book is a correspondence between the democratic values embodied in two sets of institutions: political institutions, which are the domain of representatives, and public administration, which is the domain of managers and policy workers. My claim, described in Chapter 5 as the value reinforcement hypothesis, is that the values in political institutions ought to be reflected in the values of governance structures. To make this claim, I must first consider the democratic values in a political system before turning to those embodied in governance structures. This chapter and Chapter 3 do that, and my exploration begins with accountability.

The political theorist Robert Dahl describes representative government as an institutional framework that gives citizens the "opportunity to *oppose and vote out* the highest officials in the government" (Dahl 1989, 220, emphasis added). Much of what we know empirically about how citizens are represented under representative governments is gleaned from this reactive and retrospective power of citizens over representatives. Indeed, this is evident in how we think about the functioning of our democracies in our armchair discussions of contemporary politics. If we don't like what incumbent representatives are doing, and we find ourselves as mad as hornets when we think about their performance, we can vote them out of office. Why is the retrospective sanctioning of representatives so important for understanding representative government?

The Selection View of Electoral Accountability

To be sure, there are other – if not necessarily competing – accounts of the electoral mechanism of representation, and it is helpful to the present

Theories of Electoral Accountability

discussion to consider at least one. A major alternative argument contends that, in elections, citizens might *select* the candidate that is most closely aligned with their policy positions and interests (e.g., Mansbridge 2009). On this view, accountability is still crucial to representative government, but it is not so brutally retrospective. Rather, accountability can include narrative or deliberative elements. Jane Mansbridge, the most articulate advocate of the selection theory as an alternative to retrospective sanctioning, writes that to maintain accountability "the representative *explains* the reasons for her actions and even (ideally) engages in two-way communication with constituents" (Mansbridge 2009, 370, emphasis added). One-way explanation is what Mansbridge calls narrative accountability and is similar to what a common law judge does when writing an opinion, that is, she states the reasons why she took the decision that she did. On collegial courts with a panel of judges, dissenting and concurring narratives are likewise important to document. Deliberative accountability, by contrast, comes from a give and take between a representative and the citizens that form her constituency. Mansbridge is notably reserved about the conditions under which this kind of accountability will function smoothly: "Narrative and deliberative accountability work best when the principal, even if unhappy with the result, can see that the intrinsic motivation underlying the aligned objectives remains unchanged" (2009, 384).

Because the level of explanation demanded by a selection theory of accountability is "an opportunity that few if any large-scale representative systems provide ... every system needs some monitoring of both elected officials and bureaucrats" as is essential to retrospective sanctioning (Mansbridge 2009, 385). Monitoring provides information about performance that citizens *may* use to influence their vote for or against an incumbent representative. While I will discuss monitoring in more detail in Chapter 4, this recognition that narrative or deliberative explanations cannot alone maintain accountability is important to emphasize now because it will become very important shortly. It is precisely this difficulty in achieving accountability through either selection or sanction in practice that gives champions the opportunity to claim that governance structures can help it along.

The Sanctioning View of Electoral Accountability

Mandate representation is different from this select-and-explain view. It "occurs when what politicians and voters want coincides or when politicians care only about winning elections, and to win they must *promise and implement* policies that are best for the public" (Przeworski, Stokes, and Manin 1999, 33, emphasis added). When one stops to think about this, it is easy to understand how difficult it, too, is to achieve in practice. The political theorist Adam Przeworski and his colleagues would not disagree, stating that "short of this happy coincidence, politicians may have incentives either to deviate from the mandate in the best interest of the public or to stick to it at the cost of the electorate" (Przeworski, Stokes, and Manin 1999, 33). What is more, in the selection account, such departures are the times when accountability is most taxed as well. Mansbridge notes that narrative or deliberative accountability mechanisms are important "particularly when deviating from the constituents' preferences" (2009, 370). I argue that the roles that managers and other policy workers play in turning policies into practice help to institutionalize important incentives to deviate from representatives' mandates. In so doing, they can reshape the relationship between citizens and representatives. This has the greatest consequences for democracy administered, when the democratic values of representative government are reshaped, as opposed to the nuts-and-bolts means of implementing public policies.

Understanding mandate representation requires one to address an important threshold question: What, if anything, holds politicians to their promised programs? It is not the rule of law. Manin (1997) recognizes that there is simply no formal institution in any extant representative government that requires representatives to adhere to their promised policy programs while serving in the offices to which they are elected. Citizens cannot sue their representatives for not delivering on campaign promises. Without leverage from formal rules, "[v]oters can sanction deviations from mandates only *after* their effects have been experienced" (Przeworski, Stokes, and Manin 1999, 39, emphasis added). Acknowledging this centers accountability in representative government on retrospective sanctioning and gives rise to the sanctioning approach. Because politicians are not committed to the policy programs that either they or their parties endorse during election campaigns, elections become a retrospective exercise in sanctioning incumbents. Voters' strongest leverage over government policy does not come from selecting the representative who best shares their policy views, but in giving someone else a try if the incumbent is disappointing for *any* reason.

The political theorist Bernard Manin offers a clear logic for the foregoing claims: in representative government, regular elections tie

Theories of Electoral Accountability 27

representatives to public opinion, creating a "system in which the representatives can never say with complete confidence and certainty 'We the People'" (1997, 175). Because governments can be changed if citizens do not like their performance, representatives have the incentive "to take into consideration the wishes of the electorate in their decisions" (Manin 1997, 176). Citizens need not necessarily "use their vote to express preferences about public policy; they may also elect (or not elect) on the basis of the character of candidates" (Manin 1997, 177). It is important to understand that the retrospective answerability of representatives still creates incentives for representatives to attend to the wants of citizens even when the latter are able to express policy preferences in elections "should they wish" (Manin 1997, 177). Consequently, the information that passes from citizens to representatives in an election can be seen as having two possible values. A vote to elect a candidate does not necessarily bring about the implementation of a public policy, while a vote not to reelect is a message to stop the government from implementing a "rejected" public policy (177). That message is delivered even when, for instance, some citizens condition their votes on personal dislike for a candidate, or even for the graphic design of a party logo. Manin thus concludes that "[i]n representative government negation is more powerful than affirmation" (1997, 177). The vote is a blunt instrument, but it is more profitably interpreted in the negative under the sanctioning view of electoral accountability.

In contrast to the selection approach, the sanctioning theory emphasizes that citizens simply cannot ensure that a new government will be in any way different than its predecessor. Suppose the incumbent single-party government in a parliamentary system has grappled with a foreign policy crisis through a series of very controversial decisions. The voters issue a rebuff by handing a clear majority of seats to another party at the subsequent general election. The successor government may be quite nervous about foreign involvement given the incumbent's experience. For this reason, it shifts emphasis to domestic environmental and natural resource policies, which were not topping the list of priorities on surveys during the election campaign and were given only moderate emphasis in the winning party's manifesto.

Selection does not work well in this example, but accountability does not seem to be working terribly well either, given the shift away from foreign policy. The sanctioning argument, then, observes that representatives have "an incentive to anticipate the future judgment of the electorate on the policies they pursue ... [to] ensure that their present decisions do

28   *Accountability Values*

not provoke a future rejection" (Manin 1997, 178). Given the information they have, "if citizens wish to influence the course of public decisions, they should vote on the basis of retrospective considerations" (Manin 1997, 179). The campaign promises of incumbent representatives and their challengers are not binding, but past performance informs citizens about the credibility of promises (Manin 1997, 180). Unlike the selection account, the sanctioning view places no stock in the explanations of representatives for deviations from the policy program endorsed by the voters in the prior election. If citizens go to the polls to choose their representatives prospectively, as selection theorists would have them do, Manin concludes that representatives have "complete freedom of action" in their present policy choices (1997, 177). Realizing this turns the focus of representative government from select-and-represent to accountability-and-sanction.

For accountability to work through the potential rejection of incumbent representatives, three conditions must hold. The first requires that citizens must be able to "clearly assign responsibility" to representatives for unacceptable actions (Manin 1997, 180). This condition will become critically important later in this chapter as it has two necessary elements: it must be straightforward for citizens to *identify* who is responsible for government action and also to *evaluate* whether the action was acceptable or unacceptable (Bertelli 2016).

In the *Sea-Watch 3* case with which the chapter began, the Italian government was a coalition of two parties, the *Lega* and the *Movimento Cinque Stelle*, and given that parties are on the ballot in Italian general elections, a voter may not be sure which party to sanction if she finds the blocked access of the boat to Lampedusa unacceptable. Identifiability is aided because Mr. Salvini, the interior minister, is the leader of the *Lega* party and is extremely outspoken on matters involving migrants into the country from North Africa. However, both of the other ministers who signed the Security Decree, Ms. Trenta and Mr. Toninelli, are members of the *Movimento Cinque Stelle*. Citizens' evaluation of the incident is also less than straightforward, and was made more so by the media coverage and rhetoric surrounding the incident. The Security Decree was aimed at the kind of "irregular" migration covered by the Dublin Regulation. Moreover, after a legal decision came from the Italian administrative court (TAR) as well as the ECHR, Captain Rackete of the *Sea-Watch 3* and members of her German nongovernmental organization took matters into their own hands, ramming through a blockade to dock in Lampedusa. While reasonable readers can disagree about identifiability

Theories of Electoral Accountability

and evaluability in this case, the point of the sanctioning view of representative government is that the facts of the case do not clearly compel a choice when considering that a citizen may only vote for or against a political party (Manin 1997, 180–1). What is more, citizens do not generally base their vote on just one incident.

A second condition for accountability is that citizens must be able to drive those whose policies, character, or other attributes they reject from office (Manin 1997, 181). Put differently, elections must be consequential; defeated representatives must leave and those receiving citizens' electoral support must assume their offices. This is not simply a condition that describes autocrats, but one that can happen in very healthy democracies. A recent example of a less-than-consequential contest was the German general election in September 2017. A grand coalition between the Christian Democratic Union/Christian Social Union (CDU/CSU) on the center-right led by Chancellor Angela Merkel and the Social Democratic Party (SDP) on the center-left had been in place since 2013 and the voters certainly voiced disapproval, with roughly 9 percent and 5 percent reductions in the vote shares for the parties respectively (Poguntke and Kinski 2018). Yet the coalition parties remained the two largest parties even though the Alternative for Germany party on the right received an 8 percent greater vote share than it did in 2013 and entered parliament for the first time (Poguntke and Kinski 2018). Initially, the SDP refused to enter into another grand coalition because of the electoral outcome and Ms. Merkel's CDU/CSU attempted to forge a new coalition agreement with the Green party and the classically liberal Free Democratic Party. When these coalition talks broke down because of difficulties in reconciling policies on migration and energy, SDP leader Martin Schultz was still claiming that a grand coalition would not be possible because "[t]he voter has rejected the grand coalition" (Oltermann 2017). Ultimately, things changed and the CDU/CSU and SDP came together once again to form a grand coalition agreement in March 2018 when the CDU/CSU gave the SDP the finance portfolio (Oltermann 2018). Six months after the election, the German people got the very same coalition government they had rejected at the polls.

The final condition for retrospective sanctioning is that incumbent representatives cannot have resource advantages that give them an advantage over challengers simply because they currently hold office (Manin 1997, 181). Managers and policy workers, because of their important role in implementing policies and the expertise they develop in doing so, are very well positioned to violate this condition. As a consequence, this

Accountability Values

requirement of accountability is reflected in provisions such as the Hatch Act of 1939 in the United States, which makes it illegal for, *inter alia*, "any person employed in any administrative position by the United States ... to use his official authority for the purpose of interfering with, or affecting the election or the nomination of any candidate for the office of President, Vice President, Presidential electors, Member of the Senate, or Member of the House of Representatives, Delegates or Commissioners from the Territories and insular possessions" (Public Law 76–252, Sec. 2). The act goes on to prohibit managers and policy workers from specific activities, such as promising employment as a "reward for any political activity or for the support of or opposition to any candidate or any political party in any election" (Sec. 3) as well as providing "any list or names of persons receiving compensation, employment, or benefits provided for or made possible by any Act of Congress ... to a political candidate, committee, [or] campaign manager" and "for any person to receive any such list or names for political purposes" (Sec. 6). The idea that the public administration would be politically neutral, possessed of "a wealth of knowledge and skills ... that all elected officials, no matter what their political persuasion, could call upon," has normative significance for representative government (Rourke 1992, 539). Political neutrality is an essential element of the capabilities theme in the traditional narrative of the field, yet I will argue in Chapter 6 that its value for legitimating that policy work is done in representative governments is overstated because those governments are not themselves neutral.

Having described the necessary conditions for accountability when citizens vote retrospectively and the consequences of this kind of voting for representatives, it is important to discuss two features of political systems as they are in the world today. The first is the role of institutions, specifically electoral rules and the system of political parties, in shaping the conditions of identifiability. The second is whether representative government ought to allow for deviations from an electoral mandate. I take these issues in turn in the sections that follow.

INSTITUTIONS, PARTIES, AND ELECTORAL ACCOUNTABILITY

Electoral rules include flavors of proportional representation, such as lists or single transferrable votes and of majoritarianism, such as single-member district plurality or single nontransferable votes (see Bormann and Golder 2013). A political party system captures the number of

Institutions, Parties, and Electoral Accountability

parties, electoral support through vote shares, and ideological leanings of all parties in a jurisdiction at a particular time (Boix 2007, 501). It is important to understand that both the electoral system and the party system play important roles in shaping electoral accountability. The political scientists Christopher Kam, Alexander Held, and I have examined these roles in parliamentary systems, revealing a larger impact of the party system than students of comparative political institutions had previously considered (Kam, Bertelli, and Held 2020). Before describing our claims in more detail, I should note that presidential systems, like the United States, create a more complex landscape. In federal systems, still more offices are directly elected and representatives compete with one another in policy formation. Such systems incorporate institutions to check the relative power of each actor – for instance, rules about how budgets for programmatic activity are adopted – and rely on ex-post oversight on the actions of both representatives and managers. This is crucial to the control element of the traditional narrative to which I will return in the next chapter.

Our argument builds on the sanctioning approach just described by observing that accountability in parliamentary elections can be observed in the relationship between *changes* in vote share for an incumbent party and *changes* in their governing power. If voters are to sanction a political party in government, then they must not only be able to reduce its share of seats in the legislature from what it had on Election Day, but they must also have the power to reduce the extent to which that party can exert influence over public policymaking. In parliamentary systems, governing power comes through cabinet portfolios, or areas of policy responsibility. For example, from the case of the *Sea-Watch 3* consider the portfolios held by Mr. Salvini in domestic law and order, by Ms. Trenta in national defense and by Mr. Toninelli in transportation. Crucially, it was not the Italian voters who assigned Ms. Trenta and Mr. Toninelli to their portfolios, but, rather the political parties to which they belong, and those parties did so when bargaining with each other to come up with an agreement for governing as a coalition. For this reason, parliamentary government is often described as indirect government: the people choose representatives, and then those representatives form a government across the various substantive policy portfolios.

In the parliamentary context, our argument centers on what we call the *accountability identity*, which can be written in the following way, where Δ represents the difference between the values of the particular quantities realized in the latest election result and those of the previous government (Kam, Bertelli, and Held 2020, 746):

$$\frac{\Delta \text{Portfolios}}{\Delta \text{Votes}} = \frac{\Delta \text{Seats}}{\Delta \text{Votes}} \times \frac{\Delta \text{Portfolios}}{\Delta \text{Seats}}$$

The left side represents the realization of electoral accountability; changes in votes must change the number of portfolios a party controls. The first term on the right side falls within the domain of the electoral system, and the influence of electoral rules over the relationship between changes in seats in the legislature and changes in votes at the ballot box has been widely documented by political scientists (e.g., Cox 1997; Taagepera and Shugart 1989). The second term on the right side of the accountability identity captures the influence of the party system as it relates changes in a party's seat share in the legislature to its representation in government through cabinet portfolios.

In more than 400 elections in twenty-eight countries, we show that the marginal effect of vote swings on seat share changes is greater under majoritarian than under proportional electoral rules. This is sensible because these rules are designed to influence the vote-seat transformation. Pure proportional representation intends to force $\Delta \text{Seats}/\Delta \text{Votes} = 1$, meaning that accountability depends only on the transformation of seat shares into governing power. Thus, Gamson's Law (1961) – portfolios in coalition governments are proportion to the seat shares of the constituent parties – is an obvious focal point of the literature (e.g., Fréchette, Kagel, and Morelli 2005; Morelli 1999). By contrast, majoritarian systems aim to eliminate coalition governments altogether, rendering the votes-to-portfolios relationship discontinuous. That is, a party with more than 50 percent of the votes receives all of the portfolios (Powell 2000). Kam, Bertelli, and Held (2019) find that the larger substantive effect of majoritarianism on accountability is restricted to the votes-seats relationship. It does not directly impact the seats-to-portfolios transformation.

The largest influence on the translation of seats to portfolios is when the party system displays *bipolarity*, or the ideological configuration of political parties into two distinct groups. We show evidence of this influence in two-dimensional ideological space. The mechanism for this is straightforward: when parties separate into government and opposition blocs, the number of connected minimum-winning coalitions diminishes. That is, the number of coalitions that parties *might* possibly form on the basis of their party platforms is reduced to the extent that citizens can identify both their government and the opposition to it. If they wish to

Institutions, Parties, and Electoral Accountability

sanction the government, a vote for the opposition party or bloc will achieve that ambition.

This finding is striking in an era in which "polarization" of party positions is so upsetting to many citizens, and it shows the kind of trade-offs that champions of particular electoral designs must make clear. If one wants more accountability for parliamentary government, then under the sanctioning view, bipolar party systems will help to achieve it more than changes to the electoral formula will. The pluralistic representation of diverse interests is another matter entirely, and one that I will address in Chapter 3. But it is important to see that the policy positions that underlie the extent to which a party system is bipolar, in particular about the ideological and policy positions of the parties in electoral competition, are ultimately the choices of party elites. Citizens are afforded more or less opportunity to hold governments accountable as a result of these choices.

Distinctiveness between groups of government and opposition parties quite simply provides citizens with clarity when choosing between an incumbent government and a new party that can change policy. Citizens know that a vote for the opposition party is a vote against the government. Bipolarity in parliamentary systems also limits the set of potential coalitions that incumbent parties might leverage to stay in power despite a reduction in support at the polls. Parties' ideological distinctiveness makes the compromises of coalition bargaining more difficult. Consequently, bipolarity is a crucial way in which the system of political parties can render electoral sanctions on incumbents more forceful, increasing accountability in the process.

The French political scientist Maurice Duverger based his argument regarding accountability in the configuration of parties rather than electoral rules: "Opposition under a two-party system remains distinct in spite of its moderation ... public opinion can grasp with some accuracy the difference between the points of view of the majority and of the minority and so can choose with full knowledge of the facts" (Duverger 1962, 415). But it must be said that a two-party system is not required: the Italian political scientist Giovanni Sartori's classic bipolarity condition applies to multiparty systems so long as they are constituted of two-party blocs, in and out of government, respectively (1976). While finding strong support for the importance of bipolarity, Kam, Bertelli, and Held (2019) observe that Sartori's other principal claim – that the existence of a center party weakens accountability – is far less empirically relevant (Sartori 1976).

DEVIATIONS FROM THE MANDATE AND CONDITIONAL REPRESENTATION

There is good reason for the retrospective mechanism of accountability to be privileged in representative government. Representatives ought to be allowed to deliberate about public policies after elections and to revise their programs to help, rather than hurt, the interests of the polity. Citizens are better off when their representatives can come to understand both what they want, but also what they don't know they want (Przeworski, Stokes, and Manin 1999, 39). The state of the world may change between elections and the welfare of citizens hangs in the balance.

Citizens can be quite consequentialist if they choose to be, allowing representatives to go forward with policies for which they did not vote and that they did not want ex ante, but fail to impose sanctions at the ballot box for changing course if representatives are right. Elections do not happen in the aftermath of every policy decision (Manin 1997, 182). In this sense, representative government is democratic when citizens vote retrospectively, but when they do so prospectively, they are simply choosing representatives who are not obliged to keep their promises. Manin thus claims that under prospective selection, "election is not democratic" (1997, 183). Because of this distinction, the manner in which citizens construe the voting mechanism when they engage it also has implications for the representation style representatives employ. Can representatives deviate from the policy positions for which they won their mandate? What kind of a mandate can voters conceivably endorse? I take these questions in turn in this section.

Consider a majoritarian, single-member district system such as that which assembles the United States Congress. Suppose that 60 percent of a legislative district voted to elect representative Y to the legislature. To which constituents is the representative responsible? Just the 60 percent of voting citizens who endorsed Y's candidacy? It is not difficult whatsoever to conjure an incumbent who, faced with this question, would say "I'm the representative of *all* the people in my district." Suppose Y takes this view. In order to act on it, Y would have to decide what *all* of the people want, and that would require some thinking that is independent of the electoral result because the positions of the majority that voted Y into the legislature and the minority that did not are incongruent at least across some policy domains. This problem gets even worse as the districts are amalgamated across the political geography of the country (Christiano 1996, 227).

Deviations from the Mandate and Conditional Representation 35

Compare the foregoing case to one arising in a proportional representation system under parliamentary government in which parties are assigned seats in the legislature in proportion to the vote share they received. Suppose party Z receives 30 percent of the vote. It would be straightforward to think that the leadership of party Z can focus solely on its manifesto commitments when its members act as representatives, but with 30 percent of the vote, Z must enter into a coalition with party X, which won 25 percent of the vote, in order to form a government. How should a representative from Z prioritize policy initiatives when developing a plan for the new government with X? If we assume that citizens consider parties' policy positions in a meaningful way, compromise from the manifesto will be required. If Z's representatives consider X's voters in making these compromises, Z deviates from the mandate that 30 percent of voters gave to it, and independent judgment seeps into the representation process once again. Of course, a citizen may base her vote on things other than policy positions, and suppose she chose party Z because she trusts that Z's leader would make the best coalition bargain given party and ideological constraints. Such prospective voting might, in fact, permit the foregoing deviation from the perspective of this voter, though Manin's critique of prospective selection remains intact (1997, 183). What coalition bargain would be unacceptable to the voter? The voter is likely to know it only when she sees it.

The principal-agent conception of political representation is similar to a contract in which a representative deals with one or more third parties on behalf of citizens (Vieira and Runciman 2008, 68–70). To deal with these third parties, be they foreign states or interest groups, the representative acquires information that her electors – citizens – cannot easily observe. This interaction with third parties transforms the representative into an *expert* decision maker, and the information acquired in those interactions is, in an important sense, noncontractible; it cannot be included *explicitly* in the constitutionally defined relationship between citizens and representatives (e.g., Persson, Roland, and Tabellini 1997).

Normative theorists are realistic about the coherence of citizens' priorities as they might be expressed in an election. The political philosopher Thomas Christiano argues that a representative (akin to a ship's captain) must act as a *delegate* regarding the public's (her passengers') expressed aims, but as a *trustee* on the means for achieving them: "The citizens choose the destination: the captain accepts to take them there and chooses the route and how to navigate it." The burden on the representative is to understand citizens' priorities "[a]s long as citizens are reasonably explicit about their priorities and the trade-offs among the things they want" (Christiano 1996, 171). Expressed priorities, then, are arguably more central to representatives than policy positions precisely because they reflect the aims, not the mechanisms, of public policies.

Consider a policy that brings a little benefit to a lot of people. The economists Raquel Fernandez and Dani Rodrik (1991) argue that public uncertainty about the benefits of that policy would not yield advance support for it, but, rather, an endorsement when it is implemented and the uncertainty fades away. After implementation, policy beneficiaries can form a large base of representatives who support it. Following this logic, the public may say that it prefers that the government reduce its budget deficit, but if unemployment is mitigated through social policy programs, it may be happy with the drop in unemployment as a result of social spending after all. This is because its *implied* priority was always the economy, rather than fiscal discipline. Though these economists may not be concerned about it, they are essentially arguing for a form of retrospective sanctioning in which the government can resolve uncertainty through expertise development and independent from citizen consultation. By acquiring information about the world and resolving uncertainty that voters have, the representative can learn the implied priorities of citizens. In this way, representatives develop expertise in clarifying the aims of the public and the trade-offs it makes among those aims. The political scientist Peter John and I (Bertelli and John 2013) call this *conditional representation*.

Conditional representation means that what a representative learns about the nature of citizens' priorities can condition the way she interprets expressed priorities, for instance, the results of opinion polls. That is, when representatives develop some knowledge about the process that generates expressed priorities, they can better understand what the public really wants, and not just naively act as though those numbers are the best reflection of the public's true priorities. The conditional representative is not a full-blown trustee in the sense of Edmund Burke (1912 [1790]), but, rather, an agent of citizens who must acquire information to give the public policies it faces too much uncertainty to understand that it wants (Przeworski, Stokes, and Manin 1999). Such representation is not inconsistent with being a delegate, or engaging in what the political philosopher Philip Pettit called directed representation, which does not require representatives to "track the dispositions" of citizens, but rather to be "a good indicator or model of how [represented citizens] *might have been disposed to act or speak*" (Pettit 2009, 69, emphasis added). In this, it respects the political theorist Hannah Pitkin's (1967) call for theories recommending that citizens preserve the autonomy of representatives and the citizens they represent.

Under conditional representation, if the state of the world is unpredictable to citizens, a critical part of a representative's agency relationship with them is to learn what his electors really want in an uncertain world. For instance, when mass opinion gives social welfare a lower priority than crime at a time when uncertainty about economic conditions is very high, the representative must interpret whether it should truly prioritize crime over social welfare to represent citizens' interests. If uncertainty has made crime the expressed priority, then the representative might do well to keep social welfare on the agenda because, as Manin notes, the possibility of retrospective voting in the next election gives the representative a strong incentive to take care that "present decisions do not provoke a future rejection" (1997, 178). Not responding to expressed priorities in this scenario, we claim, is evidence of expert judgment, which is precisely what the representative, as the agent of citizens, would be expected to acquire. Representatives need not respond directly to citizens' priorities about aims, expressed or implied. Political theory allows representatives to take into account that expressed priorities are collectively expressed by the voters, and are "not the faithful reflection of a pre-given mind," but require of the representative "a constructive interpretation in virtue of which the multitude is imputed a coherent mind" (Pettit 2009, 76). As they did in the accountability identity, political parties play an important role in shaping priorities.

Let me return to the example of parties Y and Z that jointly commanded a 55 percent vote share in a general election. Suppose now that the coalition they form to govern develops an accurate picture of the political economy, and concludes that citizen uncertainty masks the reality that the economy is more important than crime, though the expressed priority was the other way around because Z yielded 30 percent of the vote on a law and order platform while X got 25 percent on a set of economic growth plans in its manifesto. Acting on that information and prioritizing the economy will make the coalition appear nonresponsive, but their policy agenda is, in fact, quite representative of what the public would have expressed absent uncertainty and may work to the parties' advantage when facing the electorate again (Bertelli and John 2013a, 2013b). The conditionally representative coalition government need not be seen as deviating from its mandate, but as using its expertise – it has an entire bureaucracy of expert managers and policy workers for a start – to

38 *Accountability Values*

learn what aspects of the political economy generate citizen uncertainty about what policy areas are important. This allows the coalition to give the public what they didn't really understand they wanted (Przeworski, Stokes, and Manin 1999). Brennan and Hamlin call this political entrepreneurship, which is "proactive, identifying and promoting policies that [the representative] believes will be appreciated *ex post*, rather than preferred *ex ante*" (2000, 172).

While the bulk of empirical political scientists believe that marginal responsiveness to policy priorities and positions is what democracy demands (cf. MacKuen, Erikson, and Stimson 1989; Soroka and Wlezien 2009), political theorists distinguish representative government from such responsiveness: "there is nothing inherently democratic about the idea of representation" (Brito Vieira and Runciman 2008, 152). Normative theories of representation allow it to be "hands off" and done on a "need-for-action" basis (Pettit 2009, 72–3). Using their expertise to understand citizens' uncertainty gives conditional representatives "a means of overcoming the differences between individuals [electors] and their interests, once it is seen as something more than just a reflection of them" (Brito Viera and Runciman 2008, 137; see also Brennan and Hamlin 2000).

Consistent with the sanctioning approach to electoral accountability, representation has to be authorized (retrospectively) by citizens, and winning elections offers the conditional representative that authorization. Bertelli and John (2013a, 2013b) have shown evidence from postwar British governments that when representatives use such expertise to separate citizens' expressed priorities from the influence that uncertainty in the political economy – aspects such as economic conditions, armed conflict, and unexpected political scandals – has on those expressions, conditional representation produces electoral gains for incumbent government parties.

ACCOUNTABILITY ERRORS

Modern public administration is complicated by many actors and complex relationships among them, as the *Sea-Watch 3* case makes plain. What questions about policy work can be submitted to citizens? Throughout the foregoing discussion, I have claimed that representative government requires three basic things of representatives: identifiability, evaluability, and the possibility that they can be sanctioned by the electorate. I will argue in Chapter 5 that the values of representative

Accountability Errors

governments and the values of the governance structures which shape the policy work done for those governments should be expected to correlate. Because they are the architects of implementation, managers certainly find themselves subject to pressures that are derived from the identifiability, evaluability, and possibility of sanctioning representatives, and policy workers face these pressures as well.

Identifiability Errors

To be held accountable, a representative must be identifiable, and as I have discussed, electoral and party systems play a role in this. In the case of the *Sea-Watch 3*, citizens are presented with difficulties in regard to two accountability requirements. The coalition partners in the Italian government at the time of the incident could not have been more ideologically diverse. The most recent ideological estimates from the Manifesto Research Group's examination of the 2013 election manifestos placed the *Movimento Cinque Stelle* with a left-right ideology score at a very left −49 and the *Lega*, by contrast, much farther to the right at 3.8 (Volkens et al. 2020). This bipolarity helps to identify the *Lega* as the coalition partner most associated with the decision-making, and with Mr. Salvini as interior minister, identifiability is improved. Yet the *Movimento Cinque Stelle* defies traditional left-right characterizations (Di Maggio and Perrone 2019), and to confuse matters further, Italian parties compete in regional elections as well, and their positions within the country are not quite so coherent as one might imagine.

Figure 2.1 plots the percentage of left- and right-leaning quasi-sentences, or portions of a sentence that express a distinct idea, in the manifestos of the *Movimento Cinque Stelle* regional parties that were written for the regional elections of 2013 (Gómez, Alonso, and Cabeza 2018). When the left (solid) and right (hollow) dots are far apart in the figure, the party position is more clearly identifiable. In the northern region of Alto Adige/Südtirol, the *Movimento Cinque Stelle* is clearly a left-leaning party, making few right-leaning, but many left-leaning statements in relation to the overall averages. In the southern region of Basilicata, by contrast, the party's left-right position is less clear, with the proportions of left and right statements far below the average across regions. Sicily, the region in which Lampedusa is administratively located, is much closer to the averages of left and right statements. While that may make Sicilian citizens more likely to identify the political parties, the lack of consistency across the country is important to keep in mind.

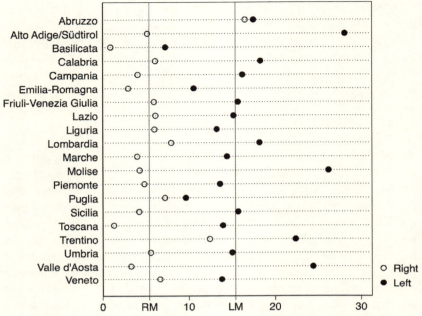

FIGURE 2.1 Left-leaning and right-leaning references in regional *Movimento Cinque Stelle* manifestos, 2012–15. LM denotes the median percentage of left-leaning (15.4%) and RM the corresponding percentage of right-leaning (5.4%) quasi-sentences in the election manifestos.
Source: Gómez, Alonso, and Cabeza (2018)

Studying a multi-level system in Spain, the political scientist Sandra León finds that policy areas that are less decentralized lead citizens to "to overstate the responsibilities of the central government, so the chances that central incumbents are held accountable are higher than that of subnational governments" (2011, 97). She argues that subnational politicians will develop a strategy to "try to avoid responsibility for bad policy outcomes by transferring blame to central incumbent, knowing that citizens regard central government as the most responsible administration in the provision and financing of public services" (2011, 100). By contrast, in policy areas in which decentralization is high, León contends that citizens tend to "overstate subnational governments' responsibilities" and that "if central government's performance remains less visible to citizens, its performance will be less subject to evaluation" (2011, 99). Under strong decentralization, the national government's strategy involves

Accountability Errors

"blaming subnational governments for outcomes that indeed remain at central government's door" (2011, 100).

Such incentives for politicians to adopt blame avoidance strategies have long been recognized (e.g., Weaver 1986), but for present purposes, what is crucial to recognize is that political institutions – the multiple levels of overlapping authority in León (2011) and in the case of the *Sea-Watch 3* – can shape these strategies. Moreover, blame avoidance strategies can coax citizens to make errors regarding identifiability. The vast array of managers and policy workers at subnational, national, and supranational levels also serve to weaken citizens' ability to identify a responsible actor.

Citizens can make two types of identifiability errors. First, *type I identifiability errors* are false positives: they occur when the "wrong" actor – that is, a policy worker or representative who was not at all (or very much) responsible – is identified for blame. In other words, citizens locate too much blame with someone who was not, in fact, the cause of a bad outcome. Locating responsibility for the arrest of Ms. Rackete, captain of the *Sea-Watch 3*, with European Union authorities would be such an error. It was the Italian authorities who made the arrest. Second, *type II identifiability errors* are false negatives: either the "wrong" actor is held answerable, or too little blame accrues to the "right" actor, who really was responsible. Of course, governance structures play an important role in shaping citizens' errors of identifiability as well. Blaming Mr. Salvini or his *Lega* party for the problems of the Dublin Regulation, which had its origins in a convention adopted by the Italian government in 1990, far before either held national portfolios, would be a type II identifiability error. The administrative organization of the prefecture, which represents the *Guardia di Finanza* that made the arrest as well as the Ministry of the Interior and other central government contributes to the kind of confusion that leads citizens to identifiability errors. What is more, the media coverage around the event is particularly well positioned to shape the accuracy of identifiability.

It is crucial to emphasize that both type I and type II identifiability errors can happen in different degrees. A type I error may identify an actor with some amount of responsibility, but who was not involved in the crucial decisions that caused an outcome. Given available information, for instance, citizens might conclude that an actor who really was responsible behaved as well as could reasonably be expected. Relatedly, a type II error can result in a state wherein citizens do not find *anyone* accountable. It may be that the truly responsible actor receives some blame when such an error is made, but it is certainly not enough. These matters of degree are significant because they are commonplace in complex governance. There really may be one or more actors in government who are truly responsible for a bad outcome, yet given the information available, citizens cannot conclude that anyone did anything wrong. If the government were just one person, the result would have been different because that single actor could bear the blame.

Evaluability Errors

Policy work must also be *evaluable* by citizens for it to become a part of retrospective accountability at the ballot box, and this is a very tricky criterion to satisfy. Much of what representatives do – and even more of what managers and policy workers do – is quite specialized, technical, and otherwise difficult for citizens, on average, to grasp. As argued by Christiano (1996), input into the means by which public policy is implemented cannot realistically be expressed by citizens at the ballot box, and it becomes a matter for conditional representation by representatives.

Revisiting the *Sea-Watch 3* case, the *Lega* party, which takes a hardline stance on immigration, has seen a steady rise in its support from citizens in opinion polls, eclipsing the *Movimento Cinque Stelle* a year earlier, and by June 2019 its approval ratings were in the mid-30 percent range, while those of its coalition partner remained steadily lower, between 16–19 percent as the incident unfolded (Scenaripolitici 2019). The Italian government at the time determined that the countries in which migrants will apply for asylum would be determined *before* any landing in Italy, and in the case of the *Sea-Watch 3*, migrants would be sent to France, Germany, Finland, Luxembourg, and Portugal (Knight 2019). Conditional representation is consistent with Italian representatives interpreting the rising popular support for the *Lega* as an interest in clear policies that resolve uncertainty about migration, and *then* facing retrospectively voting citizens in the next general election. Nonetheless, the array of choices made by managers and policy workers that shaped the event, and their compliance or noncompliance with different laws and procedures, makes evaluation more difficult.

As with identifiability, citizens can make two types of errors when it comes to evaluability. In order to understand them, imagine two voters, A and B, who are both opposed to immigration restrictions and find it unacceptable that the *Sea-Watch 3* ever entered Italian waters. Suppose A finds the front-line policy workers – the coast guard, and so forth – at fault for not blocking the *Sea-Watch 3* from entering Italian waters before the situation escalated. Citizen A would not punish the government for the errors of these policy workers. By contrast, B believes that these policy workers were just following laws, but those laws could have been changed by the Italian government or by the European Union, and this could have been done quickly and representatives at national or European levels deserve the blame. Notice that in this situation, identifiability and evaluability are bound together. They are necessary, but not sufficient, conditions for retrospective sanctioning. Voter B believes that following the law is acceptable behavior, but A does not, and these different views about *evaluability* lead A and B to *identify* different responsible actors, namely, representatives from B's, and policy workers from A's perspective.

The first kind of mistake a citizen can make, a *type I evaluability error*, arises when actions escape public evaluation, even though evaluation was possible. By contrast, *type II evaluability errors* happen when citizens can evaluate policy work as acceptable or unacceptable, but they are too uninformed, confused, or otherwise unable to properly evaluate it. Either error turns on the information that citizens have about the policy event in question.

Suppose that information through media and other easily accessible reports regarding the *Sea-Watch 3* case did not clearly address the fact that international maritime law makes the waters quite murky for front-line policy workers. International maritime law does require that the captain of a vessel, when encountering persons in danger at sea, has a duty to rescue and to transport the individuals to a safe location; no corresponding obligation is imposed on countries bordering the sea to accept the rescued individuals (Knight 2019). Thus, it was the Dublin Regulation that suggested that the obligation belonged to a member state of the European Union. To maximize ambiguity, international maritime law gave Captain Rackete broad discretion to determine what constituted emergency conditions on board the ship and it was this determination that justified her decision to force entry into the port (Knight 2019).

Given this information, neither A nor B is quite right in their evaluation. Captain Rackete had the discretion to make key choices under international maritime law before the Dublin Regulation became applicable. This made A's claim that front-line policy workers should have diffused the situation less tenable. But, international maritime law, not Italian or European law, gave the Italian authorities the legal right to refuse the *Sea-Watch 3* access to the harbor on Lampedusa, and this undermines B's claim that the government or European Union could have quickly changed the situation. If a plurality of citizens at the ballot box agreed with A and did not punish the government, they would make a type I evaluability error. Alternatively, if that plurality were convinced by B's logic and did punish the government, they would make a type II evaluability error.

In the run-up to the Italian general election of 2018, survey evidence from the Issue Competition Comparative Project (De Sio et al. 2019) suggests that the former government under the *Partito Democratico* was indeed punished for a lack of credibility regarding citizens' own positions on immigration. Fuller details of my analysis appear in the appendix to this chapter, but when controlling for a variety of factors, I found the following within-region effects evocative of the kind of retrospection that the sanctioning theory of electoral accountability envisions. If a respondent strongly believed that the government should limit the flow of refugees into Italy and also felt that the *Partito Democratico* was credible to make good on that reduction, she had a 16.6 percent chance of announcing an intention to vote for the government. My estimates show with 95 percent confidence that this chance lies between 7 percent and 26.2 percent, with similar ranges indicated in parentheses going forward. If a respondent instead felt that the governing party was not credible in making policy that limits refugees, the probability of stating an intention to keep it in power in the general election fell to just 4.4 percent (2.7–6.1 percent).

The effects were similar, but less dramatic, for those who felt strongly that Italy should accept more refugees. In this case, when a respondent perceived that the governing party was credible on her position, her probability of expressing the intention to vote for the government was a much smaller 7.4 percent (2.4–12.3 percent), and this dropped to only 1.8 percent (0.5–3.1 percent) without government credibility.

These relationships suggest that citizens were conditioning their voting intention on their own priorities, but more heavily on the capability of an incumbent party to credibly address those priorities. Thinking about electoral accountability in the case of the *Sea-Watch 3*, it would not be wholly unreasonable to believe that citizens can at least consider their policy preferences as well as the government positions on immigration when voting retrospectively. Nonetheless, it is important to understand that the relationships just discussed reflect voting intention, not the ultimate vote of these respondents on Election Day. While the correlation between intention and action is often very high, the relationship can depend on party loyalty and other aspects of self-identification (e.g., Granberg and Holmberg 1990).

CITIZENS' HEURISTICS FOR RETROSPECTION

I have argued elsewhere that to vote in a way that retrospectively assigns responsibility, a citizen can apply two simple heuristics, or rules-of-thumb, based on cues from the policy environment (Bertelli, 2016). This kind of heuristic-based theorizing has become highly influential in understanding the voting behavior of citizens in a variety of contexts (cf. Baldassarri 2013; Lupia 1994), including in normative arguments about how voters ought to behave (e.g, Kang 2002).

I fully recognize the cognitive, time, and other limitations that citizens face, and thus limit my argument to two "fast and frugal" heuristics, that the social psychologist Gerd Gigerenzer and his colleagues (1999, 14) have formulated to "limit their search of objects or information using easily computable stopping rules, and they make their choices with easily computable decision rules" (Gigerenzer, Todd, and ABC Research Group 1999, 14). What this means is that a citizen need not conduct a deep and sophisticated search for information about the behavior of representatives, managers, and policy workers, but, rather, could stop their search after finding just one piece of information. And if that piece of information is found, the process of deciding how to vote retrospectively is very simple. While my expectations of citizen engagement of policy work are not high, they do, I think, have considerable democratic importance.

Because, as we have seen, electoral accountability is stronger when citizens view the performance of representatives retrospectively (Manin 1997), the heuristics I will discuss concern a *policy event*, something that has happened about which prevailing interests in politics can offer competing views, negative or positive. The *Sea-Watch 3* incident is a clear example of a policy event. Citizens who approve of the way that the policy event was handled by representatives, managers, and policy workers may want to assign credit, but as we have also seen, the negative and retrospective act of sanctioning is also a stronger tool in elections. For this reason, I will focus my discussion of the accountability question on citizens' assignment of blame. The two heuristics that I believe are important correspond to the accountability values of identifiability and evaluability.

The *identifiability heuristic* is based on the recognition heuristic from cognitive psychology (Gigerenzer, Todd, and ABC Research Group. 1999). If available information allows a citizen to clearly identify a policy worker, then she should attribute responsibility to a policy worker, rather than to a representative. If such information does not allow her to identify a policy worker, the *default* responsibility for a policy event should adhere to one or more representatives. By available information, I mean the cues the citizen receives from easily accessible sources, such as the media reports about the *Sea-Watch 3* policy event. If these cues allow a citizen to employ the identifiability heuristic to select a policy worker, a second decision is reached.

The *evaluability* heuristic, similar to the discrimination heuristic (Gigerenzer, Todd, and ABC Research Group. 1999), allows the citizen to determine whether cues about the policy event allow for its evaluation. If they do, the citizen should blame the policy worker uncovered by the identifiability heuristic. If not, the responsibility once again goes to a representative by default.

Figure 2.2 graphically illustrates the heuristics in sequence. Suppose citizen Y reads a newspaper account, with the informational cue(s) she receives represented by the dotted line, about Captain Rackete steering the *Sea-Watch 3* into a boat from the *Guardia di Finanza*, which was captained by Officer Z. Upon reading of the incident, Y remembers that Z, a manager, was on the front line when the policy event occurred, and thus feels that Z is at least partly to blame. The newspaper story is enough for Y to use the identifiability heuristic to trigger the evaluability question, moving to the right in Figure 2.2 rather than defaulting to the politician on the identifiability question.

At this point, Y continues reading the story and learns that Captain Rackete and her German nongovernmental organization made the decision to forcibly enter the port of Lampedusa and that Police Officer X, a

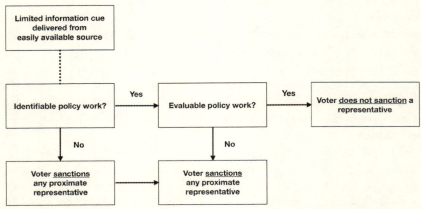

FIGURE 2.2 Identifiability and evaluability heuristics and voter sanctioning

policy worker, arrested her on landing. This single piece of information allows Y to evaluate the policy work, and she determines that Captain Rackete and her colleagues put Z and his boat in a difficult position; X's arrest was justified under the circumstances. Neither Z nor the managers in the *Guardia di Finanza* or in other Italian authorities deserve blame, Y reasons. This moves Y's decision-making once again to the right and representatives are absolved of blame.

On the basis of three pieces of information from a news story, Y makes a "fast and frugal" choice regarding accountability.

Did citizen Y make a "bad" choice? That might very well be, but it does not really matter much to my argument if she did. The theory of retrospective sanctioning allows her to make any choice she likes, and the heuristics serve a normative purpose because of this feature. Because the policy workers were identifiable and the policy work was evaluable for Y, representatives have the incentive to pay attention to what managers and policy workers are doing, if only to learn and disseminate enough information for citizens to use their "fast and frugal" heuristics to decide whether or not those very representatives deserve blame. In this framework, it is the possibility of sanction that stimulates reelection minded representatives and their political parties to scrutinize policy work. In other words, democratic accountability works better when citizens use these heuristics in a way that defaults blame to representatives when they cannot identify the important managers and policy workers involved in a policy event, or even if they can, are too poorly informed or confused by the cues they receive to evaluate the policy work involved.

In taking this view, I disagree with Achen and Bartels (2017) when it comes to blaming representatives for policy work. The rub emerges from sanctioning representatives as a default response in the identifiability and evaluability heuristics. Doing this might be tantamount to what Achen and Bartels call "blind retrospection," a malaise that makes voters act in the following way:

When they are in pain they are likely to kick the government, so long as they can justify doing so with whatever plausible cultural constructions are available to them. Only if no such constructions are available, or if no ambitious challengers emerge to articulate them, will people take out their frustrations on other scapegoats, or just suffer. In most cases, incumbents will pay at the polls for bad times, whether or not objective observers can find a rational basis for blame (Achen and Bartels 2017, 118).

While I certainly do not disagree with their findings that citizens often blame representatives for things, such as natural disasters, that are beyond their control (e.g., Achen and Bartels 2017, 128–34), my argument diverges from their colorfully worded cynicism. First, mine is not an empirical democratic argument, but a normative one. Defaulting blame to a politician is not an outcome that occurs when poorly informed voters "kick the government." It is, rather, a normatively defensible strategy to ensure that representatives pay attention to the policy work that is being done for them. In the end, representatives must either assign blame to policy workers themselves, and then do something about it, or shoulder the blame themselves. Second, unlike shark attacks or natural disasters, the government agencies, firms, and third-sector organizations that perform policy work are *sources* of information about what they are doing. Representatives ought to be monitoring what is going on in those organizations, even if they do so only when a policy event leads interested parties to sound "fire alarms" that compel representatives into action (McCubbins and Schwartz 1984).

Policy events are, in my view, not best conceived as random events as in the formal argument of Achen and Bartels (2017, 329–33), but, rather, processes about which information can be gleaned. An earthquake may come with only a few minutes of warning, but policy workers implement disaster preparedness procedures continuously, and the response to those disasters is also essential policy work. Monitoring is a good thing, I contend, because accountability is crucial to the point of public administration, and because managers and policy workers must internalize it as a value that makes democracy work (see Bertelli and Lynn 2006).

Achen and Bartels do have a response to the possibility that voters blame representatives not for an unpredictable event itself, but for the policy work done in response to it. They contend that "[i]f the voters learn in disasters what they had hitherto not suspected – namely that stronger government intervention in the economy is needed – then droughts ought to push electorates to the ideological left," but empirically they "reduce support for incumbents regardless of ideological commitments" (Achen and Bartels 2017, 136) My claim, by contrast, is that the default action of blaming politicians has the benefit of incentivizing monitoring, not choosing policies. In this way, it will improve accountability for policy work under the sanctioning, rather than under the selection view.

This kind of incentive is important regardless of the policy positions held by incumbents. Even representatives who are inclined to monitor policy work because of its substance are capable of a lapse or are forced to make trade-offs that do not reflect the priorities of citizens. And while it represents only a preliminary step, there is some evidence that citizens do employ the heuristics described above. Gregg Van Ryzin and I studied the effect of identifying a manager and providing information about program outcomes (evaluability) in a survey experiment with more than 1,100 randomly selected individuals in the United States (Bertelli and Van Ryzin 2020). We varied identifiability by randomly providing the position title of the responsible person in the federal government, and evaluability by randomly stating the outcome of a programmatic decision in a vignette. Representatives in Congress were associated with the program by stating that they had voted for it. Our results suggest that both identifiability and evaluability matter when citizens think about accountability. When the policy work was not evaluable, identifiability did not change the probability that a respondent would vote for the representative, and that probability was higher than when the policy work was evaluable. However, when work was evaluable, respondents' intention to vote for the incumbent was significantly lower when the manager was *not* identified. Without an identifiable policy worker, representatives shouldered our respondents' sanction when respondents could evaluate what was being done. That, I contend, is an incentive for representatives to monitor policy work.

BLAME AVOIDANCE STRATEGIES

If the accountability heuristics I postulate were to guide the voting behavior of citizens, then representatives, managers, and policy workers would be incentivized to blame avoidance. Table 2.1 displays how identifiability and evaluability regarding specific policy events can shape distinctive strategies of blame avoidance (Bertelli 2016, 11–3). These strategies – or, more appropriately, arguments made by representatives and managers – shape the information that citizens receive regarding a policy event.

The situation in the top left quadrant indicates policy work by an identifiable policy worker that can be evaluated by citizens, a regime of *retrospective answerability*. This regime is similar to the electoral accountability of an identifiable politician and prevails when an appointed public official is clearly connected to a straightforward policy event.

Suppose that local builder B signs a contract to design and construct an exterior ramp on the courthouse in county A after winning a competitive bid. One month after construction, a moderate rainstorm comes through the area and causes the ramp to become waterlogged because it was not

TABLE 2.1 *Accountability and the arguments of representatives*

	Strong identifiability	Weak identifiability
Strong evaluability	*Retrospective answerability* *Representatives*: Sanction the policy worker *Citizens*: Can identify and evaluate	*Source relocation* *Representatives*: Identify and sanction the policy worker *Citizens*: Can evaluate, but not identify
Weak evaluability	*Obfuscating information* *Representatives*: Monitoring, transparency *Citizen*: Can identify, but not evaluate	*Effective independence* *Representatives*: Institutional reorganization *Citizens*: Can neither identify nor evaluate

Adapted from Bertelli (2016, 12)

thoroughly sealed by B to professional standards. The ramp was closed, and the closure signs caught the eye of a reporter for the main newspaper in county A, who wrote a front-page story on the issue. In this scenario, county commissioners in A, who are identifiable as principals to that contract and share an electoral connection to county voters, are incentivized to move quickly to demand changes in the structure at no cost to the county. Responses like this combine elements of public administration scholar Christopher Hood's (2010, 201–2) strategies for presentation and spin in blame avoidance, but also lean toward scapegoating by identifying a policy worker, B, in the process (McGraw 1990, 1991).

Source relocation, which prevails in the top right quadrant, is a regime in which policy workers cannot be identified, but their work can be readily evaluated. Suppose that the construction at the courthouse in county A courthouse were more complicated, and the entire building underwent renovation. In this new scenario, builder B is one of a dozen subcontractors who work for a consortium C that managed the project. When the story broke that alleged shoddy construction, B and C were difficult to distinguish. Each tried to relocate the source of blame to the other for the work – B arguing that C insisted on excessive cost cutting in the process and C claiming that it was, after all, B that constructed the ramp. Of course, any one of the dozen builders can engage in this strategy, and they would not be likely to introduce arguments or evidence that justify the construction process and the choices made.

It is reasonable to expect that each builder would claim that another bore the blame for the policy event. This makes the strategy of the commissioners in county A more difficult as they cannot straightforwardly shift blame for the policy event ex post. The reason for this is the governance arrangement that included the consortium ex ante. This may have allowed C, B, and the eleven remaining builders to mitigate the risk of negative policy events, but it opens up the possibility of sanction for the commissioners if the voters in county A do not effectively identify a policy worker. Confronted with a host of policy workers to blame, commissioners would be expected to claim that B, or B and C together are identifiable, and move for contractual remedies against them in the hope that this will absolve the commissioners from the wrath of A's voters.

In the lower left quadrant, a regime in which identifiable policy workers whose policy work is difficult to evaluate by citizens have the incentive to present foggy arguments about the processes and outcomes of their work. Their tactic of providing *obfuscating information* does not have to be fully self-serving or understood in solely a negative light.

Returning to my example, suppose that C is one of six consortia in county A that managed large building projects and the other five consortia have faced difficulties in producing flawless projects. C's claims regarding the costs imposed by the county's byzantine rules surrounding public projects and difficult labor-management relations may be part of a genuine explanation of complexity of the event that made its way onto the front page of the local newspaper. While this representation is made in good faith, it does not alter the accountability consequences of obfuscating information.

When the strategy is successful, this kind of information complicates the commissioners' efforts to sanction C or B. It could give C more discretion if C's strategy effectively enhances its asymmetric information advantage over the commissioner (see Bertelli, 2012, 113–9). That is, C may enhance the perception of its expertise in managing construction projects, including one that led to the policy event. Moreover, C's reputation among the county's six consortia also provides information to the public, and C can use it as a gloss for processes and outcomes that lead to policy events (e.g., Carpenter 2000). In this way, reputations can enhance the citizens' difficulty in evaluating the policy work connected with a policy event. Because obfuscating information exacerbates the hidden action problem – an agent such as C or B can engage in actions that a principal such as the commissioners cannot observe – commissioners have the incentive to do more, and more extensive, monitoring of projects or increase the transparency of the processes policy work to allow other interested citizens to help with monitoring (see generally Bertelli 2012, 39–77). The consequence of poor monitoring technology in a regime of obfuscating information is that the commissioners face an increased risk that the voters of county A will sanction them at the ballot box.

When the lower right quadrant is reached, a policy worker is neither identifiable nor is her work evaluable. This regime of *effective independence* conjures an accountability failure in which the policy worker has incentives to act as though she is independent of public scrutiny and sanction. Various strategies are available to policy workers in the event that a policy event occurs and processes or outcomes are problematic for citizens. Either source relocation or obfuscating information is feasible here, as is a "rhetoric of defiance that either defends the action or reveals little information" (Bertelli 2016, 13). An example of this regime would occur if the projects that C and the five other consortia in county A were managing involved not observable construction, but, rather, environmental protection. Environmental impacts do not observe project or geographic boundaries, and each of the consortia could be to blame for a policy event that involved, say, the unanticipated degradation of a natural resource, weakening identifiability. At the same time, the technical nature of environmental science creates an impediment to the evaluation of C's policy work. In this regime, sanctioning a policy worker is very difficult for representatives, and the only thing that citizens can easily observe is their inability to do anything decisive in reaction to the policy event. Whatever the strategy, the incentive in this regime is for representatives to embark on changes to governance structures that will restore identifiability to policy workers.

CONCLUSION

This chapter begins my exploration of the essential values of representative government that policy workers and champions must consider. It has focused on the actor-relative values related to accountability. Three values are essential: the identifiability of representatives and policy workers; the evaluability of policy work; and the probability that policy events will lead to sanctioning by citizens. While elections are the vehicle for voters to hold their representatives accountable, treating representative government seriously requires that we understand that a vote cast in an election is a blunt and imprecise instrument of accountability. Write Przeworski, Stokes, and Manin, "[g]overnments make thousands of decisions that

Conclusion

affect individual welfare; citizens have only one instrument to control these decisions: the vote. One cannot control a thousand targets with one instrument" (1999, 50). What is more, they continue, citizens can use their votes for two purposes. First, "to obtain the best rulers" and, second, "to keep them virtuous"; in the end, "voters lose some control over the incumbent, [but] in exchange they elect a better government" (Przeworski, Stokes, and Manin 1999, 46).

The sanctioning view of electoral accountability places citizens in a position to retrospectively evaluate representatives. The extent to which this view obtains depends importantly on elites in political parties, who can ideologically position themselves in such a way that they provide an alternative to incumbents. Together with electoral institutions, such as majoritarianism or proportionality, these choices shape the accountability of incumbent representatives. Electoral accountability applies to the aims, rather than to the means of public policy, and conditional representation allows representatives to develop expertise in responding to the public through the interpretation of counterfactuals regarding what aims would have been expressed if some "shock" to the political economy, such as the coronavirus pandemic, had not occurred. Where policy work gets more specific, citizens can still use heuristics to hold representatives accountable for it, but they can make errors of identifiability and evaluability in the process. Overall, the mechanisms of electoral accountability are blunt, but essential to understanding how policy work can fit within systems of representative government.

Accountability values are not the only values important in representative government. Values incorporated in the process by which citizens select their representatives are essential for champions to consider as well. I turn to these procedure-relative values in Chapter 3. Once these process values are considered, I will consider the trade-offs between accountability and process values that champions explicitly or implicitly consider in the governance arrangements they envision and advocate.

Appendix: Data, Methods, and Detailed Results

The Issue Competition Comparative Project (ICCP) is a comparative international social science research project about party competition. Its data collection covers six Western European countries that held general elections in 2017–8, with country-specific analyses including Italy. The project surveyed 1,000 Italian voters using computer-assisted web interviewing. Policy issues were assessed by asking respondents to place themselves on a six-point, self-anchoring scale between two rival goals. After selecting one of the rival goals, respondents had to indicate which of the Italian parties competing in the upcoming election was deemed credible to achieve it. Thereafter, respondents were asked to report whether that goal was of high, medium, or low priority to them.

I used results from ICCP project in Italy to examine the extent to which the former Italian government under the *Partitio Democratico* (*PD*) was punished in terms of voting intention as a result of how citizens perceived the credibility of the *PD* on immigration issues and in regard to their own positions on immigration. The dependent variable, *government voting intention*, was drawn from a questionnaire item asking respondents to indicate which party they intended to vote for during the (then) upcoming 2018 Italian elections. I created a binary variable capturing intention to vote for the *PD* (coded as 1) and intentions to vote for another party (coded as 0).

The key theoretical predictors in my models are *voter preferences to accept refugees*, which assessed the citizens' own position on immigration. In the questionnaire, respondents were asked to respond on a six-point, self-anchoring scale, between "accept more refugees" (left) and "limit the number of refugees" (right). *Credibility of PD to enact preference* captures responses indicating which of the Italian parties competing in the

Appendix: Data, Methods, and Detailed Results

2018 election respondents believed to be most credible in achieving the response recorded in the voter preferences to accept the *Voter preferences to accept refugees* variable. Because the *PD* was a majority government, only its credibility was considered, resulting in a binary variable with respondents either believing the *PD* to be most credible in achieving their revealed attitudes to accept or limit the influx of refugees (1) or any other party but the *PD* (0).

To control for the influence of pocketbook (Fiorina 1978) and sociotropic attitudes (Kinder and Kiewiet 1981) on vote intention, *retrospective economic evaluation* asked respondents to evaluate the economic situation of their family during the year prior to the election on a five-point scale, ranging from "improved a lot (1)" to "worsened a lot (5)." Similarly, *prospective economic evaluation* asked respondents to evaluate the economic situation of Italy in the upcoming 12 months on a five-point scale ranging from will "improve[d] a lot (1)" to will "worsen[ed] a lot (5)."

As controls for the political leanings and engagement of respondents, additional variables were employed. *Government approval* was created using an item regarding government satisfaction in which respondents reported whether they approve (1) or disapprove or don't know about (both 0) the government's performance at the time of the survey. *Strong PD supporter* is a binary variable taking the value of 1 if the respondent strongly supports the PD and taking 0 otherwise. Strong support means that respondents indicated on one item that they felt politically closest to the PD, and classified themselves as a strong party supporter on another item. Specifically, only participants responding to the questionnaire item "Do you feel yourself to be very close to [the PD], fairly close or merely a sympathiser?" with "fairly close" or "very close" were included while respondents not feeling close to the PD or only classifying as a "mere sympathiser" were labeled "0." *Left-right self-placement* indicates the respondent's self-placement on a political left-right scale ranging from "left" (0) to "right" (10). *Interest in politics*, the self-reported extent to which the respondent is interested in politics. The scale ranges from "not at all interested" (1) to "very interested" (4).

Finally, a variety of demographic controls were included in the full models. *Age* of the respondent was calculated as the year of response (2018) minus the respondent's stated year of birth. *Female* gender was coded as 1 and male as 0 following the survey, which did not include nonbinary gender classifiers. *Standard of Living* asks respondents to place (approximately, considering all aspects) their family's standard of living on a 7-point Likert scale ranging from "poor family" (1) to

Accountability Values

TABLE 2.2 *Voter perceptions of incumbent credibility for reducing immigration and government vote intention, Italian general election, 2018*

	Base CLL	Base LPM	Full CLL	Full LPM
Voter preference to accept refugees	−0.030	0.000	−0.182**	−0.013**
	(0.055)	(0.007)	(0.078)	(0.006)
Credibility of PD to enact preference	2.464***	0.485***	1.458***	0.194***
	(0.209)	(0.042)	(0.316)	(0.042)
Retrospective economic evaluation			−0.643***	−0.017
			(0.193)	(0.011)
Prospective economic evaluation			0.526**	0.012
			(0.208)	(0.011)
Government approval (=1)			2.009***	0.239***
			(0.275)	(0.035)
Strong PD supporter (=1)			2.403***	0.538***
			(0.296)	(0.049)
Left-right self-placement			−0.131***	−0.009***
			(0.051)	(0.003)
Interest in politics			−0.302**	−0.016
			(0.152)	(0.010)
Age			0.010	0.001**
			(0.007)	(0.001)
Female (=1)			0.535**	0.026
			(0.229)	(0.016)
Standard of living			0.116	0.007
			(0.143)	(0.008)
Church attendance			0.099	0.009
			(0.079)	(0.005)
Upper- and post-secondary (=1)†			0.281	0.004
			(0.320)	(0.019)
Tertiary education (=1)†			0.582	0.027
			(0.355)	(0.024)
Small or mid-size town (=1) ††			−0.533	−0.036
			(0.325)	(0.025)
Suburbs of large city (=1) ††			−0.805*	−0.050
			(0.485)	(0.030)
Large city (=1) ††			−0.486	−0.042
			(0.403)	(0.029)
Constant	−2.456***	0.082***	−2.883**	0.058
	(0.232)	(0.027)	(1.214)	(0.074)
N	985	992	976	983
AIC	679.862	527.889	428.830	17.147

Complementary log-log (CLL) and linear probability models (LPM) presented. Robust standard errors appear in parentheses. Reference group for education level (†) is less than primary or lower-secondary school, and for urban-rural (††) rural area or village. Significance: * p < 0.10, ** p < 0.05, *** p < 0.01.
Source: De Sio et al. (2019)

Appendix: Data, Methods, and Detailed Results

"rich family" (7). *Church attendance* records the frequency of the respondents' church visits (excluding special occasions such as marriages or funerals) on an ordinal scale ranging from "more than once a week" (1) to "never" (6). The education variables I employed were created by splitting the education variable in the survey, which asks respondents to indicate their highest educational attainment into two categories – *upper- and post-secondary* and *tertiary education* – leaving *less than primary, primary, and lower* as the reference category. Similarly, the population controls are indicators for *small- or mid-size town, suburbs of large city,* and *large city* that I created from the "town size" variable in the ICCP survey, leaving *rural area or a little village* as the reference category.

To analyze the influence of policy attitudes about incumbent credibility for reducing immigration on government vote intention, I used complementary log-log (CLL) and linear probability models (LPM). The dependent variable is binary; the PD was unpopular in government, with just 15 percent of respondents indicating intention to vote for the PD. With such rare events, the CLL is more appropriate than, for instance, logistic regression because the model allows the conditional probability of vote intention to increases more slowly at lower values (Long 1997, 51–2).

All models include an indicator for which of the twenty *regions* of Italy the respective respondent lived in at the time of the survey to control for unobservable attributes at the regional level. LPM models with robust standard errors are also estimated for comparison because the within-region effects they estimate are "true" fixed effects unlike those in the CLL models. Full models include all control variables, while the base models incorporate only the theorized preference and credibility measures. All results appear in Table 2.2, while the Full CLL is the preferred specification discussed above in this chapter.

3

Process Values

Accountability values cleave to actors. They concern the relationship between citizens, on the one hand, and representatives, policy workers, and managers, on the other hand. Democratic theory is concerned with another set of values that are essential to consider in connection with governance structures. These values concern the process of aggregating the expressed preferences or priorities of citizens. They relate to procedures and define the medium for collective expression that gives representative government its claim to democratic character.

Process values are crucial for theories arguing that democracy is legitimated by the manner in which it is conducted (see e.g., Saffon and Urbinati 2013, 461–2). In this chapter, my use of the term "process" relates to the democratic process, that is, the way individual preferences and judgments are aggregated into a collective decision. These values should not be confused with those of procedural justice, such as fairness and equity, which are certainly important to understanding policy work. Surely much of the policy work done by street-level bureaucrats concerns procedural equity or equality given the applicable law. However, my focus here is on the values inherent in the political process through which citizens construct their representative government.

While there are a variety of approaches that one may take to an argument about the essential process values for public administration, mine is based on the findings of social choice theory, and in particular, on the lessons of what are known as impossibility theorems. Presented in this way, the values that I discuss will not all be achievable through the same *collective decision mechanism*, by which, I mean a voting rule such as majority rule or a Borda count. The trade-offs these values

Process Values 59

present to designers of those collective decision mechanisms that form the basis for citizens' input into representative government are crucial for champions of governance structures. I claim that champions must make these trade-offs plain when offering their arguments about how public administration might best be conducted.

The impossibility theorems of social choice stand as a challenge to champions of institutional designs at many levels, from states to study groups. Some deal with the quality of collective *judgments*. The Condorcet jury theorem, for instance, holds that for a group making a judgment for which there is some correct answer, where each member is more likely than not to choose the correct alternative, the chance of a correct decision by the group is better than by any individual member and gets better as the number of members increases (see Austen-Smith and Banks 1996). Others deal with the *outcomes* of collective decision mechanisms, such as majoritarianism. Correct decisions and majority preferences are, it must be emphasized, not the same thing. Concerning the latter, Nobel laureate Kenneth Arrow's impossibility theorem submits that any determinate social choice depends not only on the preferences of each individual in the social group but also on the mechanism through which we aggregate those preferences (see Sen 1970). Still others are concerned with the *manipulability* of voting mechanisms as a way of aggregating the preferences of individuals into a collective decision. The Gibbard–Satterthwaite theorem relates the lack of immunity of a collective decision mechanism to strategic voting, meaning that sincerely expressing a preference may not be the best way to achieve it (Gibbard 1973; Satterthwaite 1975). Estimates show that strategic voting in countries with representative governments is ubiquitous (Herrmann, Munzert, and Selb 2016; Kawai and Watanabe 2013). No prospect of a perfect way of aggregating the preferences of citizens emerges from these arguments.

Such insights led the political scientist William Riker, in his influential book *Liberalism against Populism*, to paint the bleak picture that these impossibility results make the reflection of citizens' will through representative government a fool's errand, even when there is a consensus that some collective decision mechanism, like majority voting, is clearly the best (Riker 1982). The political theorist's parry is that these impossibility theorems are, at best, not very relevant to understanding democracy. For instance, Gerry Mackie (2003) contends that the criteria – what I have been calling values – for preference aggregation in social choice theory are not necessarily desirable properties for voting mechanisms to embrace, and that alternatives exist. Moreover, Mackie relies on empirical evidence that the cycling that supports Riker's dismal view is not that frequent. An outcome capturing the will of a majority can exist, continues his possibility argument, and can even be revealed by many extant voting mechanisms. Recently, formal political theorists John Patty and Elizabeth Maggie Penn (2014), steeped in the social choice tradition, have claimed that arguments for the legitimacy of collective decision mechanisms must be about the trade-offs inherent in choosing one over the other precisely because different mechanisms will yield different outcomes for the same array of citizen preferences and priorities.

On this point, I agree with Patty and Penn. Trade-offs in these values are the centerpiece of my argument in the following chapters *because* they are inevitable. Still, the array of values and the way that they are considered in social choice theory can fly quickly above one's head. Bringing them back down to earth is not particularly helpful to the champion because it raises the possibility that Mackie's argument holds, at least as a practical matter. That is, if the values social choice theorists believe require trade-offs are not that relevant to democracy, urging that they be considered is likely to fall on the deaf ears of representatives and managers.

To address this critique, I engage the elegant argument of the political theorist Christian List (2011) that the criteria that social choice theory considers can be boiled down to just three essential values for a collective decision mechanism to subsume, or, more to the point, *not* to subsume. List (2011) provides a synthesis of the implications of impossibility theorems in social choice that is as provocative as it is useful for my present purposes. He contends that designers of collective decision mechanisms face a "democratic trilemma" in that they cannot create a system that, at once, maintains three core procedure-relative values (264).

These process values are crucial to understanding democracy administered and how it can reinforce the values of representative government. After presenting them, I provide some survey evidence of which accountability and process values European voters say are important to them and how their perceptions of those values in practice color their views of the democracies in place in their nations. This will conclude my presentation of the values I contend are important in the trade-offs made when creating governance structures. The stage will then be set to consider those trade-offs in concept and in practice.

PLURALISM

The first process value I consider is *pluralism*. This value is essentially about social coexistence, the idea that groups with cohesive interests be allowed to compete in political life for the ability to set a policymaking agenda for government. The form of pluralism at work maintains that these groups have some capacity to effectuate self-government (cf. Dahl 1956; Truman 1951). Following Christiano's (1996) argument about directed representation that I employed in Chapter 2, this power molds the content of the policymaking agenda and forms the basis of democratic input into government. The means for turning this agenda of social, economic, and other policy priorities into action rests in the hands of the government. In the notion of conditional representation (Bertelli and John 2013) discussed in Chapter 2, representatives can use their expertise to reason counterfactually, determining which priorities citizens would want if they could know as much about the state of the world as their representatives.

Because of the distinctive interests among the groups as well as their various resources for exercising political power – money, organization, religion – pluralists of this stripe take a particular view of majorities. That is, majorities are collections of minorities, and electoral institutions must preserve competition among these minorities on a regular schedule to prevent authoritarianism, dictatorship, and other forms of nondemocracy (Dahl 1956, 1971). For pluralism to be maintained, a collective decision mechanism must be designed such that "no combinations of individual attitudes must be ruled out in advance as admissible inputs to the decision procedure, so long as they satisfy some minimal constraints of formal rationality" (List 2011, 273).

Relaxing pluralism as a value in collective choice may be appropriate, List (2011) contends, when a "metaconsensus" exists among citizens or groups of citizens. This, he argues, need not be consensus" on what the right attitudes are, but on what the disagreement is about" (281).

Positive political theorists have long contended that this is possible when policy positions can be arrayed along a one-dimensional, left-right ideological ordering and a condition called "single-peakedness" adheres. Consider a collection of groups in the environmental policy space where a "left" position would place strong restrictions on pollution and other activities that harm the environment regardless of their cost to businesses and citizens, and a "right" position endorses restrictions only when their cost is low enough not to disturb the way businesses and citizens currently behave. Single-peakedness implies that a leftist in this space has an ideal package of restrictions in mind, and she dislikes policies more as they *exclude* restrictions. Correspondingly, a rightist has greater disdain for policies as they *include* more disruptive decisions. In this way, a collective decision rule such as a majority vote can collect minorities along the continuum around a compromise decision, and if these more or less leftists and rightists are distributed in society in a single-peaked distribution – a bell curve that may be skewed toward the left or right – the median position on the distribution will achieve majority support (see e.g., Bertelli 2012, 91–4).

Under what conditions does the claim of metaconsensus make sense? List (2011, 282) claims that one approach is to take "a certain level of cohesion or attitudinal homogeneity ... to be a precondition for democratic decision-making. The key idea is that democracy cannot get off the ground unless pluralism in the relevant group or society is sufficiently limited" (282). In this situation, the cohesiveness is *exogenous* to the political process and can be the product of shared community values that reduces the dimensionality of political decision-making.

The metaconsensus can also have its origins within, or *endogenous* to, the political process, and political scientists have addressed mechanisms for this rigorously and often. As List (2011, 283) puts it, the metaconsensus can be an "outcome of certain structuration processes within the democratic system." In the context of accountability, the importance of bipolarity in party competition was considered as a means of achieving metaconsensus "on what the disagreement is about" (List 2011, 281). Party system bipolarity means that elites give the people a choice of the government or an opposition policy program endogenously as they compete for votes. Indeed, this is precisely what a committee of scholars recommended in 1950 in their report for the American Political Science Association titled "Toward a More Responsible Two-Party System" (APSA Committee on Political Parties 1950). In a party system arrayed on one dimension of conflict, from left to right, electoral accountability is only concerned whether one party locates at the median, or whether there is a contest between mutually exclusive parties, or blocs of parties (Kam, Bertelli, and Held 2020; Sartori 1976). What is important to observe is that the boost to accountability provided by more bipolarity comes at the expense of pluralism through clarifying the nature of the disagreement among societal interests. This is an essential trade-off.

More broadly, two important contemporary arguments in democratic theory address the possibility of endogenous metaconsensus at the mass

Pluralism 63

public level. I will discuss these claims about epistemic and deliberative democracy in turn because versions of them are central to the claims of champions in regard to governance structures.

Epistemic Arguments

Epistemic theories of democracy contend that the legitimacy of a democratic process depends on its propensity to produce outcomes that are objectively "correct" as judged against some moral standard. (Estlund 2008, 99). The political philosopher David Estlund contends (2008, 33, emphasis added) that democratic procedures are valid if they create a situation in which "[n]o one has authority or legitimate coercive power over another without a justification that *could be accepted by all qualified points of view*," for instance, citizens on a matter of general importance or food scientists about the regulation of the packaging of spinach.

Note the connection between this and List's requirement for a collective decision mechanism to be robust to pluralism: If they are minimally rational, "no combinations of individual attitudes must be ruled out in advance as admissible inputs to the decision procedure" (List 2011, 273). When pluralistic points of view are included in the mechanism ex ante, the democratic process can endogenously produce results that are normatively and, crucially, *objectively* right. Universal suffrage, for instance, satisfies this condition more easily than rules that grant more restrictive access to collective decision mechanisms. Writes Estlund (2008, 219), "[u]nequal suffrage introduces an element of rule of some by others that is not present under equal suffrage, and so equal suffrage has a kind of default status." The point of epistemic arguments that connects them to endogenous metaconsensus is precisely that procedures are judged against their ability to improve over random choices of positions in making morally correct decisions.

A common critique of epistemic accounts of democracy is that it is not clear what is *distinctly* democratic in their construction. For instance, "[i]n a diverse community, there is bound to be little agreement about whether a decision is legitimate, since there will be little agreement about whether it meets [some] independent standard" (Estlund 2008, 99). If there is no accepted, independent standard of correctness for the problems – like determining just action – that are submitted to democracy, then "we might not have any way of knowing whether we had reached it," writes the political theorist Melissa Schwartzberg (2015, 198). And if finding the correct answer is how epistemic democracy is defined, "we must infer that when democracy fails to accomplish these ends it loses its rightful claim to authority" (199). Indeed, Schwartzberg continues, a "full-blown epistemic model relies on the claim that there is some correct decision waiting to be enacted by the collectively wise body of citizens by bringing their necessarily partial and incomplete judgments to bear through well-designed mechanisms." This is all called into question when citizens do not see the same outcome as correct, when the mechanisms for determining the correct outcome have biases that are not well understood, or when the mechanism appropriate for finding a particular correct outcome is not clear (199). If the foregoing conditions fail, citizens may only be left with procedural fairness, which is hardly an epistemic democracy (200). In one response, political theorists such as Schwartzberg (2014), Robert Dahl (1989), or Christiano (1996) relax the outcome orientation of other epistemic claims and contend that legitimately democratic decisions come from procedures that allow citizens to offer their judgments in a way that treats them equally. While others have responded to the challenge, the crucial point is that the characteristics of decision mechanisms play an important role in epistemic thinking.

Deliberative Arguments

Deliberative theories of democracy also aim toward legitimating law and policy, and given the critique just discussed, political theorists often endorse both a deliberative *and* an epistemic conception of democracy (e.g., Landemore 2013; Landemore and Page 2014). Yet for deliberative democrats, the criterion for judging outcomes need not necessarily be "correctness" in the sense of epistemic arguments (but see Nino 1996). Writes Bohman, "[t]he alternative to a substantive consensus is typically procedural, since a procedural conception of justification can support both the moral and epistemic improvement of democratic deliberation while allowing for pluralism about conceptions of the good life" (Bohman 1998, 402). The principal distinction between aggregation and deliberation in democratic decision-making is that "[t]he more public deliberation meets standards of public-spiritedness, reciprocity, mutual respect, and so on, the more participants in such deliberation are subject to the force of the better argument" (Lafont 2015, 45). Like epistemic claims, deliberative postulates have implications for the outcomes of policy work. When the citizens doing the deliberating are "informed, impartial,

Pluralism 65

mutually respectful, [and] open to counterarguments," the policies they endorse will improve on objective criteria as well (46).

Yet the feasibility of deliberative democracy in practice has led to difficulties in endorsing procedures aiming to maintain a kind of pluralism of the included. That is, when *mini-publics* – small groups of citizens that are more (a randomly selected group) or less (parents of local elementary school students) representative – are used to shape public policies, a consensus may be achieved through a deliberative process, but at the cost of legitimating the policies they produce. The political scientist James Fishkin (2011) exemplifies such a view when stating that "a democratic theory is all the more useful the *less* it requires to work on achieving several normative aims at once" (199, emphasis added). Fishkin advances a view of deliberation that is "explicitly affirming political equality and deliberation but *agnostic* about participation" (191, emphasis added). Deliberation, then, can lead to a metaconsensus, but one that prevails among participants.

The philosopher Cristina Lafont (2015, 2019) identifies problems of legitimacy and accountability in arguments for trusting the decisions of mini-publics to become public policy. Suppose that a mini-public were formed by stratified random sampling from the population, which is the strategy in Fishkin's (2011) deliberative polling. Further suppose, as problematic as it is to connect views and descriptive traits, that stratified random sampling on categories such as gender, ethnic background, and socioeconomic status is sufficient to select a group of individuals who represent the voices of the mass public. The claim to representation only holds *before* any deliberation takes place. The legitimation problem, writes Lafont (2015, 50), arises because "the efficient intervention of the deliberative filter ... makes the participants, at the end of the experience, no longer a representative sample of the citizenry at large." She continues, "[p]recisely because they have not participated in the deliberative process of becoming informed, weighing the evidence, testing their arguments in light of the counterarguments of opponents, and so on, nonparticipants have no specific reason or justification to endorse the recommendations" of the mini-public (50). As a consequence, the mini-public lacks legitimacy because it fails to permit "citizens to endorse the laws and policies to which they are subject as their own" (45).

For present purposes, it is crucial that the endogenous metaconsensus formed need not be a metaconsensus among the citizenry writ large, and this relaxes pluralism. Read in the light of Chapter 2, an *accountability* gap also results from this legitimacy problem. Because "citizens would delegate decision-making to participants in mini-publics merely because they are convinced that the latter are reliable indicators of their own considered judgments," it follows that "no space is left over for the former to hold the latter to account for their specific decisions any more than one can hold a thermostat to account for the specific temperature that it reliably indicates" (Lafont 2015, 53).

MAJORITARIANISM

The second value that a collective decision mechanism can embrace is a basic form of majoritarianism. List (2011, 273) defines this as the adoption of majority acceptance of a proposal as a necessary condition to its collective assent. In this basic form, the majority need not be sufficient to achieve collective assent, yet in so many arguments it has been considered in this stronger, sufficient manner. Indeed, Dahl (1956, 36–7) is redolent of the reach of majoritarianism in democratic thinking when he states that "the proposition that majorities should have unlimited sovereignty" is so common in political theory "that I shall not attribute the argument to any specified theorist at all."

Two conditions must be satisfied for a collective decision mechanism to be democratic. First, "whenever policy choices are perceived to exist, the alternative selected and enforced as governmental policy is the alternative most preferred." Second, "control over governmental decisions is so shared that, whenever policy alternatives are perceived to exist, in the choice of the alternative to be enforced as government policy, the preference of each member is assigned an equal value" (Dahl 1956, 37). To satisfy these criteria, majoritarianism stipulates that "the alternative preferred by the greater number is selected" (37–8). Put succinctly, to achieve rule by the people in a way that everyone votes with equal weight, a collective decision mechanism must bring forth the policy preferred by the majority against all alternative policies.

While majoritarianism is so well known as to need little explanation, the means by which a collective decision mechanism might temper it deserve more attention. Relaxing the basic sense of majoritarianism that List (2011, 284, emphasis added) conjures means that the majority can be "overruled on *some* problems on the agenda." We are all quite familiar with exogenous restrictions on majority positions, such as the enforcement of the inalienable rights of minorities to protect them against majorities.

Majoritarianism 67

Think back to the *Sea-Watch 3* example in Chapter 2. Article 14 of the Universal Declaration on Human Rights states that "[e]veryone has the right to seek and to enjoy in other countries asylum from persecution" unless those claims arise "from non-political crimes or from acts contrary to the purposes and principles of the United Nations" (United Nations 1948). Likewise, Article 10 of the Constitution of the Italian Republic states that "[a] foreigner who, in his home country, is denied the actual exercise of the democratic freedoms guaranteed by the Italian constitution shall be entitled to the right of asylum under the conditions established by law" (Senate of the Republic 1947). The policy event surrounding the landing of the *Sea-Watch 3* concerned the ability to exercise this right, which did not arise out of the democratic political process that produced the coalition government in place at the time.

Institutions that relax basic majoritarianism also exist. One example of a collective decision mechanism that does so is the Borda count, which assigns points for alternatives in the order of a voter's preferences over them. Thus, for an agenda of N alternatives (candidates, policies), a voter's favorite alternative receives N points, her next most preferred $N - 1$ points all the way down to her Nth choice, which receives 1 point. Points are aggregated across all ballots and voters and the alternative with the most points is chosen. The Borda count has the advantage of obviating the cycles associated with majority rule at the cost of choosing an alternative that need not be majoritarian and, more importantly, of strategic voting and truncating lists of alternatives on a ballot (cf. Dummett 1998; Emerson 2013). The latter concern led the economist Duncan Black (1976, 15) to warn that "even to the unsophisticated voter, the Borda count is an invitation to strategic voting." What is more, because "the scores attributed to each preference depend on the number of contestants, political strategists may field 'dummy' or 'red herring' candidates in an effort to manipulate outcomes" (Fraenkel and Grofman 2014, 189).

The manipulation problem has limited the spread of the Borda count in practice, but it is used in Slovenia for ethnic Hungarians and Italians to elect two of the ninety members of the national legislature. According to an expert on elections quoted by Fraenkel and Grofman (2014, 188), the impetus for the system was the existence of opposing interests within the Italian and Hungarian minority populations: "If plurality or majority system [sic] were used, these groups would confront each other and one would win over the other. With Borda, usually the winner is the person who is most acceptable to all and who is not an extremist." Moderation

68 *Process Values*

seems particularly important given the overrepresentation of these minority groups. Each member of the Slovenian parliament has approximately 20,000 electors, though the minority Hungarian representative has 6,000 and the minority Italian representative only 2,000 (Toplak 2006, 826–7). What is more, the minority group members also have a *second* vote for one of the eighty-eight remaining members of the legislature (Toplak 2006, 827). Moreover, these two nonmajoritarian representatives have been pivotal. For instance, the 1996 election gave a bloc of right-leaning parties a majority of seats (forty-five of the eighty-eight), but both nonmajoritarian representatives were affiliated with left parties, and, as a consequence, a right-leaning government failed to materialize (Toplak 2006, 827). The Borda mechanism in Slovenia does not require all of the candidates to be ranked on the ballot, and the number of ballots that list only one candidate is so large that it has led Hungarian representatives to encourage a change in the electoral formula (Fraenkel and Grofman 2014, 196).

Nonmajoritarian electoral rules are certainly not concentrated in Slovenia. A wide range of peaceful governments worldwide employs various examples of these institutions (see generally, Lublin 2015).

Finally, List (2011) reckons with another endogenous restriction on majoritarianism that is based on a reflective equilibrium, defined by the philosopher John Rawls (1971, 48, emphasis added) as a "state ... reached *after* a person has weighed various proposed conceptions and he has *either revised* his judgments to accord with one of them *or held fast* to his initial convictions (and the corresponding conception)." The version of reflective equilibrium envisioned by List (2011, 285) "may begin by taking the majority attitudes on all propositions as its provisional attitudes and then identify the most plausible – perhaps the least invasive – way to revise them to achieve overall coherence." Majoritarianism in such a mechanism is only a starting point for collective decisions.

COLLECTIVE RATIONALITY

The final value in the democratic trilemma is *collective rationality*. For this value to be incorporated, a collective decision mechanism must be able to deliver "what may count as a full solution to any problem brought to it" (List 2011, 274; see also List and Pettit 2011). It has two components. *Consistency* requires that the decisions produced are not contradictory, and this includes the intransitivities in the impossibility results discussed above (List 2011, 266). *Completeness* mandates that the

Collective Rationality 69

collective decision mechanism must form a judgment when issues are introduced; that is, it cannot produce a *non*decision.

One exogenous means of relaxing the completeness component – and therefore collective rationality – requires partitioning the decision-making agenda into items that require a decision and those that do not, taking a majority vote only on the former (List 2011, 287). In the reality of legislative decision-making, institutions are created to address such problems. The political scientist Kenneth Shepsle recognized this practical deficiency in social choice results decades ago: "[t]he theorems of majority rule typically begin with an undifferentiated set N of decision makers. A central feature of all legislatures, however, is differentiation. [The United States Congress] is more accurately described not by N but rather by a family of subsets of N (committees), with each agent in N a member of at least one such subset" (Shepsle 1985, 11).

The relationship between congressional committees and the floor has been considered carefully as an agency problem. In developing a formal approach to the power of committees over a legislative majority, the political scientist Keith Krehbiel distinguishes the distributional power of committees "to get a majority to do what *is not* in the majority's interest with respect to a single issue" from the informational power used when a committee "credibly transmits private information to get a majority to do what *is* in the majority's interest" (1991, 76, emphasis added) Such authority is exercised by partitioning the decision agenda and applying majority rule in both the committee and floor *before* the policies adopted pass to a nonmajoritarian bureaucracy for implementation, further partitioning the choices involved (see Bertelli 2012, 78–120 for a general treatment; for specific arguments, see e.g., Epstein and O'Halloran 1999; Huber and Shipan 2002).

Because delegating the authority to make policy equips one governance structure that I consider in Chapter 4 – namely, bureaucracy – I will discuss this in more detail momentarily. At this point, however, it is vital to intuitively grasp the kinds of relationships presented in Figure 3.1.

On the left side is committee delegation. Representatives, who choose by majority rule, delegate authority to a group of their own membership to address a particular issue. For instance, on January 3, 2019, the Committee on Science, Space and Technology of the US House of Representatives issued a report on a Senate bill it was delegated the *authority* to study further and to make recommendations. The bill (S. 141) was designed to "to direct the establishment of a national framework to address current and future space weather challenges and

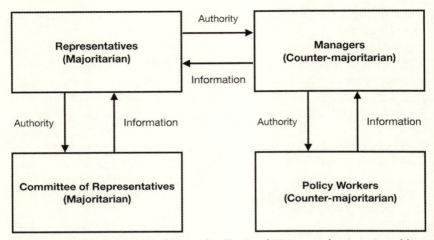

FIGURE 3.1 Agency relationships and collective decision mechanisms in public policymaking

needs, to coordinate efforts to monitor, prepare for, avoid, mitigate, and respond to space weather events, and to improve the lead time, accuracy, coverage, and timeliness of space weather forecasts" (Committee on Science, Space, and Technology 2019, 7).

To collect *information*, the committee "[o]ver the past six years ... held two hearings and one markup relevant to this bill" (Committee on Science, Space, and Technology 2019, 7). The committee ultimately commended the bill, with some changes from the Senate version, to the House floor for approval. One amendment proposed by Representative Edwin Pearlmutter (D-Colorado), which was approved via unanimous voice vote, "elevates the National Space Council to coordinate federal agency responsibilities and implementation of space weather research and forecasting and encourages involvement with the academic community and commercial sector" (10). An amendment to substitute another bill and end consideration of the Senate version introduced by Representative Eddie Bernice Johnson (D-Texas) was majority defeated by a roll-call vote of 13–19 (10). The report provides cost estimates for implementing the bill, stating that "enacting S. 141 would not increase net direct spending or on-budget deficits in any of the four consecutive 10-year periods beginning in 2029" (15).

The right side of Figure 3.1 represents the familiar scenarios described in Chapter 1. Representatives formally grant authority to managers to implement a legislated policy goal, and these managers, in turn, delegate some of that authority to policy workers inside or outside of government.

The information rationale for delegation allows each of the agents (committee, manager and policy worker) to learn information that can reduce uncertainty about the state of the world (Bertelli 2012, 85), and this helps the principal (representative) do, as Krehbiel noted, "what *is* in the majority's interest" (Krehbiel 1991, 76). By contrast, this information can be used to move the majority "to do what *is not* in the majority's interest with respect to a single issue" (Krehbiel 1991, 76). Such informational and distributional power can be used in each of the agency relationships depicted. One key feature to note is that while representatives' delegations to committees do not abandon majoritarian collective decision mechanisms, as the vote on Representative Johnson's substitute amendment makes clear, this may not true once authority is passed into the hands of managers.

The consistency component of collective rationality can be endogenously relaxed as well, and doing this is useful for champions when designing governance structures. One way that List (2011) considers doing this is through what the legal scholar Cass Sunstein (1995) called the "incompletely theorized agreement." His definition of the concept is worth quoting at some length.

Participants in legal controversies try to produce incompletely theorized agreements on particular outcomes. They agree on the result and on relatively narrow or low-level explanations for it. They need not agree on fundamental principle. They do not offer larger or more abstract explanations than are necessary to decide the case. When they disagree on an abstraction, they move to a level of greater particularity ... [For instance,] people may invoke many different foundations for their belief that the law should protect labor unions against certain kinds of employer coercion. Some may emphasize the potentially democratic character of unions; others may think that unions are necessary for industrial peace; others may believe that unions protect basic rights. (Sunstein 1995, 1735–6)

A trade-off thus arises in regard to collective rationality. The agenda for decision-making need not be partitioned as a means of relaxing completeness if a collective decision can be reached by allowing different explanations for the same choice. Relaxing one or the other of these criteria can influence the overall process value.

Table 3.1 summarizes the foregoing discussion. The process value listed in the leftmost column is defined and then connected with the strategies for relaxing the value I have described. In Chapter 4, I will show how governance structures embody these trade-offs through a series

Process Values

TABLE 3.1 *Process values*

The three values in List (2011) and the strategies for relaxing them to address the democratic trilemma

Value	Meaning	Strategies for Relaxing
Pluralism	Competition among cohesive groups	Metaconsensus; epistemic view of process; deliberation
Majoritarianism	Majority assent necessary for collective assent	Institutions such as Borda count; reflective equilibrium
Collective rationality	Achieve both consistency (noncontradiction) and completeness (avoid nondecision)	Partition agenda into obligatory and nonobligatory decisions; incompletely theorized agreements

of examples. But before doing so, I think it is important to consider some empirical information about how citizens view the importance of the values we have been discussing to their own conception of democracy. It may well be easier for champions to relax a value if it is not that important to citizens in relation to others.

WHAT DO CITIZENS WANT FROM THEIR DEMOCRACY?

In their empirical study of American voters' attitudes about democracy, political scientists John Hibbing and Elizabeth Thiess-Morse (2002) identify a deep distinction between the way that ordinary citizens and political elites, including representatives, see democracy in America. Elites, they find, "tend to believe that the ideal democracy is characterized by an excited commotion, with diverse ideas and new proposals being offered and tested in the stimulating crucible of public debate" (157). By contrast, citizens "believe that Americans generally agree on overall societal goals" and "are convinced there is a reasonable way of proceeding that can be divined by hard-working, unbiased, intelligent people" (156). Some ordinary Americans "are not eager for candidates to offer any proposals at all"; "[m]any others do not believe politics should entail a competition of ideas" and still more "are not convinced a legitimate opposition is central to good government" (157). In general, citizens' agreement on what they want from public policies precludes an interest in political debate, "since the best way to achieve those things will be readily

What Do Citizens Want from Their Democracy?

apparent to those who study the problems in an unbiased way, and since the little details of policy are not that important anyway" (157). Their views of the policymaking process make clear that they do not want "processes in which people who are making political decisions are able to feather their own nests" (158).

This portrait of mass attitudes toward the job of representatives diverges, intriguingly, from normative arguments insisting that the collective decision mechanism in a democracy *must* be a decision forum for the most significant societal disagreements (e.g., Saffon and Urbinati 2013). Hibbing and Thiess-Morse (2002, 152) identified an American voter who wants basic majoritarianism and collective rationality to be privileged over pluralism – "Americans generally agree on overall societal goals" – and doesn't want to be that actively involved in how those goals get met. Moreover, their political elites are reluctant to believe in relaxing pluralism and see the collective decision mechanism as much more active, a place in which representatives have some agency and in which collective rationality might be relaxed if their programs are put in place.

This is all the more striking given the views of American citizens about pluralism. Hibbing and Thiess-Morse report that while 70 percent of respondents did not believe that the representative government in place "does a good job of representing the interests of all Americans," their "displeasure with the current system ... tends not to spring from perceptions that minority views are going unheard but, rather, from perceptions that minority views are *dominating* the political scene" (Hibbing and Thiess-Morse 2002, 152, emphasis added). One of their focus group participants got at the heart of this perception, stating that "... the demonstrators come in front of the White House or wherever. They pitch their little thing and confuse the whole issue" making it difficult for representatives to achieve policy objectives (153). The argument in this book adopts Christiano's (1996) view that, through elections, citizens have the ability to choose social and policy aims and also the trade-offs that might be made among them by representatives in making laws and also in policy work. The citizens in these focus groups articulate an interest in effectuating the representation of the aims of the majority that won the last election.

The attitudes of citizens can change across time and place. A look at data from the 2016 European Social Survey shows a somewhat different kind of good democratic process in the minds of European citizens in twenty-nine countries. I statistically analyzed how *expectations gaps* in democratic values – the difference between the importance of a value to

Process Values

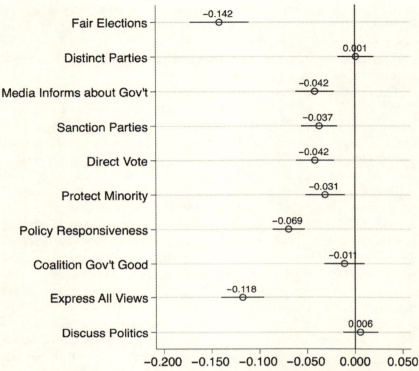

FIGURE 3.2 How expectations gaps for democratic values influence citizens' evaluation of their national democracies, Europe, 2016. Dependent variable: "How democratic do you think [your country] is overall?" Ordinary least squares regression coefficients represented by dots with 95 percent confidence intervals as dark horizontal lines. Estimates are within country and standard errors are clustered by region within each country.
Source: European Social Survey

citizens and the extent to which that value is achieved by their own representative governments – contribute to citizens' views of how "democratic" they perceive their countries to be. Full details of the analysis are provided in the appendix to this chapter, but an above-the-fold presentation of the key relationships appears in Figure 3.2. When expectations gaps grow in the values listed on the left, citizens perceive that their representative governments are less democratic, which manifests itself in statistically significant *negative* relationships when the horizontal uncertainty estimate bands do not cross the vertical line at zero.

Conclusion

75

The largest impacts are uncovered when citizens' expectations of fair elections and the expression of pluralistic views are not being met; that is, one accountability (probability of sanction) and one process value (pluralism) seem to be most important. Gaps in expectations about accountability appear to be captured mainly in the idea that policy should respond to citizens' wants (policy responsiveness) and that this should be checked through a functioning electoral mechanism (fair elections and the sanctioning of political parties), but the expectations gaps regarding distinctiveness of political party positions and coalition governments (identifiability) make no difference to citizens' assessments of democracy. The extent to which the media provides information about the government (evaluability) is consequential for citizens.

The process value of pluralism to the meaning of democracy is further supported by expectations about the extent to which minority interests are protected. Yet it would be difficult to interpret this as supporting the relaxation of majoritarianism in favor of pluralism given that the influence of expectations gaps regarding direct votes on policy issues is influential to citizens' views about functioning democracy, while the discussion of politics at the heart of deliberative claims is not.

CONCLUSION

Like the accountability values in the previous chapter, the three process values of collective decision mechanisms that I have discussed in this chapter, as well as the strategies for relaxing them summarized in Table 3.1, are important for understanding how public administration can reshape democracy. A conundrum arises because all pluralism, majoritarianism, and collective rationality cannot be simultaneously incorporated in a single collective decision mechanism. When champions must incorporate such a mechanism in their governance structures, this becomes their predicament as well, and this will be important throughout the remainder of the book.

Citizens have their own views about the importance of these values. My analysis of survey data reveals that European citizens may expect more from their systems than those systems can provide. Respondents systematically perceived less democracy in their country when their expectations about a wide range of accountability and process values were not met. And those they don't observe, as in connection with the bipolarity of their party systems or coalition governments, are consequential to accountability. Nonetheless, these citizens do clearly expect that their countries can do better in making elections fair, fostering pluralism, and making responsive policies. The expectations gaps of citizens and their influence on how well they think that democracy is working are useful to keep in mind in Chapter 4. Specifically, relationships like those depicted in Figure 3.1 can create opportunities for champions to use governance structures in a way that helps representative government to meet the expectations of their citizens.

The way in which trade-offs among accountability and process values are made must be well conceived and argued, of course. To understand those arguments more clearly, I change my focus from describing particular values of representative government to developing a framework for understanding how they are made manifest in governance structures. This shift will give the champion the leading role among my characters in Chapter 4, and the value trade-offs champions make will be exemplified in a variety of settings.

Appendix: Data, Methods, and Detailed Results

The European Social Survey (ESS) conducts face-to-face interviews with cross-sectional samples from the mass public. It is administered every two years with newly selected participants mapping attitudes, behavior patterns, and beliefs of the European populations. Table 3.3 shows the countries covered and the number of respondents from each in the estimation sample. The questionnaire from the ESS in 2012 (sixth round) consists of a core module, designed to collect time-series data on changing attitudes and values across Europe (including items measuring topics of enduring interest to the social sciences and socio-structural variables), and a rotating module. Items in the rotating module vary on a yearly basis and are selected following an open call for proposals where researchers may apply for new modules or request the repetition of old ones.

In 2012, the rotating module included questions on the "understanding and evaluation of different elements of democracy" (Rotating module Q#: E1–E45). Participants were asked about "how democracy is working in general." Respondents indicated their perceived importance of specific features of democracy in general (including items on fair elections, party distinctiveness, etc.) on a ten-point scale ranging from 0 ("not at all important for democracy in general") to 10 ("extremely important for democracy in general"). Subsequent questions asked respondents about the way they "think democracy is working in [their country] today" in regard to each item on a ten-point scale ranging from 0 ("does not apply at all") to 10 ("applies completely").

I used responses to these questions to examine how *expectations gaps* for democratic values influence citizens' evaluation of their national

Process Values

TABLE 3.2 *Components of expectations gaps, European Social Survey, 2012*

Value	Evaluation	Importance	Mean	SD
Fair elections	"How important do you think it is for democracy in general that national elections are free and fair?"	"national elections in [your country] are free and fair"	1.72	2.86
Distinct parties	"How important do you think it is for democracy in general that different political parties offer clear alternatives to one another?"	"different political parties in [your country] offer clear alternatives to one another"	2.21	3.08
Media informs about gov't	"How important do you think it is for democracy in general that the media provides citizens with reliable information to judge the government?"	"the media in [your country] provide citizens with reliable information to judge the government"	2.76	2.79
Sanction parties	"How important do you think it is for democracy in general that governing parties are punished in elections when they have done a bad job?"	"governing parties in [your country] are punished in elections when they have done a bad job"	2.75	3.43
Direct vote	"How important do you think it is for democracy in general that citizens have the final say on the most important political issues by voting on them directly in referendums?"	"citizens in [your country] have the final say on the most important political issues by voting on them directly in referendums"	3.37	3.47
Protect minority	"How important do you think it is for democracy in general that the rights of minority groups are protected?"	"the rights of minority groups in [your country] are protected"	2.24	2.96

Appendix: Data, Methods, and Detailed Results

Value	Evaluation	Importance	Mean	SD
Coalition gov't good	"How important do you think it is for democracy in general that the government is formed by two or more parties in coalition?"	"How often you think the government in [country] is formed by two or more parties in coalition?"	0.65	2.70
Policy responsiveness	"How important do you think it is for democracy in general that the government changes its planned policies in response to what most people think?"	"How often you think the government in [your country] today changes its planned policies in response to what most people think?"	3.78	3.02
Express all views	"How important do you think it is for democracy in general that everyone is free to express their political views openly, even if they are extreme?"	"To what extent do you think everyone in [your country] today is free to express their political views openly, even if they are extreme?"	1.55	2.55
Discuss politics	"How important do you think it is for democracy in general that voters discuss politics with people they know before deciding how to vote?"	"voters in [your country] discuss politics with people they know before deciding how to vote"	0.91	2.92

Expectations gaps are formed by subtracting evaluation from importance. N = 13,958.

democracies. Expectations gaps are the difference between the importance of a value to citizens and the extent to which the value is achieved by their representative government. Specifically, this is the difference between respondents' perceived importance of a specific feature of democracy in general and the extent to which they believe the respective feature to apply in their country.

The dependent variable *Citizens view of democratic perceptions in own country*, is drawn from a questionnaire item in the politics core module (B18e) asking respondents to indicate "how democratic do you think [your country] is overall?" on a ten-point scale ranging from 0 ("not at all democratic") to 10 ("completely democratic"). The main independent variables in my models are the ten expectations gaps, generated subtracting the respondents' evaluation of their representative government on the achievement of a specific democratic value from the importance they attach in general to that same value.

To control for respondents' political leanings and engagement, their *Left-right ideology* is a self-placement from 0 ("left") to 10 ("right"). As there was no binary classifier capturing a self-reported vote cast in the last national election, I generated one using the values of 1 (respondent voted) and 0 (respondent did not vote). Moreover, I included demographic controls in my models, including the gender of the respondent coded as 0 ("female") and 1 ("male"), age, and finally, the years of full-time education completed ("about how many years of education have you completed, whether full-time or part-time?" – reported as full-time equivalents and including compulsory years of schooling).

Because the dependent variable is a ten-point response scale, I estimate two types of models. Linear probability models include country-level fixed effects with standard errors clustered on the respondent's region.

TABLE 3.3 *Country coverage, European Social Survey, 2012*

Country	N. Respondents	Country	N. Respondents
Albania	299	Ireland	584
Belgium	740	Israel	625
Bulgaria	329	Iceland	280
Switzerland	740	Kosovo	154
Cyprus	209	Italy	234
Czech Republic	296	Lithuania	445
Germany	1,239	Netherlands	663
Denmark	535	Norway	443
Estonia	742	Poland	508
Spain	594	Portugal	234
Finland	980	Russia	438
France	756	Sweden	509
United Kingdom	254	Slovenia	199
Hungary	315	Slovakia	335
		Ukraine	279

Numbers of respondents listed for each of the countries are those in the estimation sample. N=13,958.

Appendix: Data, Methods, and Detailed Results

TABLE 3.4 *How expectations gaps for democratic values influence citizens' evaluation of their national democracies, European Social Survey, 2012*

	Linear probability models		Ordered probit models	
	Base	Full	Base	Full
Fair elections	−0.148***	−0.142***	−0.070***	−0.073***
	(0.017)	(0.016)	(0.010)	(0.009)
Distinct parties	0.020*	0.001	0.010*	−0.001
	(0.010)	(0.010)	(0.005)	(0.006)
Media informs	−0.029***	−0.042***	−0.015**	−0.022***
	(0.011)	(0.010)	(0.006)	(0.006)
Sanction parties	−0.040***	−0.037***	−0.022***	−0.022***
	(0.010)	(0.010)	(0.006)	(0.006)
Direct vote	−0.038***	−0.042***	−0.020***	−0.025***
	(0.011)	(0.010)	(0.006)	(0.006)
Protect minority	−0.023*	−0.031***	−0.013**	−0.019***
	(0.013)	(0.010)	(0.006)	(0.006)
Policy responsiveness	−0.059***	−0.069***	−0.028***	−0.037***
	(0.009)	(0.009)	(0.007)	(0.007)
Coalition gov't good	−0.010	−0.011	−0.003	−0.005
	(0.011)	(0.011)	(0.005)	(0.006)
Express all views	−0.133***	−0.118***	−0.066***	−0.063***
	(0.011)	(0.011)	(0.006)	(0.007)
Discuss politics	−0.004	0.006	−0.000	0.004
	(0.010)	(0.009)	(0.006)	(0.004)
Live in democracy		0.345***		0.203***
		(0.017)		(0.022)
Voted last election (=1)		0.012		−0.002
		(0.051)		(0.035)
Left-right ideology		0.084***		0.044***
		(0.017)		(0.012)
Age (years)		−0.006***		−0.003***
		(0.001)		(0.001)
Education (years)		0.014***		0.007*
		(0.006)		(0.004)
Female (=1)		−0.104***		−0.050*
		(0.037)		(0.026)
Constant	7.329***	4.175***		
	(0.054)	(0.196)		
Variance of country RE			0.146***	0.130***
			(0.038)	(0.032)
Variance of region RE			0.056***	0.047***
			(0.013)	(0.014)
Observations	15,081	13,958	15,081	13,958
AIC	62,898.633	55,976.454	60,482.466	53,732.509

Linear regression (LM) and random-effects ordered probit (OP) models presented, cutpoint estimates for OP models not reported. LP models include country-fixed effects with robust standard errors clustered on the region in parentheses. OP models report robust standard errors. Significance: * $p < 0.10$, ** $p < 0.05$, *** $p < 0.01$.

Ordered probit models are estimated with random effects at both the country and region level. Base models include only the expectations gaps, while full models include the control variables discussed above. The full ordered probit model on the far right of Table 3.4 is my preferred specification on the basis that it achieves the minimum Akaike Information Criterion (AIC).

4

Governance Structures and Democratic Values

The democratic values discussed in Chapters 2 and 3 provide a useful, if surely not exhaustive, guide to the potential influences that policy workers can have over democracy. In this chapter, my task is to illustrate how these values are represented in four basic governance structures in contemporary public administration. To be sure, these basic structures have many hybrid variants in practice, but understanding the value they capture illuminates much about the values of contemporary governance. With this structural emphasis, my focus shifts to champions, the institutional designers among the characters in this book. The architecture of their democratic influence comes in the form of governance structures, such as the rules and hierarchies of bureaucracy, or the mechanisms for consensus in participatory structures.

When champions propose structures, they make trade-offs across the democratic values that I have been discussing. In this chapter, I make two essential claims in this regard. First, these trade-offs are unavoidable, resulting in what I call the champion's dilemma. Between List's trilemma of process values in Chapter 3 and the relationship of these process values to the accountability values in Chapter 2, champions simply cannot respect the full measure of values in representative government. Second, as a technical matter, these trade-offs need not *necessarily* be consistent with the institutions of representative government in the jurisdiction they seek to reform. But if they are not, do they really allow policy workers to use what discretion they have to act responsibly? The importance of responsible policy work in the traditional narrative of public administration cannot be overstated: it is its fundamental problem.

84   *Governance Structures and Democratic Values*

After introducing these ideas and examining in this chapter what the democratic trade-offs in basic governance structures look like, the question of consistency between governance and political values becomes the subject of the rest of this book. I hypothesize and find some evidence of a positive correlation between governance and political values in Chapter 5. Whether there should be consistency of governance and political values is the crucial normative question that can link the champion's dilemma to the fundamental problem of public administration, and I take it up subsequently in Chapter 5.

THE CHAMPION'S DILEMMA

Taken together, the unavoidable nature of value trade-offs and the lack of a mandate for technical consistency admit a *champion's dilemma*: no choice of governance structure is neutral to democratic values and must enhance some of those values at the expense of others. Compromise is a necessity, not an option. Seen in a more epistemic light, a champion may argue that this state of play is just fine because the compromise of values can help to produce "good" policy. That is, confronting the champion's dilemma means that democracy administered improves as a result of such trade-offs. Making democratic trade-offs in this way, the argument goes, is simply practical. Moreover, if "good" policy is defined as "correct" in some sense, some champions contend that the public is benefited by less democracy because it can give them "correct" policy outcomes. This is reminiscent of the epistemic democratic theory of Estlund (2008) that I discussed in Chapter 3, and I will call such claims "epistemic" in this chapter as well.

An alternative view to these pragmatic and epistemic claims – and my normative contention in this book – is that democracy administered *well* means respecting the trade-offs of the system of representative government that exists in the jurisdiction in question. Though surely not a problem only for designing governance structures, champions rarely have the authority to effectuate a "constitutional moment" (Ackerman 1998). That is, their governance structures are not the product of a robust deliberation with broad participation. Consequently, the process by which these structures are created does not lend enough legitimacy to hold them up against the political system. Instead, the claims of champions are based on pragmatic or epistemic grounds that separate "efficient" and "effective" administration of policy work from the values of the representative government that made these policies in the first place.

The Fundamental Problem of Public Administration

My goals in making this argument are threefold. First, I want to challenge champions to be explicit about the value trade-offs that lurk in their structural designs. Second, I want to encourage a research agenda in the field of public administration that can reveal a nuanced understanding of how the values of government and governance relate to one another. Third, I want to invite champions to consider explicitly the relationship between the values of representative government in political systems and their governance structures because a mismatch can have consequences for both. As representative governments differ in their values, so, too, do governance structures. In some Scandinavian nations, public administration has its own constitutional position. The German *Rechtstaat* connects public administration directly to maintaining the rule of law. The next chapter considers empirical connections between political and governance values, while Chapter 6 argues that seeking a complementarity between political and governance values, to the extent that doing so does not violate the law, defines responsible value reinforcement in practice. But first, to understand the importance of value trade-offs to the traditional narrative of control and capability in public administration. I begin by relating the champion's dilemma to the fundamental problem of situating public administration within a system of representative government.

THE FUNDAMENTAL PROBLEM OF PUBLIC ADMINISTRATION

The champion's dilemma, with its inevitable value trade-offs, cannot be more important in contemporary public administration. For scholars such as Pollitt and Bouckaert (2004), who see the reform of governance structures as key to understanding contemporary public administration, it is the core concern of the field. In my view, they are right. The champion's dilemma reaches these heights because it confronts what Laurence Lynn and I (Bertelli and Lynn 2003, 2006) consider to be the paramount concern for democracy administered: managers' responsible use of judgment. Crucially, responsibility, both in theory and practice, is necessarily defined in terms of representative government. Managers use their judgment to decide what the law and the state of the world require of them when administering public policies. The managers' role is not merely subordinate to that of representatives. It is not principally a technocracy of expertise nor a reputation for pragmatism or a commitment to epistemic correctness. How managers use their discretionary authority in ways that are both representative of public wants and effective in some practical sense is the *fundamental* problem of public administration. Solving it means balancing so many epistemic and pragmatic justifications with democratic values; this is what links the champion's dilemma with the fundamental problem of public administration. Delegation of power in a representative democracy is a transmission of democratic values from representatives to managers. It is not just a grant of authority and the discretion to use it. The champion's dilemma binds when designing or reshaping these delegations, and that cannot be done without thinking about the values in representative government that have been the subject of the last two chapters.

Accountability to Representative Government

The notion that delegation conveys values is evident in what is perhaps the most enduring debate in the scholarly field of public administration. At the beginning of the 1940s, when public administration in the United States was caught between the New Deal's growing cadre of federal managers and World War II, Herman Finer and Carl Friedrich debated the responsiveness of governance structures to the fundamental problem of public administration. At the core of the debate was the role of managers' own beliefs about policy and, of course, about democracy. Think for a moment about the champion's dilemma in this environment. Designing structures that privilege accountability too much could mean enabling an authoritarian, while those that privilege the professional values and expertise of managers could lead to a technocracy that could place representative governments in more peril as the world raced toward a war of unprecedented scale. The debate between Friedrich and Finer was playing out in a heady period for champions.

Finer contended that structures should be set up such that managers' own beliefs are *immaterial* to the exercise of discretion. He argued that responsible administration is "working not for ... what the public needs, but of the wants of the public as expressed by the public" (Finer 1941, 337). The Finerian response to the champion's dilemma is to enhance accountability to representative government and to rely on its political institutions to express the popular will in domains that concern managers. If citizens are to be the masters of managers, this "mastership needs institutions, and particularly the centrality of an elected organ, for its expression and the exertion of its authority" (337). The Finerian position particularly emphasizes the enhancement of identifiability and evaluability whereby representatives "are to determine the course of action of the

The Fundamental Problem of Public Administration 87

public servants to the most minute degree that is technically feasible" (336) and increasing the probability of sanction wherein representatives wield "the power to exact obedience to orders" (337).

In this argument, Finer resolves the champion's dilemma wholly by insulating the trade-off in process values enshrined in an existing scheme of representative government. Leaving process value trade-offs to constitutional designers, Finer strengthens the accountability of managers to representatives, and this allows representatives to be, in turn, accountable to the people. Finer's position can be heard in many postwar responses to the fundamental problem of public administration. For instance, the political scientist John Millett contends that guided by responsibility to representative government in a Finerian sense, management "abhors the idea of arbitrary authority present in its own wisdom and recognizes the reality of external direction and constraint" (Millett 1954, 403). This position has echoes of Christiano (1996) in that it *does not* preclude the means of democracy administered from being in the hands of managers. It *does* require that their means of making policy be consistent with the aims that the public chooses when it elects representatives, who can engage in direct or conditional representation as they wish. The Finerian focus is on removing "arbitrary authority" from managers as in American administrative law (Bertelli and Lynn 2006, 80–92). Policy workers' efforts to use the strategies in Figure 2.2 to induce accountability errors would also be problematic on this view. Retrospective answerability for policy work to representatives is paramount.

The accountability values privileged in the Finerian argument are likewise evident. Consider the argument of the political scientist J. Roland Pennock that "responsibility involves the identifiability of particular individuals or groups who are the effective causes of whatever the government does" (Pennock 1952, 797). Crucially, he continues, "for the government as a whole to be accountable to the electorate is not enough, but that the voters should be able to identify the responsible authorities and hold them accountable as a group for their deeds and misdeeds" (797). Both identifiability ("identify the responsible authorities," not just "the government as a whole") and evaluability ("for their deeds and misdeeds") are evident in Pennock's claim.

Finer's view is also quite explicit in a contemporary positive theoretical literature grounded in the principal-agent problem that examines the extent of administered policy that will remain unsanctioned by representatives (cf. Bendor and Mierowitz 2004; Epstein and O'Halloran 1999; Huber and Shipan 2002). In this literature, democracy administered *well* implies that policy workers and managers (agents) make policies that coalitions of representatives (principals) intend. Because managers have the ability to make trade-offs about the use of resources and their influence over policy outputs and outcomes, they, rather than policy workers, are the implicit focus of this literature. The accountability values of Chapter 2 are tools and the process values of Chapter 3 escape systematic treatment. The result is a literature that reads too much like the economics of contract to be fit for purpose. Put simply, while control and capability are considered, these positive theories are just not very good for understanding value reinforcement.

This literature on the "political control of bureaucracy" has two notable aspects which can be understood by seeing the problem of accountability of managers to representatives for the use of discretion as performance on a contract. The contract – which "solves" the principal-agent problem – in question is a piece of duly enacted legislation. That is, managers are mandated by representatives to take actions, but the criteria for using their judgment in doing so is not well specified. The use of managerial discretion is thus necessary for the functioning of government. Legislation, in this manner, specifies an incomplete contract that leaves accountability in representative government in the hands of managers.

Positive theories respond to this problem in two ways. First, they ask whether representatives might give managers the incentive to improve accountability by manipulating the values we discussed in Chapter 2 as a part of the structure of legislation. This kind of action is known as *ex ante* control (of managers) because it occurs before managers exercise the discretion afforded by the legislative contract. Second, positive theorists address the effectiveness of observing the discretionary actions of managers on the relationship between the policy goals of the representatives who agreed to the terms of the legislation and the administered policies that managers have undertaken. Observations by representatives – through monitoring, audits, the review of performance information, testimony and so forth – are called *ex post* controls on managers because they can only happen after the discretionary behavior that legislation enables.

Perhaps the seminal argument of the control literature is due to McCubbins and Schwartz (1984). They relate ex ante controls to the pulling of a fire alarm, warning representatives about what managers are doing. To do this, legislation "establishes a system of rules, procedures and informal practices that enable individual citizens and organized interest groups to examine administrative decisions . . ." (McCubbins and

The Fundamental Problem of Public Administration 89

Schwartz 1984, 166). Citizens and interest groups hold the key to accountability. When the actions of managers are on display, they have the incentive to tell representatives about what those managers are doing. Chapter 2 explained that accountability in representative government is stronger in sanction than in selection. Representatives should expect to hear from citizens and interest groups only when they are unhappy with the actions of managers. Seen through this lens, the voting heuristics discussed in Chapter 2 are a low-information variant of fire alarms with direct consequences for representatives at the ballot box. My claim there has echoes of the responsibility argument in Pennock (1952) discussed above. Citizens can sound the alarm – or even extinguish fires – at the ballot box, I argue, and on the basis of "fast and frugal" heuristics (Bertelli 2016).

By contrast, McCubbins and Schwartz use police patrols as the metaphor for ex post control over managers. As when police officers walk their beats, peering into darkened alleys and observing things on the street as they pass, representatives legislate a process that "examines a sample of executive-agency activities, with the aim of detecting and remedying any violations of legislative goals and, by its surveillance, discouraging such violations" (McCubbins and Schwartz 1984, 166). The difference between these tools is not between formal and informal mechanisms. It is a question of timing – do the controls happen before or after managers take discretionary action? The well-known conclusion of this argument is that fire alarms enable more oversight than police patrols because they unlock the energies of citizens, specifically, those organized into interest groups. It is of great moment that interest groups can help representatives to avoid the expense and inaccuracies associated with examining the behavior of managers after the fact.

The process values maximized in this formulation are all *implicit* in the theory. Majoritarianism – if indeed majority rule is how the political principal is chosen by citizens and how it makes its collective decisions – might be privileged, but it would just as well be relaxed if the plural principal, say, a coalition of representatives, used a Borda count to congeal its members' preferences. A kind of pluralism is also privileged, but it is one centered on organized interests with the incentive to make efforts to sound fire alarms (Lowi 1979). Authors in this literature are agnostic to the representation of citizens' varieties of views by the groups sounding fire alarms. And in all of these theories, policy is an abstraction: the policy space can be that of environmental or national defense or trade, it does not matter. Unless policy is multidimensional, as between social

and economic policies, no trade-off is required. When assuming a unidimensional policy space, theorists relax collective rationality through the
partitioning of the decision agenda, and they need not specify how this
partitioning is achieved to motivate their analyses.

An example of an explicit accountability argument in the political
control of bureaucracy tradition can be found in Fox and Jordan
(2011). They argue formally that if representatives have more information than citizens about how managers will use their discretion to shape
public policies and managers are expert enough to make a policy, in fact,
benefit citizens, then public administration descends into politics itself.
When these information and expertise conditions – capability conditions –
are met, Fox and Jordan explain, "[W]e have a condition in which voters
can't distinguish delegations that are beneficial or costly for them and well
intentioned politicians are willing to mask the truth. This undermines
accountability" (Fox and Jordan 2011, 843–4). They argue that when the
policy motivations of representatives and the citizens they represent are in
alignment, representatives grant authority to managers who also share
those motivations.

Given their unidimensional policy space, I can choose my example
arbitrarily, partitioning the decision-making agenda of representatives and
citizens. Consider an anti-fracking representative of a district in
Pennsylvania where fracking – high-pressure drilling to release natural gas
from rock – has improved labor demand substantially. This representative
would be motivated to entrust regulatory tasks to managers who are
not in favor of limiting fracking because of its environmental impact.
Alternatively, if party pressure leads the representative to oppose fracking,
the managers she prefers will be biased such that her opposition is an artifact
of administration, not a lack of alignment with her constituents. The tool
with which representatives sculpt accountability in this example is identifiability, in particular, through a formal grant of authority to the manager. The
unidimensional space relaxes collective rationality, and the primary process
value might implicitly be majoritarianism because the model considers a
"single representative voter" (Fox and Jordan 2011, 831). Yet the model
need not specify the process of representation to be solved, leaving it
agnostic, for instance, to pluralism-majoritarianism trade-offs.

Autonomy from Representative Government

Carl Friedrich's response to the fundamental problem of public administration is different, chiefly because he feels that managers' beliefs are

The Fundamental Problem of Public Administration   91

inescapable. Believing implicitly that managers' jobs are part of representative government itself, he argues that "public policy is being formed as it is being executed, and is likewise being executed as it is being formed" (Friedrich 1940, 6). Through this argument, Friedrich plucks what has become a lingering epistemic chord in public administration, one – in his words – in which a policy violates a sense of managerial responsibility "if it can be shown that it was adopted without proper regard to the existing sum of human knowledge concerning the technical issues involved" as well as "for existing preferences in the community, and more particularly its prevailing majority" (12).

The Friedrichian trade-off is very different from the Finerian one. It relaxes pluralism with an epistemic view that policy work has essential technical elements that can be done *right*, which, in turn, removes those issues from the agenda of the democracy, easing the collective rationality value. It also brings the process value of majoritarianism into the foreground, by allowing for a technical metaconsensus to relax pluralism. The accountability value of evaluability ("existing preferences in the community") is also strengthened and considered subject to majoritarianism ("more particularly its prevailing majority"). Friedrich's trade-off clearly reshapes representative government, weakening the probability of sanction by equating policy work with policymaking, which has become another truism in our scholarly field, that is, the impossibility of a politics-administration dichotomy. Most dramatically, Friedrich allows managers to determine for themselves the meaning of a citizen's majority position, rather than relying on representatives to do that. On these things, Finer cannot help but disagree.

This position is at work in arguments that managers engender reputations for efficient, effective administration among politicians and stakeholders and lessen accountability as a result (cf. Bertelli and Busuioc 2020; Carpenter 2010, 2001). In such situations as the increasing reputation of the United States Postal Service in the nineteenth and early twentieth centuries, Carpenter notes that "[d]elegation now became bargaining. The agent became a co-equal player in national policy battles" with representatives (Carpenter 2000, 125). This epistemic, rather than technical, metaconsensus achieves the same goal of relaxing pluralism. The position is also a part of contemporary theories of expertise acquisition, such as the interpretation of political scientists Sean Gailmard and John Patty (2013, 2007) – the model itself shares essential features, like unidimensional policy, with the foregoing political control literature – that the leeway to acquire expertise in furtherance of their own policy objectives is a currency through which policy-motivated managers are rewarded for their policy work. The political scientists Gary Miller and Andrew Whitford contend that the political agency relationship between citizens and representatives can lead to a problem with the Finerian adherence to representative government. Representatives, on this view, engage in hidden action (moral hazard) that cannot be easily checked by citizens. Consequently, they argue, "[w]hen legislators' preferences are perverse, bureaucratic accountability can only magnify those preferences" (Miller and Whitford 2016, 47). That is, representatives' hidden action, say, through intransparent interest group influence, is the source of the perversity. Strengthening accountability values in the Finerian approach generates these problems, while a Friedrichian focus on expertise and managers' view of the public interest can rein them in. Miller and Whitford (2016, 47) continue, "[B]ureaucratic autonomy may be the means of controlling political moral hazard." They are silent on how this reshapes or reinforces the values of representative democracy.

Drawing from the seminal work of the public administration scholar Frederick Mosher (1968), arguments under the banner of representative bureaucracy also capture a Friedrichian sense of autonomy. Mosher contended that managers and policy workers can be directly, but passively representative of citizens when their socioeconomic characteristics such as race, gender, disability, and so forth reflect those of citizens more generally. He also recognized an active form of direct representation wherein the use of managerial discretion benefits citizens in particular socioeconomic groups with which managers or policy workers identify. A broad empirical literature led by public administration scholars such as Norma Riccucci shows evidence of both forms of representation as well as a symbolic variant in which citizens believe that policy work is more legitimate when they share the characteristics of the policy worker or manager doing it (see e.g., Riccucci and Meyers 2004; Riccucci, Van Ryzin, and Lavena 2014). In this narrative of legitimacy through direct representation, the accountability value of identifiability and the process value of collective rationality remain important. Direct representation relates to identifiable characteristics and identities have influence over all problems on the agenda of managers and policy workers. Pluralism is an essential process value here, and majoritarianism is weakened. Yet like the epistemic arguments discussed above, the mechanisms for relaxing majoritarianism or collective rationality are not carefully considered, though in their broad empirical application from education to policing and beyond, representative bureaucracy arguments *implicitly* partition the decision-making agenda.

In sum, the Fredrichian response to the fundamental problem of public administration is dramatically different than the Finerian reflection of representative government as it permits managers to do much more to reshape democracy than does the latter argument. In the Finerian rationalization, limiting managers is the key to respecting representative government, and any perversities in the political agency relationship between representatives and citizens are the province of the electoral and party systems, as discussed in Chapter 2. Democracy administered is a constitutional-level concern that managers should be constrained from altering. In a Friedrichian regime, reputation, expertise and a direct form of representation can allow managers and policy workers to reshape political agency in the representative governments they inhabit.

EVALUATING GOVERNANCE STRUCTURES DEMOCRATICALLY

Champions create governance structures that have both normative and positive consequences for the beliefs and behaviors of policy workers and managers. They must respond to the champion's dilemma by making arguments about the potential upsides and downsides of the structures they prefer. How can we evaluate governance structures in terms of democratic values? I contend that this question must be addressed systematically, or we will not have an accurate picture of how governance structures enable or constrain democracy administered. The remainder of this chapter is an attempt to work out a framework for this kind of inquiry.

Figure 4.1 summarizes my framework for understanding structural responses to the champion's dilemma; I find this framework useful for making a systematic assessment of the value trade-offs implicit in governance structures. The columns distinguish structures that enhance accountability values described in Chapter 2 from those that obviate them. *Accountability-enhancing* structures strengthen the connection between managers' actions and representatives' policy goals. *Accountability-obviating* structures rely not on elections, but instead on small groups of citizens, on managers' own knowledge, on the economic market, and so forth to achieve accountability to citizens.

The rows of Figure 4.1, correspondingly, distinguish governance structures that enhance or obviate the process values discussed in Chapter 3. *Process-enhancing* structures create a means of respecting the conditions

	Accountability-enhancing	**Accountability-obviating**
Process-enhancing	**Controlled Agency** (Bureaucracy)	**Representative Agency** (Participatory Governance)
Process-obviating	**Managed Agency** (Managerialism)	**Independent Agency** (Privatization or Quasi-Government)

FIGURE 4.1 Governance structures and accountability – Process value trade-offs Structures in parentheses are examples of the agency type.

of procedural democracy when gathering feedback from citizens to inform and assess managers' actions. *Process-obviating* structures replace institutional means for respecting the criteria of procedural democracy with managers' own judgments.

The champion's dilemma recognizes that all governance structures make trade-offs between and among process and accountability values. The nub of the Friedrich-Finer debate lies in the difficulty that representatives have in impressing belief systems about the basic structure of representative government on managers and policy workers. This normative argument – that is, the claim that the values of representative government ought to be correlated with the belief systems of policy workers – connects the champion's dilemma to public administration's fundamental problem, the responsible exercise of discretion by managers and policy workers. The cells in Figure 4.1 identify regimes of value trade-offs and associate them with specific classes of governance structures. In doing so, Figure 4.1 characterizes the trade-offs in these canonical regimes in what I think is a helpful way.

The remainder of the chapter will define the core structures represented in each cell. Each of these will also be considered in practice through an extended example, which provides an opportunity to illustrate the values and means for molding them as discussed in Chapters 2 and 3.

CONTROLLED AGENCY

Controlled agency structures, like those governing the Charlottesville public safety agency and the *questore* with which this book began, are the most Finerian institutional designs. With one stroke, they do two crucial things. First, they enhance accountability values that link accountability for policy work to the accountability of representatives, who, in turn, are accountable to citizens through representative government. Second, they enhance the process values of the representative governments in which they are situated, but do not alter the existing balance of process values. In particular, if systems are majoritarian, controlled agency structures privilege majoritarianism among the values discussed in Chapter 3. If representative governments are constructed through proportional electoral formulas, then controlled agency structures correspondingly focus on pluralism. Other flavors of electoral formulas have this relationship to a greater or lesser extent. It is important to my case that the reader not confuse the level at which these value balances are struck. The trade-offs inherent in electoral institutions occur at the constitutional level, and they "control," so goes the metaphor, the democratic belief systems that govern agency relationships unless policy workers' beliefs are altered by governance structures.

Bureaucracy is one controlled agency structure that deserves special attention because of its privileged position within representative governments. In describing the ideal type of bureaucracy, the sociologist Max Weber contends that bureaucracy is "the purest type of exercise of legal authority" (Weber 1964 [1921], 333). In representative government, this allows the rule of law to bind policy work to representatives, who hold their positions because of election. In keeping with the literature on the political control of bureaucracy, a coalition of representatives is the "supreme chief" to which accountability flows for policy work. Weber writes, "Only the supreme chief of the organization occupies his position by virtue of appropriation, *of election*, or of having been designated for the succession" (Weber 1964 [1921], 333, emphasis added). The rest of the managers and policy workers in a bureaucracy are chosen by appointment, and this is because "[t]here is no such thing as a hierarchy of elected officials in the same sense as there is a hierarchy of appointed officials" (333).

It is useful to consider Weber's rationale for why representatives cannot themselves populate these hierarchies. A cast of representatives might seem to help the Finerian position of democracy administered through the strictest possible accountability to representatives. It also could be a way to steer clear of the agency loss from delegating power to managers and policy workers. Neither of these views is correct.

Weber's first claim is that "election makes it impossible to attain a stringency of discipline even approaching that in the appointed type" (Weber 1964 [1921], 335). This "stringency of discipline" accumulates expertise, including technical expertise, as well as any reputation managers and policy workers have either individually or collectively in their organizations for "good" policymaking and has been the subject of the bulk of the literature in public administration. This is a capability argument, and, indeed, Weber goes on to say that control over the "bureaucratic machinery ... is possible only to a very limited degree to persons who are not technical specialists" (338). He is explicit that "the trained permanent official is more likely to get his way in the long run than his nominal superior, the Cabinet Minister, who is not a specialist" (338).

Seen through this lens, bureaucracies can fail as controlled agency structures precisely because they allow for a "stringency of discipline" that results in subordinate power. "Bureaucratic organizations," that is, managers and policy workers, "or the holders of power who make use of them," namely, representatives, "have the tendency to increase their power still further by the knowledge growing out of experience in the service" (Weber 1964 [1921], 339). For bureaucracy to be a controlled agency structure, it must tend toward empowering representatives at the top of the hierarchy so that "stringency of discipline" does not overtake the Finerian emphasis of accountability values. This is a strong position *against* the use of epistemic arguments to justify "good" policymaking. It is unambiguously a claim about control. It shows the extent to which the process trade-offs of Chapter 3 are not entrusted to policy workers in regimes of controlled agency.

A second problem with a hierarchy of elected officials is also instructive. If, as would be required, "it is open to a subordinate official to compete for elective honours on the same terms as his superiors, and his prospects are not dependent on the superior's judgment" (Weber 1964 [1921], 335). When a subordinate makes direct appeals to the public in elections, a problem for legitimate authority occurs: those appeals can challenge the authority of her (also elected) superior. This undermines accountability by significantly relaxing identifiability: is the citizen to hold the superior or subordinate accountable when both are incumbents tied to policy work and offer competing retrospective and prospective narratives about it? It may be somewhat ironic – yet also possibly quite obvious to

Controlled Agency

observers of multilevel government, for instance, American federalism, the European Union, or the history of the long ballot – that the direct election of politicians at different levels of hierarchical responsibility would lead to the failure of bureaucracy as a controlled agency structure. Analytically speaking, however, the reason for the failure in this case is the relaxation of identifiability and its knock-on effect on the probability of sanction (see e.g., Cheibub 2006, 353).

An important way of understanding bureaucracy as a controlled authority structure is through its potential to provide policy-neutral expertise. That is, if managers and policy workers demonstrated an "ability to do the work of government expertly, and to do it according to explicit, objective standards rather than to personal or party or other obligations and loyalties" it would be possible to "[t]ake administration out of politics" and to achieve controlled agency as a result (Kaufman 1956, 1060). Specifically, policy-neutral policy workers forebear from epistemic claims-making and resist the pressures of metaconsensus and the expediency of incompletely theorized agreements where perspectives are either sidelined or left unreconciled. As the foregoing fable of the all-representative hierarchy makes clear, the focus of neutral competence is *upward* information flows from policy workers to managers and ultimately to representatives. If neutrally competent information flows upward, the argument goes, then political control can flow downward and bureaucracy remains a controlled agency structure.

The Impossibility of Neutral Controlled Agency

In an illuminating essay, the political scientists Hammond and Paul Thomas (1989) argue that neutral competence in a bureaucratic hierarchy is impossible. This is because its elements cannot collectively be achieved in the same way that basic majoritarianism, robustness to pluralism, and collective rationality cannot be mutually fulfilled by champions facing the democratic trilemma (List 2011) of Chapter 3. To establish a terminology, Hammond and Thomas (1989, 161) consider a hierarchy with four levels: a director at the top, followed by regional headquarters, state headquarters and finally field officials at the "street" level of the organization. These labels are common to American federal agencies, but the levels of the hierarchy are generic. Casting the actors in the roles of my characters of this book, the director and the regional and state office heads are managers who must aggregate information from street-level policy workers. The higher the level of the manager, the more information she

98 *Governance Structures and Democratic Values*

has to aggregate. Within this hierarchy, choices are made between policy alternatives "starting with the bottom-level field officials who make recommendations to higher-level managers, with the director making the ultimate decision" (Hammond and Thomas 1989, 160).

Hammond and Thomas "call a structure neutral if, given some initial pieces of information or advice forwarded by the bottom-level field officials, changes in the intervening structure *do not change choices made by the director*" (Hammond and Thomas 1989, 160, emphasis added). Alternatively, a hierarchy is biased if changing the structure without changes in the initial information from field officials leads the director to different choices. When certain conditions are met, neutrality can be assured, but if they cannot all be met simultaneously, trade-offs ensue just as in the case of process values in Chapter 3. The following are required a hierarchy to be neutral. If *one* of these conditions fails, the hierarchy is biased.

- *Objectivity*. No street-level policy worker can disfavor a policy alternative to the extent that she would not recommend it (Hammond and Thomas 1989, 163).
- *Unified decision rule*. Managers at each level of the hierarchy must employ an aggregation rule – that is, a rule that determines what decision a manager will make given the pieces of advice that are presented by subordinate policy workers – that gives all alternatives the possibility of being chosen (163–4). Moreover, the aggregation rule that managers and directors use must be precisely the same: "One might think of a manual or rulebook that specifies in complete detail what aggregation decisions must be made, given all possible combinations of recommendations from subordinates" (164).
- *Turflessness*. There can be no "jurisdictional" requirements that serve to limit the alternatives that can be considered. The organization cannot have units that consider a particular set of alternatives their "turf," and, consequently, "turf wars" between branches of the hierarchy cannot reduce the number of alternatives (cf. Herrera, Reuben, and Ting 2017).
- *Path independence*. The single aggregation rule used by managers cannot produce different results when their subordinates are grouped in different ways. Put differently, the rule must produce the same results regardless of the organizational "path" that information follows from subordinates to managers.

- *Informativeness.* Consider the situation when a subordinate policy worker has no advisory opinion to offer to managers. When such a neutral recommendation is aggregated with a non-neutral alternative – that is, a recommendation to do X rather than Y – the non-neutral advice prevails and the manager's decision is to do X (Hammond and Thomas 1989, 166–7).
- *Balance.* Suppose the following scenario arises: subordinate A says "do X" and subordinate B says "do Y." In such cases, managers must take "no official position" (167). By contrast, when a manager is presented with "a unanimous recommendation from his immediate subordinates, he must agree to their wishes" (168).

It is useful to think of how clearly these requirements work against the novel trade-offs of process values by policy workers. Informativeness, balance, and objectivity preserve the possibility of pluralism or majoritarianism by deactivating any influence of a metaconsensus among policy workers or their reliance on epistemic claims about the benefits of bureaucratic procedure. The unified decision rule avoids the intransparent reshaping of policy workers' advice resulting from deliberations internal to their organization, helping to mitigate accountability errors. Turflessness and path independence preserve the scope of collective rationality – that is, a food safety agency has a broad legal mandate in regard to food safety as defined in a delegating provision of law, but policy work cannot exceed that mandate – preventing policy workers from reshaping it through internal information flows. Of course, failures of these conditions happen all of the time, but recognizing them is an important way of understanding why bureaucracy fails to achieve controlled agency. Consider the following example.

The BAMF-Affäre

Germany is a federal state with a parliamentary system of government. Some policy areas are delegated to state or local governments in the German constitution, which also distinguishes two types of agencies (*Bundesverwaltung*): direct (*unmittelbare*) and indirect (*mittelbare*) (Bach 2012, 167). Direct agencies comprise the federal administration and include the ministries, the German Federal Court of Auditors, and various other federal agencies, including the Federal Agency of Migration and Refugees (BAMF) (Pötzsch 2010). BAMF has no legal independence from the German state and falls within the portfolio of the interior minister, Horst Seehofer at the time of the events described below (Federal Office for Migration and Refugees 2016). Funding for BAMF policy work comes entirely from the interior ministry, which exercises functional and legal control over BAMF and must be informed about its operations (Federal Office for Migration and Refugees [BAMF] 2017).

Formally speaking, BAMF should be an excellent example of controlled agency. Its policy work includes asylum proceedings and refugee protection; it also coordinates refugee integration at the national level and conducts migration research for advising federal representatives (Federal Office for Migration and Refugees [BAMF] 2016). In addition to BAMF's headquarters in Nuremberg, the agency has various offices across the German states. These regional offices are centers for asylum procedures, namely, for completing applications, conducting interviews, and rendering decisions on cases (Federal Office for Migration and Refugees [BAMF] 2016). Accordingly, the connection between the regional offices, BAMF's federal office, and the interior ministry is the kind of hierarchy that Hammond and Thomas (1989) study.

The story of BAMF also involves several policy events, and returning to Figure 2.2 in Chapter 2 and its depiction of the arguments that representatives make can help explain some of the nuance regarding the accountability values at stake. In the regional office at Bremen in 2018, a set of events occurred that one newspaper called "the culmination of a long history of mishaps and problems in the federal agency" (Herrmann 2018). In the wake of the refugee crisis of 2015, BAMF registered hundreds of thousands of refugees, struggling all the while to keep up with the inflow. The result was overcrowded arrival centers and long waiting lines for asylum seekers and migrants. Manfred Schmidt, the former head of BAMF, had previously warned about the chronic overload and backlog of the agency, but the need for additional personnel went unheard by political superiors (Dummer, Klingst, and Lobenstein 2018). This raises the possibility that the objectivity criterion – and perhaps balance as well – was relaxed. Schmidt ultimately tendered his resignation to Interior Minister Thomas de Maizière.

Schmidt's interim successor, Frank-Jürgen Weisse, striving to "implement what politics demands from him" (Herrmann 2018), accelerated asylum proceedings with the support of a larger budget and more employees. Yet Weisse received an internal critique from the agency's Staff Council, which, in an open letter to the public, bemoaned a "departure from the rule of law" (Süddeutsche Zeitung 2015, 1). Specifically, the letter noted the lack of a viable means of checking the identity of Syrian asylum seekers (Süddeutsche Zeitung 2015). These claims about the rule of law are notable because they enhance the process values in German representative government. Managers, the Staff Council effectively contended, do not have the ability to reshape the laws made by representatives. What is more, the letter implied that questions about the objectivity and balance criteria of the administrative hierarchy remained, undermining its neutrality.

As with Schmidt's BAMF before it, the interior ministry behaved in accordance with a regime of retrospective answerability (see Figure 2.2). This is precisely what a champion would hope would happen in a controlled agency structure. Weisse left the agency in January 2017 (Steiner 2016), making way for Jutta Cordt to attempt to address a backlog of 435,000 open asylum cases and to reassess potentially erroneous decisions (Herrmann 2018).

A few months later, both BAMF and the German armed forces (in the portfolio of the defense minister) found themselves in the spotlight. Austrian officials arrested a German soldier in February 2017 as he attempted to leave the airport in Vienna with a pistol he had previously hidden in a vent. After checking his fingerprints, the officials were surprised to discover that the soldier had been officially registered as an asylum seeker in Bavaria (Grunau 2017). Further investigation revealed that the man in question was a right-wing extremist who allegedly planned a terrorist attack on high-ranking "refugee-friendly" politicians in Germany, including the minister of justice and the vice president of the *Bundestag*, Claudia Roth. Officials believe that the soldier's false identity as a Syrian refugee was intended to be a focal point for public blame in the aftermath of the planned attacks (Grunau 2017).

Highly identifiable, Defense Minister Ursula von der Leyen felt political pressure, as did Jutta Cordt at BAMF, who acknowledged to the press that "blatant mistakes in every procedural step" had been made, but that there had been "no deliberate manipulation" by agency managers or policy workers (Grunau 2017). After an internal inquiry in the midst of election campaigns, Cordt and Interior Minister De Maizière held a press conference in which they promised that about 100,000 asylum decisions from 2015 through 2016 would be reevaluated (Mayr 2017). As would be expected from a controlled agency structure, the policy event created by the soldier's unsuccessful attempt to recover the handgun in Vienna led to behavior that remained consistent with retrospective answerability, namely, Cordt's *mea culpa*.

In April 2018, another scandal shook the agency. In the Bremen regional office, prosecutors' investigations uncovered approximately 1,200 errors in cases granting asylum as well as possible corruption. This fed a media frenzy that ensconced the "BAMF-*Affäre*" in German political debate for weeks (Adelhardt and Peters 2019). The former head of the Bremen office was accused of accepting bribes and determining thousands of asylum applications without a legal basis, particularly when the applications were submitted by three lawyers with whom she had a personal relationship (Adelhardt and Peters 2019). The alleged favoritism violated the unified decision rule and path independence criteria because the Bremen office was clearly determining asylum cases on a different basis than the other offices.

Public outcry made manifest a variety of questions about political responsibility, identifying the coalition government, particularly Interior Minister De Maizière and his successor, Seehofer. But this time, the strategy was source relocation (see Figure 2.2). Corruption is easily evaluable by the public as unacceptable, and Seehofer denied culpability by limiting his identifiability, arguing that the policy event did not take place during his ministerial tenure despite his involvement in the refugee crisis while serving as prime minister of Bavaria (Strauch 2018). Nonetheless, he promised a "ruthless inquiry" (Herrmann 2018). Seehofer swiftly closed the BAMF office in Bremen, sacking the highly identifiable Jutta Cordt and publicly calling the affair a "huge scandal" despite the fact that prosecutors' investigations were still in the early stages (Adelhardt and Peters 2019). Other politicians joined Seehofer in voicing still legally unsubstantiated opinions that corruption reigned in Bremen (Katzenberger 2018). The accountability in the German political system was seeping into the interior ministry and BAMF.

In two special sessions, the Federal Committee on Internal Affairs inquired into the BAMF scandal, finding serious deficits of staffing – evident in substantial accumulated overtime and canceled trainings – and a reduction in quality standards for asylum proceedings. The inquiry found that these antics were not isolated in Bremen, but had been occurring in other branch offices because they prioritized speed over thorough process as regional offices combated their backlogs (Lückoff 2018). With public evaluability increasing, Seehofer reacted at once, announcing a thorough reform of the BAMF (Lückoff 2018). Nonetheless, most of the accusations against the former Bremen office chief could not be proved. After reassessing 18,000 positive asylum decisions in Bremen, the interior ministry admitted in a parliamentary inquiry that it revoked only forty-seven. Prosecutors also could not find evidence to support the bribery allegations (Adelhardt and Peters 2019). This cast doubt on the violations of the unified decision rule and path independence criteria, rendering BAMF a rather controlled agency and the *BAMF-Skandal* more of a *Skandälchen* in the end.

The BAMF case depicts a hierarchy that fails some neutrality criteria, but which maintains the retrospective answerability of managers and policy workers to representatives that controlled agency structures seek to achieve. Information flows from the media and other sources, and, crucially, the strategies of representatives and managers can work to maintain controlled agency. Among the structures discussed in this chapter, only controlled agency is unabashed in its focus on accountability to representatives who are, in turn, accountable to citizens as the process values in specific forms of representative government demand. In the remaining structures, champions make important design trade-offs that place the equipoise of democratic values in the purview of managers.

MANAGED AGENCY

A managed agency structure allows the process values of representative government to be relaxed while maintaining accountability to representatives. It does this by shifting the focus of accountability from the procedures by which policy work is done to the outcomes it produces. In this way, managed agency permits managers to deploy resources and enlist policy workers in ways that improve the efficiency and effectiveness – where outcomes are the linchpin – of public administration. Perhaps the most celebrated feature of managed agency is that outcomes are measured and managers face incentives to perform well on those measures. That is, the focus of accountability in managed agency is an outcome, not the process of achieving it.

As is true for all governance structures, champions of managed agency must confront the fundamental problem of public administration, and they do so by focusing on the aims that citizens demand from the policies their representatives enact. Citizens want better-educated children or shorter waiting times for medical procedures and small business licensing. Representatives are accountable to citizens for prioritizing and achieving these aims, but they can employ managers and policy workers to help determine appropriate means of doing so. Champions of managed agency want to allow managers more flexibility than the process-enhancing element of controlled agency affords them. Doing this can benefit representatives, who gain more leverage on the counterfactuals of what citizens would want in policy domains, improving their conditional representation. The capability argument for "letting managers manage" is their refrain and the key to the process-obviating nature of managed agency. Trade-offs in process values become possible for managers and champions alike.

Ingredients of Managerialism

So much has been written about managed agency over the past forty years that it hardly seems prudent – or even possible – to review the relevant literature here (see generally Curry and Van de Walle 2018; Lægreid 2014; Pollitt and Bouckaert 2004, 2011). More fruitful for present purposes is to set out the principal elements of these structures. In a highly influential article, Hood (1991) describes the key features of managed agency in his discussion of managerialism and the New Public Management, labels used for the introduction of such structures internationally.

- *Identified discretion.* Managed agency promotes the active use of discretion by "named persons at the top" of the organization (Hood 1991, 4). This enhances the accountability value of identifiability by associating performance in regard to outcomes with a particular manager.
- *Targeted aims.* Managed agency requires goal definition and "targets" or other "indicators of success, preferably expressed in quantitative terms, especially for professional services" (Hood 1991, 4). Doing this promotes evaluability as an accountability value and allows representatives to track the progress of managers on the aims for which citizens hold them accountable in elections.
- *Targeted rewards and sanctions.* In managed agency, "[r]esource allocation and rewards [are] linked to measured performance" and this facilitates the "breakup of centralized ... personnel management" (Hood 1991, 4). This feature enhances accountability by raising the likelihood of sanction for outcomes. Crucially, it focuses reward and sanction on the particular aims to which managers are attending, rather than applying them "bureaucracy-wide" across policy aims and organizations.
- *Disaggregated aims.* Champions of managed agency encourage the disaggregation "of formerly 'monolithic' units" and the formation

of "units around products, operating on decentralized 'one-line' budgets and dealing with one another on an 'arms-length' basis" (Hood 1991, 5). This crucial feature partitions the decision-making agenda and relaxes collective rationality requirements that face, for instance, government ministries as a whole.

- *Competitive contracting.* Managed agency incorporates a "[m]ove to term contracts and public tendering procedures" as a means to promote competition (Hood 1991, 5). This enhances both identifiability (of contractors) and evaluability (against contractual targets or market prices) of their policy work.

- *Incentives for personnel.* The pursuit of "greater flexibility in hiring and rewards" is a common claim by champions of managed agency (Hood 1991, 5). Focusing incentives on identifiable policy workers can both help managers achieve their targeted aims and promote all of the accountability values – identifiability, evaluability, and the probability of sanction – discussed in Chapter 2.

- *Efficiency.* Perhaps the most celebrated aspect of managed agency is its "[s]tress on greater discipline and parsimony in resource use" (Hood 1991, 5). Champions argue that this strategy allows targeted rewards and sanctions to work, enhancing evaluability and the probability of sanction, and allows representatives to direct limited resources toward more of the aims for which citizens hold them accountable.

Managed agency influences two process values most clearly. By targeting and disaggregating aims, it has the ability to obviate both pluralism and collective rationality, depending on the way in which it is championed. The focus on performance targets and efficiency can be seen as a reflection of a metaconsensus among citizens and representatives. For instance, if citizens generally want to spend less time in line at the driver's license bureau, obviating pluralism by making wait times the key object of a performance target can make sense. In the case of measuring school performance on the basis of test scores, the notion of a metaconsensus about school outcomes is more difficult to justify. Other aspects of a student's education might be important to groups of citizens. Moreover, collective rationality is obviated by the disaggregation of aims, removing their correlations on the decision-making agenda. If wait times are more acceptable in another policy domain such as the licensing of medical care providers, managed agency allows for a specific focus on driver licensing, rather than considering the length of wait times in a more contentious, abstract sense.

An Escape from Prison Bureaucracy?

The United Kingdom is a parliamentary system and a constitutional monarchy. It is an iconic example of a high-accountability system of indirect representative government: British citizens elect their representatives in Parliament via a majoritarian electoral formula in single-member constituencies; these representatives, in turn, select a government led by the prime minister to assume executive authority. British elections display so much accountability in contrast to their majoritarian counterparts because the party system has offered few opportunities for coalition formation; in fact, in the postwar period there has been just one coalition government, the Conservative-Liberal Democrat coalition between 2010 and 2015. Of the twenty-eight parliamentary democracies studied by Kam, Bertelli, and Held (2020), the United Kingdom has the highest accountability. Strikingly, when accountability is measured, as discussed in Chapter 2, as the influence of vote share on cabinet portfolios changes from one election to the next, this influence is twice that of Australia, the next-most accountable system. Germany, the source of my controlled agency example with its mixed-member proportional representation system, ranks eleventh. I will call this measure the accountability index as we proceed, and Table 4.1 in the appendix to this chapter ranks the scores of countries examined by Kam, Bertelli, and Held (2020). Accountability in the United Kingdom has become somewhat more diffused as authority has been granted to devolved elected governments in Wales, Scotland, and Northern Ireland, which have indirectly chosen executives of their own who lead government departments composed of civil servants, weakening identifiability (James et al. 2012).

In the national government, ministerial departments require direct political oversight and are led by government ministers who are chosen by the prime minister. Ministers are "responsible for the actions, successes and failures of their departments" (UK Government 2019) and are supported in their policy work by various junior ministers and civil servants. Subordinate to these ministerial departments are *executive agencies* that focus on specific policy aims. A ministerial department makes decisions about funding and strategy for executive agencies, requiring frequent reporting as they do their policy work. Since the governments of Margaret Thatcher in the 1980s and 1990s, executive agencies have been perhaps the archetypal form of managed agency. They embrace most of the characteristics – and both of the process value influences – discussed above (see e.g., James 2003a, 2003b). This governance structure appeals to a metaconsensus on efficiency in policy work that obviates pluralism as a value: efficiency may not be what every citizen wants, but the disagreements about efficiency, equity, justice, fairness, and so forth among groups of citizens and political parties are well known.

Executive agencies are headed by competitively selected managers, operate under their own budgets, and have some independence from regulations and ongoing oversight from their parent departments; these things combine to create identifiable discretion for the manager and the agency. The agency's accountability, as well as that of the manager, is to the parent department for performing specific activities whose outcomes are measured against performance targets, targeted aims chosen by the parent department (Efficiency Unit 1988, 9). The incentives for personnel are strong, with a portion of the manager's pay and tenure dependent on performance targets and accountability directly located in the "corporate unit" of the executive agency, rather than in the parent department (9, 17–8).

The aims of a ministerial department are disaggregated, relaxing the process value of collective rationality when executive agencies are created, which is a reaction to the finding of Thatcher's Efficiency Unit (1988, 4) that "the greater diversity and complexity of work in many departments" contributes to what the report called "ministerial overload." Consider the parent Ministry of Justice headed by Robert James Buckland, MP, Secretary of State for Justice at the time of this writing (UK Ministry of Justice 2019). Buckland assumed office in 2019 and is the sponsoring minister of the executive agencies subordinate to the ministry, including Her Majesty's Prison and Probation Service (HMPPS), which administers correctional services in England and Wales. Originally created in 2004 as the National Offender Management Service (NOMS), this executive agency combines probation and prison services, representing two different management units within the HMPPS agency structure (Her Majesty's Prison and Probation Service 2019).

As an executive agency, the HMPPS operates prison and probation services "separately from, but subject to the structural and resource choices of a primarily policy-focused department," in this case, the Ministry of Justice (UK Cabinet Office 2018, 4). As a matter of law, the HMPPS is a business unit (House of Commons Justice Committee 2012) of the Ministry of Justice, legally part of the parent department, but administratively distinct (UK Cabinet Office 2018). At this writing, the HMPPS is led by Dr. Jo Faraar, who reports directly to Secretary of State Buckland, who, in turn, is accountable to Parliament for all matters concerning the HMPPS. The Ministry of Justice determines the policy framework (that is, the aims) for HMPPS in addition to its strategic objectives, approves the agency's corporate plans and reports, and appoints Dr. Farrar and other members of the management team (UK Cabinet Office 2018). Two directors general of the HMPPS Agency Board, one responsible for general prisons, the other for general probation, report to the secretary of state for the Home Office – the cabinet and the prison minister, a post within the Ministry of Justice (Her Majesty's Prison Probation Service 2019; UK Cabinet Office 2018).

Another key position that connects Parliament with the Secretary of State for Justice and the HMPPS is the permanent secretary and principal accounting officer of the Ministry of Justice. The permanent secretary, the most senior civil servant in the ministerial department, is responsible for running the day-to-day operations of a department and is directly accountable to Parliament for the "allocation and spending of any funding or income that the Executive Agency receives" (UK Cabinet Office 2018). The permanent secretary's responsibilities also include advising the secretary of state "on an appropriate framework of objectives and performance measures for the Executive Agency ... on an appropriate budget for the agency ... and on how well the agency is achieving its strategic objectives and whether it is delivering value for money" (UK Cabinet Office 2018, 6).

As noted, the executive agency structure weakens pluralism by focusing on efficiency as the paramount goal of its procedure and also on collective rationality through its partitioning of a ministerial department's agenda. This allows the majoritarianism of the British electoral system and accountability to the representatives that citizens select through it to stand as its most important democratic values.

Figure 4.2 shows the direct lines of accountability for targeted aims that permeate this managed agency structure. Direct reporting by both administrators, senior civil servants, and cabinet ministers to Parliament reflect the high-accountability nature of indirect government in Westminster systems. They also mitigate identifiability errors should an unfortunate policy event take place. In addition to distinctive areas of responsibility for public aims, that is, the disaggregated aims, the synergy between executive agency and department enhances the identification of managers and representatives, complementing the accountability of British government. This structure also maintains an aspect of neutrality that I discussed in the last section: it promotes turflessness because accountability for the "turf" of HMPPS is shared

Managed Agency

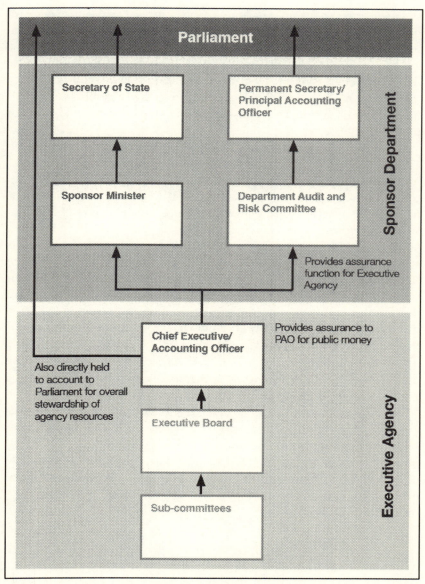

FIGURE 4.2 Accountability in United Kingdom executive agencies.
Reproduced from UK Cabinet Office 2018, 7, © Cabinet Office, 2018. This information is licensed under the Open Government Licence v3.0. To view this licence, visit http://www.nationalarchives.gov.uk/doc/open-government-licence/

by the entire sponsor department. By contrast, path independence becomes questionable because the information that flows through civil servants (on the right side of Figure 4.2) and representatives (on the left side of Figure 4.2) can be different; information about resource use that comes directly to Parliament from the executive agency manager (on the far left in Figure 4.2) can diverge more still. This figure reveals several trade-offs deducible from this specific form of managed agency.

The loss of path independence in this framework is the cost of identifiability of the direct reports to Parliament, while promoting turflessness works against that same value, opening the agency to strategies of source relocation when policy events occur. Consider the efforts of former Home Secretary Michael Howard to distinguish operational and policy responsibility for prisons, thereby acquitting himself of any responsibility for a policy event. After a series of escapes by Irish Republican Army prisoners from the Parkhurst top security prison on the Isle of Wight in 1995 and the Whitemoor prison in Cambridgeshire in 1994, citizens and Labour opposition parliamentarians called for the resignation of both Howard and Derek Lewis, the director general of the executive agency then known as HM Prison Service. Following a subsequent inquiry into prison security, management failure and inefficiencies in the executive agency were uncovered (Turpin and Tomkins 2007). A report by Sir John Learmont mused on an agency experiencing "a chapter of errors at every level and a naïvete that defies belief" (Mills 1995).

Highly identifiable, Lewis was quickly shown the door in 1995, while Howard remained atop the Home Office, acquitting himself of any blame related to the report's findings through a source relocation strategy. Lewis later filed a lawsuit accusing Howard of "blurring the demarcation lines of responsibility," undermining the process-obviating gambit of disaggregating aims, and identifying Howard as the source of the departmental misconduct (Mills 1995).

REPRESENTATIVE AGENCY

Representative agency is the first of the accountability-obviating structures in Figure 4.1. It is a regime in which citizens provide direct input to managers regarding both policy aims and the means of implementing them. The goal of representative agency is to facilitate collective decisions that legitimate subsequent policy work. Two key differences between representative agency and an incarnation of direct democracy are found in the representativeness of the citizens involved in decision-making and the partitioned agenda that obviates collective rationality. Representative agency structures often make use of the mini publics discussed in Chapter 3, groups of citizens who are chosen from more representative means like random sampling or through less representative processes such as open self-selection. This weakens pluralism when compared, for instance, to universal suffrage in elections. Champions of representative agency often justify the trade-off in representativeness on the basis of the benefits of citizen involvement and couch their arguments in the language of deliberative or pragmatist democracy. Such claims seek to justify the restrictions on pluralism by championing the epistemic policy benefits and deliberative processes on which these structures rely.

In all their varieties, representative agency structures obviate the accountability values in representative government through a challenge to the articulation of policy aims through elections and the representatives who gain authority from those elections. Select citizens enter policy decision-making processes about both aims and means, and specific process values of democracy are embedded in these processes. List's (2011) "trilemma" in Chapter 3 means that champions must make trade-offs among majoritarianism, pluralism, and collective rationality. Put simply, by obviating accountability in extant systems of representative government, champions face the same trade-offs as do the constitutional designers of political systems.

Bringing Citizens Back In

In a useful and provocative essay, the political theorist Mark Warren (2009, 6) outlines four basic features of representative agency structures. First, these structures are a "response to democracy deficits." Second, they are often "elite-driven." Third, their "evolution is often de-linked from electoral democracy." Fourth, they reshape the notion of constituency "based on the 'all affected' principle" rather than adhere "to predefined and relatively static territorial constituencies." I will take each of these elements in turn.

Champions of representative agency challenge representative government in a variety of ways. There is a disjuncture between geographic constituency and policy aims, particularly in this age of gerrymandering and globalization, that gives the electoral constituencies a rather arbitrary flavor when thinking about particular policy aims (cf. James 2015;

Rehfeld 2005). Particulate matter in the air and virus strains in humans are diffused without regard to the boundaries of electoral constituencies, and poverty and inequality exist both between and across them. In technical policy domains, representatives are poorly equipped to act. They delegate broad policymaking discretion to unelected managers who, in turn, appear to weaken accountability to representatives in order to engage in policy work that circumvents perverse results for citizens (e.g., Miller and Whitford 2016). That is, managers must fulfill the aims, from immigration reforms to financial security, that citizens entrust to their representatives, and do so despite the policy preferences of representatives, rather than because of them. Completing this rosy picture, the influence of special interests in our globalized world disorients managers and representatives alike from citizens' policy aims.

Representative agency structures arrive on this landscape as a means of bringing the citizen back into policymaking, for the particular purpose of rationalizing, connecting the aims and means of policy work. A champion of these structures, the political theorist Archon Fung states this plainly:

> [T]he strongest driver of participatory innovations has been the quest to enhance *legitimacy*. The hope is that such innovations can increase legitimacy by injecting forms of direct citizen participation into the policy-making process because such participation elevates perspectives that are more closely aligned with those of the general public and because that participation offsets democratic failures in the conventional representative policy-making process. (Fung 2015, 515, emphasis added)

It may feel ironic – though it is analytically quite straightforward to see – that representative agency structures are "very much about elite responses" (Warren 2009, 7). Managers and policy workers face the failures of representative government squarely and daily. In their quotidian policy work, they "find that the legitimacy generated by electoral democracy does not carry over to issue-segmented constituencies"; that "any given policy generates opposition which derails their capacities to plan"; that "they are short on information and enforcement capabilities, which often only can be expanded by engaging with advocates"; and that representatives are "powerful enough to impose solutions, but often in ways that are clumsy and costly" (Warren 2009, 7). Thus, managers play a stimulating role in processes meant to reinvigorate citizens' involvement with policy work.

Champions of representative agency structures, together with managers, can detach policy work from representative government, legitimating it more directly. Fung contends that "the principal reason for enhancing citizen participation in any area of contemporary governance is that the authorized set of decision makers – typically elected representatives or administrative officials ... lack the knowledge, competence, public purpose, resources, or respect necessary to command compliance and cooperation" (Fung 2006, 67). What is interesting is that representatives do not always disagree with this assessment, and they can be willing participants in weakening the electoral accountability of policy work. Warren notes that "elected governments have become increasingly aware that electoral legitimacy does not translate into policy-specific legitimacy" (2009, 8). Representatives and champions alike can thus find their way to view representative agency structures as *supplementary* to electoral democracy, shoring up its functional weaknesses" (8, emphasis added). The success of this supplemental role lies in the appropriate trade-offs among process values.

Of course, representatives are motivated by electoral fortune, and representative agency can help them with blame avoidance strategies as they reduce their identifiability with any negative policy event, while allowing them to claim credit for positive policy events according to the strategies in Chapter 3. In this way, the obviation of accountability values weakens the accountability of representatives to citizens, but in a way that appeals to them. Moreover, the reshaping of constituencies discussed above molds political accountability as well, with representatives less identifiable as a result. This influence, of course, is particularly relevant in single-member district systems with majoritarian electoral formulas, such as the United States or the United Kingdom. Particularly in such systems, the creation of representative agency can help to protect incumbent representatives.

It is important to contemplate that weakening accountability values in representative government does not occur because of the elite-driven nature of policy work in representative agency. What does matter most, I argue, is that these structures obviate the link between representatives and citizens because they concretize weighty choices regarding process values. This creates a more difficult task for champions because the process value trade-offs discussed in Chapter 3 have to be made *within* the representative agency, rather than rely on the form of representative government in the political jurisdiction in which it operates. The result is an appeal to a form of democracy that elides representative government.

The types of citizen participation used in representative agency structures exhibit quite a bit of variation, which Fung (2006, 67) helpfully surveys. One source of variance is how well participants *represent* the diversity of stakeholders or citizens more generally. The bulk of representative agency employs "the least restrictive method of selecting participants: They are open to all who wish to attend" (67). While pluralistic in the abstract, this criterion effectively privileges higher income and educational attainment and tends to exclude "those who have special interests or stronger views" (67). One alternative is to "selectively recruit participants from subgroups that are less likely to engage" such as bringing economically disadvantaged populations into the process of community policing but weakening pluralism by relying on consensus that arises in deliberations among a narrower set of interests (67). Relying on open self-selection can also disqualify majoritarianism through a lack of representation of the broader cast of citizens (67). To enhance pluralism, another selection mechanism is random selection for participation, which "is the best guarantee of descriptive representativeness" (68). A third option, which effectively obviates pluralism, and likewise collective rationality, by partitioning the decision-making agenda into specific domains and placing in the hands of a nonrepresentative citizens group, is to involve "[l]ay stakeholders" or "unpaid citizens who have a deep interest in some public concern and thus are willing to invest substantial time and energy to represent and serve those who have similar interests or perspectives but choose not to participate" (68). The process value implications are quite stark when only participation is considered, but champions do not make this choice in isolation.

A second source of variance among representative agency structures can be found in the extent to which the participants themselves *make decisions* that shape policy work. Fung observes that the "vast majority of those who attend events such as public hearings and community meetings do not put forward their own views at all," and are, rather, there to "receive information about some policy or project" as well as to "bear witness to struggles among politicians, activists, and interest groups" (2006, 68). This weakens pluralism. By contrast, one alternative mechanism enhances collective rationality at the expense of majoritarianism and pluralism by involving "professional stakeholders" who "are frequently paid representatives of organized interests and public officials" as a means of enhancing involvement in decisions about policy work (2006, 68).

Other mechanisms work to enhance collective rationality. Fung observes that this usually centers on "aggregation and bargaining" wherein "participants know what they want, and the mode of decision-making aggregates their preferences – often mediated by the influence and power that they bring – into a social choice" (2006, 68). Such a structure could, depending on the nature of the aggregation and bargaining

Representative Agency

processes, enhance majoritarianism or pluralism, but not both, and it might allow for incompletely theorized agreements, particularly if experts are in the mix who can agree to disagree about competing rationales behind policy work. Alternatively, some representative agency structures are deliberative in that they "employ procedures to facilitate the emergence of principled agreement," which involves "the clarification of persisting disagreements, and the discovery of new options" (69). Deliberation involves "a process of interaction, exchange, and – it is hoped – edification precedes any group choice" and a commitment by participants to "aim toward agreement with one another ... based on reasons, arguments, and principles" (69). Doing this can enhance pluralism and collective rationality at the expense of majoritarianism, for instance, if an initial majority "learns" endogenously in deliberation or if an ultimate decision can be reached while participants disagree about the reasons that justify it. Pluralism is weakened if, as the philosopher Cristina Lafont (2019) has argued, the interaction itself renders the participants unrepresentative of the broader polity.

A final way in which representative agency structures differ is in their *influence* over the policy work and the choices of managers, a control argument. Much of this influence is, in practice, indirect, impacting "members of the public or officials who are moved by the testimony, reasons, conclusions, or by the probity of the process itself" (Fung 2006, 69). While "[m]any (perhaps most) public policies and decisions are determined not through aggregation or deliberation but rather through the technical expertise of officials" without citizen participation, several mechanisms are employed. The "advice and consultation" of public participants can influence agency decision-making and help to enhance either collective rationality – unless they serve to partition the decision agenda – or pluralism, seeking to balance epistemic benefits against less pluralistic selection criteria. Similarly, some structures involve participants "in a kind of cogoverning partnership" that teams them up with managers, policy workers and even representatives "to make plans and policies or to develop strategies for public action" (Fung 2006, 69). I will return to this notion of collaborative governance momentarily, but it is straightforward to see the possibility of incompletely theorized agreements among ardent stakeholders and an epistemic view that their agreements, given the pluralism of stakeholder types, produce "good" policies. They could certainly make specific collective choices while agreeing to disagree about the rationales for them.

Representative agency requires champions to engage in a commutation of process values when establishing a decision-making process and defining the representativeness of participants and their influence over policy work. To justify this constitutional-level activity, some champions appeal to the fundamental problem of public administration and representative agency as a way of addressing it. For instance, the public administration scholar Tina Nabatchi contends that a deliberative form of representative agency is mandatory because "public administration has historically accepted among its responsibilities educating citizens about government and governance and promoting and maintaining democratic practices" (Nabatchi 2010, 377) Moreover, the historical use of controlled and managed agency is, Nabatchi argues, a core element of the problem: "public administration has contributed to [democratic] deficits with its long-standing embrace of bureaucratic ethos; the field's focus on managerialism and instrumental rationality has eroded its abilities to consider and implement effective citizen engagement processes" (377). That is, controlled agency has made it difficult for managers to balance competing interests as an element of responsible behavior (Bertelli and Lynn 2003, 2006a, 2006b).

This elite view from the manager's perspective has a strong counter-majoritarian streak. Taken in a light least unfavorable to representative government, the claim here seems to be that managers should engage citizens directly because they have been *overly* accountable to representatives in the sense of the legal scholars Jacob Gersen and Matthew Stephenson (2014). That is, managers behave in the way representatives believe they should, though they, in fact, think representatives would be better served if they did something else. What results is managers' "gaming" of targeted aims (cf. Burgess et al. 2017; Propper 2003), bureaucratic inertia (cf. Congleton 1982; Robinson and Meier 2006), and so forth. Bringing citizens into processes where the nexus of aims and means is debated is meant to avoid such unintended consequences by obviating accountability.

A more compelling rationale for representative agency, I think, is rooted in the philosophy of pragmatism. Particularly valuable is the account of the political scientist Christopher Ansell, which focuses on the representative agency structure of collaborative governance "in which public agencies engage with various stakeholders to jointly deliberate about public problems" (Ansell 2011, 167; but see Dorf and Sabel 1998; Moffitt 2014, 12–3). Ansell's case is built from a political theory that "might prefer a situation where power is widely distributed and diffused so that no single person or institutional role has a large power advantage," a celebration of pluralism (Ansell 2011, 127). Recognizing that "institutions often concentrate power, the solution might be a Madisonian separation-of-powers strategy for taming power" or "it might also ... emphasize the importance of third parties as arbitrators and integrators," a role to which managers and policy workers are apposite, but which is also countermajoritarian (127).

Collaborative governance is appealing from this vantage in that it "binds stakeholders together into problem-solving 'publics' that have the capacity for joint learning" (Ansell 2011, 167). This governance structure constitutes "a deliberative approach and, at a minimum, requires an exchange of perspectives" and "depends on the ability of stakeholders to be able to authentically reflect upon the perspectives of opposing stakeholders" (169), which helps to legitimate this form of representative agency as participants "establish a joint sense of ownership over this collaborative process" (178). It can also weaken majoritarianism through a type of reflective equilibrium or weaken pluralism as deliberation works well but makes the deliberators less representative of citizens more broadly (Lafont 2019). In this sense, as an institution, collaborative governance shares some of the spirit of consensus democracy, which "aim [s] at restraining majority rule" through shared, dispersed, limited, fairly distributed decision-making authority, and, especially, delegated authority to stakeholders in the collaborative (Lijphart 1984, 30). Importantly, Ansell sees managers and policy workers from controlled agency structures "as often the main barrier to a fuller development of collaboration ... guarding their traditional prerogatives and procedures" in a way that "will prevent effective collaboration or turn it into ritual" (Ansell 2011, 183) This is grounds for obviating identifiability and the probability of sanctioning these public officials.

Ansell concludes his championing of collaborative governance with an admirably straightforward admission of its role in reshaping democracy: "[t]he success of collaborative governance therefore depends on a broader transformation of the role of public agencies in democracy" (2011, 183). This differs strikingly from the argument represented in Nabatchi (2010) that deliberation can make up for what is broken in controlled agency. In collaborative governance, the criteria for neutrality in controlled agency give way to a deliberative process that barters the majoritarianism of electoral results for pluralism. The success of this trade-off depends on how deliberative the collaborative (i.e., the collective decision mechanism) really is in practice. The existence and reach of pluralism and collective rationality values within the collaborative are also crucial to judging the trade-off against majoritarianism. Obviating accountability to representatives places process values in the hands of managers, and the legitimacy of governance hangs in the balance.

Some champions of representative agency understand the extent to which they must confront the fundamental question of public administration. Bryson, Crosby, and Bloomberg are exemplary in recognizing that, in representative agency, the role of managers is more expansive than in controlled and managed agency. This is because *managers* must now make trade-offs in process values: "they are presumed able to help create and guide networks of deliberation and delivery and help maintain and enhance the overall effectiveness, capacity, and accountability of the system" (2014, 448). The result is that "[t]he nature of discretion also changes" because "government delivers dialogue and catalyzes and responds to active citizenship in pursuit of what the public values and what is good for the public" (448). In the scenario they describe, accountability in representative government is not doing enough work to uncloak the aims of citizens. Consequently, champions or managers seek to design and implement a new mechanism to help reveal a fuller picture of those aims, and this new mechanism must be legitimate from the perspective of citizens. To do this, the collaborative governance research program of the planning scholar John Bryson and his colleagues examines how policy makers and managers make value trade-offs (Page et al. 2018) and carefully explore the purposes behind direct citizen engagement (Bryson et al. 2013).

Budgets of the People, by the People, for the People

In the Federative Republic of Brazil, politics operate within a presidential and multiparty system, whereas power is exercised at the federal, the state, and the municipal level (Brazil 2019). The president at this writing, Jair Bolsonaro, is head of state and government, with the power to appoint the executive, that is to say, the ministers of state responsible for portfolios in education, foreign affairs, health, and so forth (Brazil 2019). Brazil is also federalist, with twenty-six semi-autonomous states and the Federal District centered on the capital, Brasilia. At the state level, executive power is vested in a governor, appointed secretaries, and a unicameral legislature (Pires 2017). Additionally, each municipality within the Brazilian states is recognized as a minor federal unit with an autonomous government. Citizens of each municipality directly elect a

Representative Agency

mayor with comparably autonomous agenda-setting power (Wampler 2008) and a legislative body called the *Câmara de Vereadores* (Avellaneda and Gomes 2017). This multilevel structure reduces identifiability in Brazilian representative government (e.g., Niedzwiecki 2016).

This government structure emerged in 1988 during the adoption of Brazil's seventh constitution since independence and was accompanied by the inclusion of participatory measures at the municipal level and ballot initiatives at the national level (Brazil 2019; Wampler 2007b). One such measure is participatory budgeting, which enables citizens to participate personally and through elected delegates in a representative agency structure for allocating resources to specific projects, or for determining general spending priorities (Shah 2007).

Participatory budgeting places citizens in a process that both defines the aims for public administration and considers the means for implementing them, and it incorporates trade-offs in process values. As with other representative agency structures, participatory budgeting moves beyond representative government and the importance of neutrality in controlled agency structures. Here, the citizens are immersed in decision-making, and the means, a champion would contend, need not achieve neutrality because accountability to representatives is obviated given the participation of citizens.

Participatory budgeting initiatives in Brazil are varied in their designs, despite sharing basic similarities (Wampler 2007a, 26). The character of participatory budgeting and its success or failure are dependent on the sociopolitical setting of the municipality. The most basic aim of participatory budgeting – broad and representative participation by the municipal society – is constrained by limitations in literacy, education, and policy expertise. Citizens' expectations about the participatory budgeting process can become exaggerated, leading to frustration and the capture of processes by elites (Moynihan 2007). Moreover, the reluctance of governments to shift meaningful decisions to the community can be a political constraint that weakens collective rationality (Moynihan 2007). Other limitations also follow when representatives do not relinquish authority to participatory budgeting processes. For instance, representatives have been known to manipulate these processes in conjunction with managers in municipal agencies "to advance their own agendas" (Wampler 2007b, 65) and when they allocate insufficient funding, projects may not achieve their aims (Wampler 2007a).

Porto Alegre in the Brazilian state of Rio Grande do Sul is possibly the most successful instance of participatory budgeting in the country

(Wampler 2007b, 87). Several decades of participatory budgeting initiatives were set in motion amidst municipal bankruptcy and administrative corruption (Wampler 2000; Fung and Wright 2001). By the mid-2000s, most political parties in municipal elections were running on platforms that included participatory budgeting (Moynihan 2007), and the governance structure enjoyed strong mayoral support that increased the success of projects (Wampler 2007b). Such support is crucial because the participatory budgeting process in Porto Alegre is launched by the mayor, who "is responsible for initiating the budget bill" (Moynihan 2007, 67).

The sixteen regions of Porto Alegre biannually deliberate an agenda that includes previous spending decisions and elect delegates to represent them in processes that encompass multiple regions (Moynihan 2007). Regional meetings are open to the public, and turnout is incentivized because it determines the total number of delegates each region is allowed to elect (Moynihan 2007). Participants can also propose specific projects, such as sidewalks or community centers, within each region, though project feasibility is determined by policy workers. Neighborhood groups compete for projects, encouraging citizens to participate in hopes of getting their project or delegate into the next round (Bovaird 2012).

Once elected, delegates meet weekly "to assess the region's spending priorities" (Moynihan 2007, 68). They are then tasked with informing citizens in their region of the outcomes of their deliberation, and must also elect two more delegates to represent their region in the citywide Participatory Budget Council (Moynihan 2007). This body, during its weekly assemblies, is educated at the behest of representatives and managers in municipal agencies, who organize workshops and programs to teach delegates about budgeting, and to provide support in understanding and analyzing the merits of proposals (Moynihan 2007). After about three months of these weekly meetings, delegates present a list of proposals to the mayor, who may "accept the budget or ask the council for revisions (a request that the council can override with a two-thirds majority)" (Moynihan 2007, 68). The original or revised submission of the Participatory Budget Council is then included in the overall municipal budget and voted on by municipal legislature (Moynihan 2007).

The amount of spending allocated to participatory budgeting processes and the ability of the government to commit to the passed budget are crucial determinants of project success (Moynihan 2007). Porto Alegre is exemplary in its spending and budgetary commitment; in a municipal comparison from 1996 to 1998, despite the comparably small budget, it achieved the highest per capita spending of US$201, compared with just

US$11 in the coastal city of Recife, and "was able to meet nearly 100 percent of its commitments" (Wampler 2007a, 35).

In sum, the citizens of Porto Alegre have a representative agency structure that allows them to shape general spending priorities and to fund specific projects. The city boasts broad participation by citizens with lower socioeconomic status. Participatory budgeting rules and their oversight are firmly in the hand of citizens, and the municipal government abides by them (Wampler 2008). During the participatory budgeting process, citizens are assisted by representatives and managers; the process is accessible and comprehensible by the citizen participants. Furthermore, representatives show a credible commitment to the projects chosen by participatory budgeting, "implementing the public works they select in a timely and transparent manner" and even submit their "own policy initiatives for approval by [participatory budgeting] participants" who have a veto over them (Wampler 2007b, 128).

All of this has happened largely under Workers' Party governments, whose institutional reforms have increasingly sidelined the municipal council, Porto Allegre's legislative body, and increased the executive discretion of the mayor, who still retains "final legal authority" over the participatory budgeting process (Wampler 2004, 89). Because participatory budgeting has been popular with Workers' Party voters, this mayoral veto is used sparingly (Wampler 2004). Participatory budgeting in Porto Allegre requires "the good will and benevolence of the municipal government" (Wampler 2004, 90). Representative agency in Porto Allegre also benefited from a nonbipolar structure of the party system, specifically "a set of weakly institutionalized local opposition parties that failed to resist forcefully" did not make electoral accountability of the Workers' Party likely (Goldfrank 2007, 151).

Blumenau, located in the southern state of Santa Catarina, was founded by German colonists in 1850 and gives a very different account of participatory budgeting as a representative agency structure. Wampler (2008, 72) goes so far as to call it an "Emasculated Participatory Democracy" in which citizens and representatives were "unable to use contentious politics to pressure the government to dedicate more time, energy, and resources" to the participatory budgeting process (73). Participatory budgeting in Blumenau began in 1997, similarly motivated by financial difficulties and a corruption scandal. Yet any ambitions for social inclusion or citizen participation gave way to the demands of activist groups (Wampler 2008).

Participation in Blumenau was high initially, around 10 percent of adults. The resources available were comparatively larger than in Porto Allegre, yet the ultimate decision to deploy them remained with the mayor (Wampler 2007b, 144, 2008). When an opposition party managed to gain control over four Blumenau regions where participatory budgeting was ongoing, it became politically risky for the mayor to consign project decisions to a process that allocated less than 1 percent of the municipal budget (Wampler 2007b, 2008, 72). The rules of participatory budgeting in Blumenau are almost identical to those of Porto Alegre. Both processes have two rounds in which citizens vote for both policy proposals and delegates (Wampler 2007b). While the role of the Participatory Budget Council in Porto Alegre was limited, its cousin in Blumenau "was charged with making final budgetary decisions regarding which projects" should be reported to the mayor (Wampler 2007b, 160). Additionally, project implementation in Blumenau requires citizens in communities directly affected by projects, like the residents of a street to be paved, to contribute 20 percent of the project's cost through neighborhood associations, either through money or physical labor. A crucial difference between the cities is that the government of Blumenau does not credibly commit to these rules, and has developed a reputation for contravening them (Wampler 2007b). The participatory budgeting experiment in Blumenau has struggled from this lack of commitment to it on the part of mayors. This made the process rather pro forma, leaving those who actively participated disillusioned (Wampler 2008).

Participatory budgeting in Brazil has the potential, as in Porto Allegre, to bring distinctive groups of citizens into structured decision-making arenas, but it obviates accountability values in meaningful ways. Group distinctiveness, as in the discussion of bipolarity in Chapter 2, increases identifiability for participant groups, that is, one group wants a street repaved, while another seeks a new sewage system. The process also enhances evaluability for citizens because it educates participants about the budgeting process as well as the projects that are ultimately undertaken. Yet it weakens the identifiability of representatives, and this is most dramatic in the case of the mayor of Blumenau. In the framework of Figure 2.2, blame avoidance is possible even when representative government creates incentives for retrospective answerability to citizens who are informed through the participatory budgeting process (Bertelli 2016). This process reorganizes accountability for the projects in which it is involved, transferring it from representatives and policy workers to citizens, who have no one to blame but themselves, mitigating the

Representative Agency 123

consequences of their accountability errors. In Blumenau, this makes retrospective voting a more favorable proposition for the mayor, and can even allow the continuation of the kind of corruption that made participatory budgeting initially appealing there. In Porto Allegre, the commitment of representatives and managers to the process allows this form of representative agency to obviate accountability in representative government but also to replace it with direct participation that is far less of a blunt instrument for citizens than the ballot box.

Process values are clearly on view as well. Pluralism operates differently in the two cities. Some neighborhood groups, as in Blumenau, are highly organized, and build consensus before the deliberative process of participatory budgeting can have an impact. Because these groups of citizens vary in their levels of literacy, policy expertise, and education, more skilled group organizers can weaken pluralism in this way. While suffrage is universal even at the micro-region level, access to the collective decision mechanism is effectively constrained by requirements of literacy and time. Participants in the mini-public are, in this way, not broadly representative when compared with all citizens who have access to elections. This representation gap gets more pronounced at later stages when delegates are elected by the mini-public, and this happens as participation becomes more consequential with delegates deliberating and voting on spending. Delegates later in the process engage much more with policy workers and representatives, and in so doing, endogenously become less representative (Lafont 2019).

While these things relax pluralism, the participatory budgeting process also influences majoritarianism as well. Even in Porto Allegre, where group organization has less impact on the agenda, the nested hierarchy of votes – electing delegates before proposing projects to the mayor – has features that could introduce a reflective equilibrium, but one that prevails among participants who are not representative of the population. Accountability values may work counter to this situation, but only partially. Although delegates are identifiable and required to present their choices to larger and more representative groups of citizens (enhancing evaluability), sanctioning them might be difficult and accountability errors are possible, if not likely.

Collective rationality is enhanced at the outset of participatory budgeting, which begins with open public meetings that can set the decision agenda for regions. The Participatory Budget Council, though, shares key features with the legislative committees described in Chapter 3. It holds the power to present representatives with amended proposals, which may be less representative of initial citizen interest. This can partition the initial agenda, relaxing the completeness component of collective rationality. The process, which allows two project proposals to move forward from the initial meetings, and incompletely theorized agreements can help to produce a kind of resolution in which citizens agree to disagree about why they should be pursued. In the coastal city of Recife, for instance, neighborhood groups frequently present projects benefiting distinct constituencies that disagree on why projects are worthwhile, but vote for *both* proposals to move them to the next round (Bovaird 2012). Finally, the local focus of participatory budgeting may result in different processes for participation, at different times, in different policy domains, and across sub-national jurisdictions (Feldman and Khademian 2000, 151).

Champions of participatory budgeting believe that it has the potential to "improve state performance" because it establishes an institution to "constrain and check the prerogatives of the municipal government" while bringing citizens into policy work (Wampler 2007, 21). Such statements reveal the obviation of accountability values in representative government. The political scientist Brian Wampler (2007a, 21) contends that participatory budgeting can enhance "the quality of democracy" as participating citizens gradually and through their engagement in the process deepen their understanding of government, their own civic responsibilities, duties, and rights and the policy process. Champions often strike such chords, suggesting that participatory budgeting can make up some ground in systems where representative government underperforms. The public administration scholar Donald Moynihan (2007, 58) makes the epistemic claim that "participation is particularly important because it fosters good governance," which includes increased accountability, government legitimacy, and performance. But doing all of those things *well* belies the champion's dilemma. The extent to which it "promotes transparency" for representatives seeking to understand public aims and citizens seeking information about policy work, and generally "helps individuals become better citizens" (2007, 58) depends on the considerations I have raised above.

INDEPENDENT AGENCY

To say that the idea of placing policy work at arm's length from politicians has been an important theme in research and practice is an exercise in useful understatement. It is an indispensable idea in the study of

Independent Agency

institutional political economy. Consider, first, the observation of Nobel laureate Douglass North (1993, 12) that "[i]nstitutions are the rules of the game and organizations are the players." Organizations, such as the legislatures in which representatives work and the various loci of managers and policy workers, both make and react to the rules, which are embedded in the governance structures at issue in this chapter. Vital to my present discussion is that representatives can create structures – such as managed and representative agency – that enable policy work while reducing the "micro-managing" of accountability and process values through oversight. Can representatives profit from tying their hands entirely, thereby allowing policy work to proceed without imposing *any* constraints via accountability mechanisms or process value trade-offs? Can representatives resist the temptation to circumvent the rules of independence? These are the problems of independent agency.

Independent agency is a governance structure in which representatives make a commitment to refrain from intervening in policy work. It moves beyond managed agency because it does not permit representatives to insist on particular outcomes, obviating the accountability values of representative government. Consider an independent central bank, which has as its *raison d'être* the choice of conservative monetary policies (Barro 1973). The delegation itself is a targeted aim. Independent agency also does not require citizen participation to legitimate the process value trade-offs that champions of representative agency envision. Bartering process and accountability values is the choice of managers and policy workers in these structures.

Credibility and Independence

In an instructive essay, the political scientist Kenneth Shepsle (1991, 247) observes that commitments to independent agency can display "motivational" and "imperative" forms of credibility, that is, the extent to which representatives' "promise, pledge, vow, covenant, guarantee, or bond" not to meddle in policy work is and will be reliable. *Motivational* credibility means that the promise aligns well with the incentives that representatives themselves face. As I write, the coronavirus pandemic is unfolding across the world, and when representatives commit to placing decisions about quarantines, vaccine development, and the distribution of medical supplies into the hands of "experts" – managers in public health organizations, as well as physicians, nurses, and other essential policy workers – the value of their commitment is motivational. Neither representatives nor citizens want more deaths than their agents.

Commitment, by contrast, is *imperative* when there is no mechanism for representatives to intervene: "not because it is compatible with contemporaneous preferences but rather because performance is coerced or discretion to do otherwise is disabled" (Shepsle 1991, 247). That is, the rules of independent agency dictate that representatives have no discretion to intervene in relevant policy work. Imperative credibility has two problems. First, it may not be easy to verify whether the imperative really exists, such as when the enabling statute does not carefully explain the conditions of independence (247). Second, if both representatives consistently demand and the managers in an independent agency structure similarly adhere to a particular course of policy work, it may be difficult to see commitment as good for citizens. To illustrate, Shepsle invokes Nobel laureate Thomas Schelling's (1978) facts of the "chicken" game, in which two drivers rapidly converge toward a one-lane bridge: "If *both* drivers ... disconnect their steering wheels and tie down their accelerators ... no one will deny their credible commitments, but the optimality of the result is surely in question" (Shepsle 1991, 247, emphasis original).

The reality of independent agency is far from pure motivational or pure behavioral commitment. Representatives "credibly commit themselves to standing rules of procedure not by making it *impossible* to suspend such rules but only by making it difficult"; that is, the value of independent agency "resides in the salutary effect on *current* behavior induced by *future* expectations" (Shepsle 1991, 249, emphasis original). If citizens expect their government to act in a particular way, that is, the commitment to policy work of a certain character is credible, they will plan their activities in economy and society accordingly. Alternatively, if citizens do not perceive a credible commitment, they may act against their own collective interest, substituting individual motivations for coordinated actions.

Nowhere is this clearer as I write than when President of the United States Donald Trump draws a bead on the quintessentially independent Federal Reserve System (see generally Fernández-Albertos 2015; Keefer et al. 2003). For instance, amidst the expanding coronavirus crisis on March 10, 2020, the president wrote on Twitter: "Our pathetic, slow moving Federal Reserve, headed by Jay Powell, who raised rates too fast and lowered too late, should get our Fed Rate down to the levels of our competitor nations. They now have as much as a two point advantage, with even bigger currency help. Also, stimulate!" President Trump's strategy of source relocation points identifies Chairman Powell and makes clear evaluation claims to his Twitter followers. But these tweets reveal that the commitment may be imperative, but it is certainly not motivational. Furthermore, the behavior of markets seems to suggest that imperative credibility is in serious doubt. Bianchi, Kind, and Kung (2019) find that the average impact of these tweetstorms on market expectations relative to the federal funds rate for overnight bank lending is negative, statistically significant and approximately 0.1 percentage points. They write, "the tweets do not simply affect expectations about the timing of changes that markets were already anticipating, but instead move market expectations about the stance of monetary policy" (Bianchi, Kind, and Kung 2019, 14), which implies "that markets do not perceive the Federal Reserve Bank as a fully independent institution immune from political pressure" (15).

The Costs of Independence

The political scientist J. Andrew Sinclair and I deployed the transaction-cost politics framework constructed by the economist Murray Horn (1995), a former top finance official in New Zealand, to theorize how agency independence relates to accountability in representative government (Bertelli and Sinclair 2018). Horn (1995, 13–4) identifies four costs to politicians that accrue from the choice of governance structures. Bargaining costs relate to negotiations about the nature of policy work between representatives and organized interest groups of citizens. They increase as these negotiations become more difficult. Commitment costs have to do with the structure of representative government, rising as new coalitions of representatives find it easier to revise or replace the policies of their predecessors. Agency costs accumulate in the relationship between representatives, managers, and policy workers. These costs are greatest when managers and policy workers find it either difficult or unpalatable to do the policy work that representatives ask of them. Uncertainty costs are tied up with the predictability of outcomes that policy work can effectuate. When citizens and organized stakeholder groups are less clear about what the costs and benefits of policy work might be, these costs rise. Each of these costs is due to the nature of governance structures as well as the form of representative government that is in place.

128 *Governance Structures and Democratic Values*

Horn (1995) contends that champions should minimize these costs when designing governance structures. Managed agency structures would be well suited when bargaining, uncertainty, agency, and commitment costs are all low so that outcomes could be defined in a way that citizens, representatives, managers, and policy workers would consider to be "good," such as lower waiting times at driver licensing centers. That would justify relaxing pluralism as a process value via metaconsensus on the "good" aim, as with efficiency in managed agency. Managerial flexibility could then help effectuate those outcomes efficiently and effectively. This is the main improvement over controlled agency, which also is appropriate in that cost environment. However, high-accountability political systems, such as that of the United Kingdom, increase commitment costs because a new government could more easily abandon the policies of the previous one, weakening the case for managed agency if citizens' metaconsensus was a false or fleeting one.

Both controlled and representative agency allow for the expertise of managers and policy workers to be marshaled into service when uncertainty costs are high. Representative agency leverages this environment differently, and seems most appropriate when bargaining, agency, and uncertainty costs are all high, but commitment costs are low. Champions can leverage the ease of negotiation in the policy environment by incorporating it into policy work, reducing agency costs by bringing representatives, managers, and citizens into the same governance structure to do policy work that does not clearly translate into widely accepted "good" outcomes. This justifies the obviation of majoritarianism. Still, representative agency works best when representatives can commit to the structure, and separation-of-powers political systems with more checks-and-balances – the United States or Brazil – are more encouraging environments for these structures (Tsebelis 1995).

Independent agency is an extreme structure in terms of Horn's (1995) transaction-cost framework, and I think it is better understood in what it does to reorient these costs. Independent agency obviates all of the accountability values of Chapter 2. It shields representatives from citizens by rendering them less identifiable (Bertelli and Sinclair 2018, 695). In the case of monetary policy, which President Trump identifies with the Federal Reserve in the tweeted rhetoric of my example, markets are responding to a shift in the probability of sanction: independent agency obviates it, but presidential rhetoric seems to bring it back enough to change investor behavior.

Independent agency removes representatives from bargaining with groups of citizens. If policy work is not done transparently, so that organized groups of citizens can understand it, evaluability is curtailed and uncertainty costs rise. Moreover, if bargaining in the legislative arena is not replaced with a mechanism for citizen participation like those championed in representative agency structures, both bargaining and uncertainty costs can rise as citizens struggle to relate policy work to outcomes that are not clearly related to the aims and trade-offs reflected in its choice of representatives in the last election (Bertelli and Sinclair 2018, 695).

The canonical function of independent agency is to reduce commitment costs – even for representative governments like that of Britain, where they are constitutionally high – by making it difficult for politicians to overrule the policy choices of managers through the mechanism of imperative commitment (Bertelli and Sinclair 2018, 695). By pulling policy work away from representatives, independent agency obviates accountability values. What is more, it does not necessarily replace the accountability relationship between managers and representatives with more direct connection between citizens and representatives as in representative agency. In confronting the champion's dilemma, the architects of independent agency design a structure that, on its face, undermines representative government.

Because it collectively obviates the accountability and process values in representative government, representatives must have a very good reason for enacting laws that permit agency independence. The need for policy-specific, technical expertise exercised at arm's length from the influence of electorally motivated representatives is the paramount reason, and it embraces an epistemic claim about "correct" policy. The limit of independent agency structures presents itself when private entities do policy work without any more oversight from representatives than other private activity must withstand, for example, avoiding criminality. In such cases of *privatization*, the economic market or the mission of the organizations involved are surrogates for representative government in connecting the policy aims of citizens with the means by which they are provided. In the case of contracting for trash collection services, reliance on market forces is a straightforward argument. Citizens are in consensus: they want their trash to be collected and to pay the least amount of money possible to have this done. Their aim for this policy domain is efficiency (e.g., Savas 1977). Market competition can help independent agents achieve this goal under such conditions. This form of market accountability replaces that of representative government when policy work is privatized (e.g., Borowiak 2011).

In other scenarios, the case for independence is more (or less) clear cut. The US Organ Procurement and Transplantation Network was established by Congress as "a *private* nonprofit entity that has an expertise in organ procurement and transplantation" for precisely these reasons (42 U.S.C. 274(b) (1) (A), emphasis added). It may strike the reader as preposterous on its face that representatives, and managers in a controlled agency relationship with them, should be responsible for keeping "a national list of individuals who need organs" (42 U.S.C. 274(b)(2)(A) (i)), and "a national system ... to match organs and individuals ... especially individuals whose immune system makes it difficult for them to receive organs" (42 U.S.C. 274(b)(2)(A)(ii)). The reason for this consensus of unease is a rather profound question of motivational credibility – can representatives resist efforts by major campaign contributors should they or their loved ones face death in the absence of a transplant? The National Organ Transplant Act works to increase imperative credibility by locating the network out of government entirely – in a nonprofit organization – with federal funding provided through contracts (42 U.S.C. 274(a)). However, the Secretary of Health and Human Services, who serves in the US president's cabinet, has authority to consider "critical comments" that arise from operation of the network (42 U.S.C. 274 (c)). The statute also requires an element of public participation in that the network's board of directors must consist of "representatives of organ procurement organizations ... transplant centers, voluntary health associations, and the general public" (42 U.S.C. 274(b) (1) (B) (i)). While technical expertise and political distance are essential, the network does not operate with complete independence.

It is often observed that independent agency is more of a continuum in practice. In the United States, Datla and Revesz (2013, 769) observe that "there is no single feature, structural or functional, that every agency thought of as independent shares" and that agencies should more profitably be "seen as falling on a spectrum from more independent to less independent." Scholars have recorded these features in large datasets, translating them into quantitative measures of the independence continuum for the United States (Selin 2015), Europe (Gilardi 2002, 2005), and countries around the world (Hanretty and Koop 2012; Jordana, Fernández-i-Marín, and Bianculli 2018). This variation should not be surprising given the limits of representative government as managers and policy workers become more independent.

Art's Length

Because of the high commitment costs embedded in its high-accountability form of representative government, the United Kingdom is an interesting context in which to examine the nature of independent agency (cf. Bertelli 2008; Bertelli and Sinclair 2015; Bertelli, Sinclair, and Lee 2015; Durose, Justice, and Skelcher 2015; Tonkiss and Noonan 2013). Non-Departmental Public Bodies (NDPBs) are not part of a specific ministerial department (UK Cabinet Office 2011). NDPBs have, with limited exceptions, their own legal personality, but the ministers of their "sponsoring" departments are directly accountable to Parliament (UK Cabinet Office 2011).

There are four different types of NDPBs: advisory, consisting of external experts advising ministers in specific areas of policymaking; tribunal, having jurisdiction over a specialized field of law (Schuppert 2010); independent monitoring boards overseeing the management of prisons and hospitals (Ellison 2018); and executive, the subject of this section. Executive NDPBs receive government funding to "carry out a wide range of administrative, commercial, executive, and regulatory or technical functions which are better delivered at arm's length from Ministers" (UK Cabinet Office 2011). The relationship between the sponsoring department and NDPB is formally defined to facilitate responsibility for policymaking, financial and risk management, and value for money (UK Cabinet Office 2006). Regular reviews ensure a continued need for the executive NDPB's functions to be independent, and the body must be transparent, publishing an annual report and public accounts (UK Cabinet Office 2011).

In its advice to ministerial departments, the Cabinet Office suggests that the independence of executive NDPBs may be appropriate to ensure that advice and expertise of nondepartmental bodies are removed from partisan politics. The government makes the epistemic argument that these bodies are suited for providing independent expertise regarding "technical, scientific or other complex issues," such as funding decisions and ethical problems in policymaking (UK Cabinet Office 2006). Figure 4.3 shows the decision-making process that the Cabinet Office recommends for determining whether an independent agency is appropriate for a particular kind of policy work. The threshold question is whether the government needs to provide the service, and if the answer is no, the private market, the nonprofit sector, or other means are given responsibility by default. As in the case of executive agencies, the question

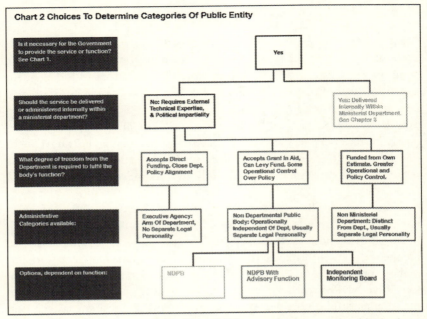

FIGURE 4.3 When ministers should establish a nondepartmental public body in the United Kingdom.
Reproduced from UK Cabinet Office (2011). © Cabinet Office, 2011. This information is licensed under the Open Government Licence v3.0. To view this licence, visit http://www.nationalarchives.gov.uk/doc/open-government-licence/

begins by disaggregating the decision-making agenda, relaxing collective rationality. Once again, nongovernmental provision is the most extreme form of independent agency because it leaves accountability and process values to the discretion of policy workers with no formal relationship to representative government beyond the terms of a contract or grant-in-aid program (cf. Carman 2009; Dicke and Ott 1999; Ott and Dicke 2001; Romzek and Johnston 2005). Moving farther down the decision tree shapes the structure of independent agency.

The second question in the figure is paramount for justifying independence. Impartial and expert policy work must be at stake, and this invites epistemic justification or appeal to a metaconsensus, such as regarding the neutrality of a judicial proceeding. If not, accountability values take precedence and a controlled agency structure is preferred. If independent agency is justified, the inquiry turns to how much independence is warranted, and the Cabinet Office is explicitly concerned about budgetary

Independent Agency

133

independence. A direct funding line creates the least independence, while a grant-in-aid increases the discretionary authority of NDPB managers in resource allocation. The ability to fund policy work through collecting its own revenues, as when a museum charges for admission to special exhibits, gives NDPB managers even more independence. Figure 4.3 also shows that each of these budgetary models maps into different legal frameworks and ultimately to different classifications of bodies. The systematic framework in place in the United Kingdom brings the question of imperative commitment and the reality that independent agency lies along a continuum into sharp relief.

One area in which greater independence has been justified is the funding of art and cultural endeavors. The subjectivity of determining what is "good" and "bad" in this arena even led the art historian E. H. Gombrich (2006, 1–2) to a practice of "self-denial" in his work "lest the well-known masterpieces to be crowded out by [his] own personal favourites." A metaconsensus on "good" art is unlikely to exist, but that may make it possible to appeal to another, namely, that art is important for its own sake. The Arts Council England was constituted as an executive NDPB working at arm's length from the Department of Culture, Media, and Sport. Since 2002, it is responsible for developing and investing in "artistic and cultural experiences that enrich people's lives" (Arts Council England 2019). Since 2011, the Arts Council also supports "activities across the arts, museums and libraries" (Arts Council England 2019), including dance, music, and literature. This includes grants to local authorities, arts organizations, and direct funding for artists (Bertelli et al. 2014, 348–9).

Funding for the Arts Council's policy work comes from government grants-in-aid the National Lottery (Arts Council England 2015). The planned activity for 2018–2022 consists of $391 million in grant-in-aid awards and an additional $83 million from the lottery (Arts Council England 2018). The creation of a lottery with the arts being its main beneficiary was far from uncontroversial, and became a point of friction among citizens, managers in the NDPB, and the Department of Culture, Media, and Sport, and representatives. Those buying National Lottery tickets are largely in the working class, and lottery money substantially supported an $88 million grant to the Royal Opera House at Covent Garden in 1995, causing a backlash by newspapers and politicians criticizing that Covent Garden is not accessible to those paying for its programming (Riding 1995). One headline in *The Sun* read, "It's the greedy beggars' opera," opinion polls registered public opposition, and the chief music critic for *The Times* wrote that the wealthy disproportionately benefited from the grant to the opera house (Riding 1995). Any claim to metaconsensus around *l'art pour l'art* is not without controversy, but majoritarianism can be devastating to it.

The Arts Council responded to the criticism in their 1995–1996 annual report by including the text of a speech by its chairman to the House of Commons highlighting the benefits, but also the difficulties, associated with lottery funding and outlining a way forward (Arts Council of England 1996). The cultural politics of theater were also affected by the lottery earmarking, with accusations of a bias toward the "high arts" and activities in London (Lacey 2004). Only "a handful" of the 159 organizations that received funding were "tiny and regional" (Riding 1995) despite denials by the Arts Council that smaller projects were not "crowded out" by big grants to prestigious institutions (Arts Council of England 1996). Clearly, this would undermine pluralism. Studying grants from the Arts Council between 2003 and 2006, my colleagues and I found evidence that areas with more swing voters received more grants, revealing a pattern consistent with distributive politics (Bertelli et al. 2014). Such criticism continued throughout the next decade, and was accompanied by budget cuts to the NDPB over the past ten years, most notably a reduction of 29.6 percent in the grant-in-aid following the 2010 comprehensive government spending review (BBC 2010).

Following this fiscal restraint, a parliamentary select committee concluded in 2011 that the NDPB was able to "function well" despite "significant spending reductions on its own administration" leading representatives to "question whether the Arts Council had previously been spending an unnecessarily high amount on its own administration" and finding that "it was previously spending far too much on itself" (House of Commons: Culture, Media, and Sport Committee 2011, 17). This aspect of an agency's policy work – administrative versus programmatic spending – is highly evaluable. The Arts Council, supported by "senior figures in the arts" and an official report, defended its recent achievements in the hearings (Higgins 2011). Yet the relationship of Arts Council managers and representatives continued in a Liszt-Wagner fashion – complex, difficult, and occasionally resentful. In 2017, after a new wave of criticism revisited the disproportionate funding of London institutions, grants to the Royal Opera House, the Southbank Centre, the National Theatre, and the Royal Shakespeare Company were cut by 3 percent for 2018–2022 (Pickford 2017). Arts Council Chairman Sir Nicholas Serota emphasized an increase of 4.6 percent in funding outside London between 2015 and

Conclusion 135

2018 to skeptical representatives and citizens (Pickford 2017). Opera funding gained more criticism in 2018 on familiar grounds of pluralism. The leader of UK Music, which represents the commercial music industry, accused the Arts Council of being "too posh for pop" and complained that the disproportionate funding of opera crowded out other types of music (Dugher 2018).

The policy work of the Arts Council does not achieve the ideal of independent agency, and this is because the obviation of accountability values – identifiability, evaluability, and the probability of sanction – is far from complete. The Arts Council, not representatives or managers in the Department of Culture, Media, and Sport, are identifiable with funding decisions. Their policy work is evaluable, not in its intricacies, but in the distribution of funds across the landscape of arts and cultural organizations in Britain, and between administrative and programmatic spending. Recent reductions in the grant-in-aid show that representatives do not restrain themselves from sanctioning the NDPB.

The Arts Council thus illustrates two important elements of independent agency. First, both motivational and imperative commitment to independence is essential. The size of the grant-in-aid is a crucial choice that representatives retain, and this mechanism reduces the independence of the NDPB. Second, in the high-accountability British government, representatives have significant commitment costs, and this shows in their relationships with managers in the NDPB. The Arts Council operates at arm's length from the sponsoring department's minister in day-to-day agency operations, giving them process independence, but remain accountable to the minister for policy work in a general sense. By comparison, the executive agency responsible for prisons considered in the managed agency section of this chapter is accountable for achieving outcomes that are defined by a sponsoring minister. HMPPS has significant autonomy over process values, while the Arts Council has additional independence in choosing the aims of arts funding. Yet the low commitment costs of the British system can make it worthwhile for representatives, particularly when citizens and the media apply pressure, to take back accountability for policy work. The result is independence that is weakened by low motivational commitment.

CONCLUSION

This chapter began with the core challenge of creating structures of governance in systems of representative democracy. No structure can preserve all of the accountability and process values at the same time, and trade-offs must be made that still allow policy workers to use their discretion responsibly. Democracy administered is therefore subject to the value trade-offs required by the champion's dilemma. In normative terms, the choices of champions must confront the fundamental problem of public administration. I think that much of the contemporary literature that champions the agency structures described above is not clear enough about the value trade-offs involved. My framework for analyzing how champions respond to this dilemma, and how representatives and policy workers use their discretionary authority in those structures permits what I believe to be a fresh look at some very heavily studied phenomena.

The examples of this chapter included information about levels of accountability in countries in which they were situated. In Chapter 5, I engage in a more systematic analysis that relates accountability values in representative government to the values of governance structures. This begins my treatment of the question of whether the latter should reinforce the former. I begin Chapter 5 by hypothesizing that it should – a hypothesis that could be drawn from a variety of theoretical approaches. Yet this claim of value reinforcement is more than supported in the data. In Chapter 6, I argue that it deserves a place in the legitimating narrative of public administration.

Appendix: The Accountability Index

The Accountability Index (ACI) is drawn from Kam, Bertelli and Held (2020) and reflects electoral accountability in parliamentary government. It represents the marginal effect of changes in vote share for parties in government on changes in their share of cabinet portfolios, or in the terms of the accountability identity from Chapter 3, $\delta\Delta C/\delta\Delta V$. Equations 4–6 in Kam, Bertelli and Held (2020, 750) show precisely how this is calculated from our data.

The meaning of the ACI is straightforward. When votes for parties in government increase (decrease), the share of that party's participation in government through cabinet portfolios correspondingly increases (decreases). The normative claim that the ACI is an index of electoral accountability "is that incumbent parties that lose votes should participate less in policy making" (Kam, Bertelli and Held 2020, 757). Meeting this condition has two requirements, namely that "the electoral system must ensure that losses in votes translate into losses in seats" and also that "the party system must ensure that losses in seats translate into losses in cabinet portfolios" (757). Analyzing 400 elections in twenty-eight parliamentary democracies, we found that both proportional and majoritarian systems, which have different underlying values of representation, both "generally do a good job in ensuring a strong, positive votes-to-seats relationship" (758). Where electoral accountability is prone to breaking down is when "the party system fails to translate losses in seats into losses in cabinet portfolios," and this happens more often as the bipolarity of the party system decreases (758).

Table 4.1 presents all countries in the study ranked by their ACI values.

Governance Structures and Democratic Values

TABLE 4.1 *Accountability in parliamentary governments*

Rank	Country	ACI	Rank	Country	ACI
1	United Kingdom	10.38	15	Latvia	1.97
2	Australia	5.22	16	Iceland	1.96
3	Finland	4.86	17	Sweden	1.95
4	Canada	4.46	18	Greece	1.87
5	New Zealand	4.36	19	Norway	1.86
6	Japan	3.93	20	France	1.82
7	Portugal	3.68	21	Austria	1.81
8	Spain	3.41	22	Netherlands	1.64
9	Belgium	3.06	23	Luxembourg	1.42
10	Israel	2.61	24	Poland	1.32
11	Germany	2.52	25	Estonia	1.29
12	Hungary	2.23	26	Italy	.88
13	Denmark	2.16	27	Slovakia	.27
14	Ireland	2.08	28	Czechia	−1.70

The ranking and values of the ACI in the countries included in Kam, Bertelli and Held (2020) are presented.

5

The Value Reinforcement Hypothesis

Do governance structures systematically differ across systems of representative government? Are responses to the champion's dilemma constrained by the accountability and process values rooted in national political systems? I will argue that addressing the former question essentially requires an attempt to answer the latter. The value trade-offs that governance structures make can come into tension with those embraced by the system in which they are situated. Building on the analytic framework in the previous chapter, I make a simple, testable claim that can enable this positive research agenda, and which, I maintain, is an important channel for studying public administration in representative governments in a way that is both contemporary and comparative.

I call this claim the *value reinforcement hypothesis*. Governance structures reinforce the values of the representative governments they serve. If a political system embraces pluralism and collective rationality as process values, its governance structures will enhance those process beliefs. If a government faces strong electoral accountability, its governance structures will emphasize accountability values, making identifiable managers likely to face sanctions for their performance. Correlations such as these would be observed if the hypothesis has potential for guiding a positive research agenda.

To simplify the discussion that follows, I will refer to values in the political system as *political values* and values in governance structures as *governance values*.

The value reinforcement hypothesis expects a correlation between political and governance values. Two classes of causal mechanisms can underlie this correlation, and these mechanisms can have many varying forms. An *institutional reinforcement mechanism* focuses on representatives, who respond to the incentives of the political system and that emerge from its collective decision mechanism. That is to say, representatives are chosen in majoritarian or proportional elections, which create different incentives. Specifically, the relevant incentives are those of electoral accountability discussed in Chapter 2 and of democratic process in Chapter 3.

Institutional reinforcement mechanisms can be *formal*. Representatives enact laws that enable specific governance structures. These structures, in turn, incentivize managers to help representatives respond to the incentives of their form of representative government. When a statute requires a form of representative agency, it can specify these mechanisms, for instance, the requirements for membership on and partisan balance of advisory committees, or the decision rules and procedures by which citizen participation bodies make collective choices.

Pamela Clouser McCann, Giulia Leila Travaglini and I have focused on a subset of these formal provisions of law that we call *nonfiscal partnerships* in which the United States Congress has required state and local authorities to interact with authorities in forms of representative agency (Bertelli, Clouser McCann, and Travaglini 2019). Nonfiscal partnerships are an important contrast to the direct granting of funds to subnational governments, which are overseen by federal-level managers. An example is section 254(a) (1) of the Telecommunications Act of 1996 (Pub. L. No. 104-104) which enables the Federal-State Joint Board on Universal Service "to recommend changes to any [Federal Communications Commission] regulations ... including the definition of the services ... and a specific timetable for completion of such recommendations." The membership of the Joint Board must include one "State-appointed utility consumer advocate nominated by a national organization of State utility consumer advocates." The Joint Board "shall, after notice and opportunity for public comment, make its recommendations" and section 245(a) (2) requires the Federal Communications Commission to "initiate a single proceeding to implement the recommendations from the Joint Board."

The institutional reinforcement mechanism that we propose to explain the choice of nonfiscal partnerships over grants of money has three components. First, faced with a choice between granting money to subnational authorities and requiring nonfiscal partnerships, the latter are preferred when congressional representatives have less conflict over policy aims with federal managers than with relevant subnational

The Value Reinforcement Hypothesis 141

representatives (Bertelli, Clouser McCann, and Travaglini 2019, 380). This is a control argument grounded in American federalism and reminiscent of Weber's problem of the all-representative bureaucracy described in Chapter 4. Identifiable representatives at subnational levels who share aims can be trusted to spend federal money, but nonfiscal partnerships use representative agency to temper the ambitions of those who do not share aims. Second, when the outcomes of policy work are difficult to predict because the means for producing them is unclear as a technical matter, nonfiscal partnerships are more likely. This is a capability argument. Representative agency is valuable to federal representatives because it can stimulate the development of capability for performing subnational policy work. Third, when the enacting coalition of representatives in Congress is likely to disintegrate after the next election, nonfiscal partnerships are less likely to appear in legislation because they would allow the next group of representatives to undermine the aims of the statute. This is another control argument. Grants of money, under these conditions, are easier to restrict.

The control and capability mechanisms described in Bertelli, Clouser McCann, and Travaglini (2019) suggest how representative agency can be value-reinforcing; in this case, it would reinforce accountability values. When the technology for producing "good" outcomes is uncertain, Congress can benefit from incorporating managers from inside and outside government because of the epistemic benefit of these collaborations. But this is tempered by the accountability values embedded in congressional elections. Representative agency is a risk for highly identifiable congressional representatives when it incorporates the views of managers and subnational representatives into collaborations that could produce outcomes for which their supporters might sanction them at the ballot box. Partnerships, through their increased capability, could make policy work sufficiently evaluable to allow citizens to see the policy conflict for themselves. It is important to note that our approach shares the limitations of other formal models of delegations from representatives to policy workers discussed in Chapter 4, and the core of that critique applies here as well. Our model does not explicitly incorporate value trade-offs and can only speak to them by implication.

Institutional reinforcement mechanisms can also be *informal*, based on unwritten norms and practices of policy workers and representatives, including those that guide the interaction between the two. The comparison of New Public Management in the Netherlands and the United Kingdom in the next section will suggest several possible institutional reinforcement mechanisms. These mechanisms posit that policy workers' informal rules of conduct, the internal procedures of decision-making, embrace governance values that correlate with political values.

A *behavioral reinforcement mechanism* is centered in the democratic belief systems of policy workers. Governance structures reinforce values by shaping managers' beliefs about those values. Similar to belief systems in the mass public (Converse 2006 [1964]), the democratic belief systems of policy workers are constrained, namely, a change in one value makes it necessary to change another. For instance, suppose the managed agency structure in the HMPPS described in Chapter 4 made Director General Derek Lewis orient his beliefs toward accountability for outcomes. Now suppose that Lewis passed these values down to his subordinates through written and verbal communication as well as informal interaction. Then, the HMPPS would reinforce values through a behavioral mechanism, and the managerial communications and style that Lewis took up would be the appropriate focus of a study seeking to assess a causal claim of behavioral reinforcement.

Behavioral reinforcement mechanisms are overwhelmingly informal, but can be shaped through formal means, such as the language of a law. Suppose that in the nonfiscal partnership example above, the Joint Board developed informal norms that complemented the system accountability values. The Federal Communications Commission has many features of an independent agency structure; a norm of making specific recommendations and confronting existing regulations could shift accountability back to Congress. Behavioral reinforcement mechanisms can be found in the practices of managers and policy workers as they perform policy work. For instance, the political theorist Bernardo Zacka (2017) conducts an ethnographic study of street-level managers in social service agencies that reveals how policy workers within them balance competing values of efficiency, fairness, responsiveness to the aims of policies and respect for the clients they serve. The policy workers he observes make trade-offs in ways that give them distinctive characters. Some are indifferent and relax respect, some are "caregivers" at the expense of responsiveness or efficiency, and still others are "enforcers" who privilege responsiveness. It is these practices of policy workers that contain behavioral reinforcement mechanisms.

The value reinforcement hypothesis is evocative of the political scientist Harry Eckstein's argument about the cultural reinforcement of democracy. Representative governments perform better – that is, they are more durable and legitimate, maintain order, and meet challenges with effective policies – when patterns of authority in a society are congruent with patterns of authority in the governance of that society (Eckstein 1966, 1971).

Contemporary public administration scholarship acknowledges value reinforcement, but it has not congealed around a systematic comparative agenda to study it. In this chapter, I review an existing literature and also conduct a novel analysis of existing data to show that correlations between political and governance values do exist. First, I illustrate institutional reinforcement through the findings of a robust literature on the implementation of New Public Management reforms across countries. My focus is the United Kingdom and the Netherlands, which differ significantly in terms of electoral accountability. Second, I illustrate behavioral reinforcement through quantitative evidence from a large-scale survey of managers in eighteen European parliamentary governments.

Testing causal claims regarding value reinforcement is an important next step once correlations are observed. Institutional and behavioral reinforcement mechanisms provide a useful comparative lens on the traditional narrative of public administration. Where an institutional mechanism operates, theories of control and capacity work well. Where a behavioral mechanism is in place, managerial responsibility can be shaped informally through the practices of policy workers. And where both operate at once, scholars might be able to assess how well managers and other policy workers are addressing the fundamental problem of public administration. The penultimate section of this chapter outlines such a research program. Moreover, I maintain that causal claims regarding value reinforcement have a normative foundation in the nature of the state that cannot be ignored in this positive research program, and I present a normative theory in Chapter 6.

VALUE REINFORCEMENT AS A POSITIVE CLAIM

The introduction of New Public Management (NPM) reforms were explicitly motivated by accountability and a desire "to cut the costs of government and make it work better for citizens or users" (Hood and Dixon 2015, 2). Lægreid (2014, 1) observes that the "shift from a bureaucratic ethos of office to a managerial regime" was a marked change from controlled agency in regard to "*who* is accountable" and "*for what*" they must answer (see generally Bovens 1998). That is, managed agency is meant to restrict managers' autonomy over the aims of policy; outputs or outcomes are determined ex ante by representatives, and managers are held accountable ex post for achieving them (Laegrid 2014, 2–3). Cost reductions and performance improvements were linked to managed agency "to bring greater business efficiency to government" (Hood and Dixon 2015, 1). The NPM strategy also includes an important measure of independent agency, stimulating the construction of agencies in which managers operate at arm's length from representatives, such as in the Non-Departmental Public Bodies (NDPBs) in the United Kingdom discussed previously.

This mixture of managed and independent agency facilitated blame-avoidance strategies, shifting identifiability from representatives to managers. Representatives are "left with a strategic role – setting broad goals but keeping their hands off the day-to-day business of running the machine, which should be delegated to professional managers. They [are] to act as chief executives, or even chairmen of the board, not 'fixers'" (Pollitt and Bouckaert 2012, 168). Identifiable managers, rather, are "held accountable through incentives and performance systems" (Lægrid 2014, 4). What is more, output and outcome metrics create a "citizens as customer" focus that unlocks a "dual accountability of civil servants to politicians and consumers" that creates sometimes competing principals for managers and policy workers (8). In this way, NPM is formally an intriguing structure for representatives, who can train managed and independent agencies on the aims that the public wants, and allow managers the flexibility to innovate the means to achieve them.

Accountability and Process Values in New Public Management

NPM reforms reshape representative government significantly, obviating process values, on the one hand through managed agency, and accountability values through independent agency on the other. The managed agency component strengthens identifiability and the probability of sanction, but not necessarily evaluability as it "lets managers manage," holding them accountable only for the result of that process. Recalling the framework in Figure 2.2, obfuscating information strategies are anticipated because both representatives (for policy aims) and managers (for outputs or outcomes) are identifiable, but the means for doing policy work is weakly evaluable by the public. The citizen-as-customer orientation of NPM makes managed agency itself an institutional strategy of source relocation and places it in the hands of representatives. Executive agencies in the United Kingdom, such as HMPPS in Chapter 4, are an excellent example because they operate "separately from – but within a policy and resources framework set by – a primarily policy-focused department" (UK Cabinet Office, 2018, 4). That is, when policy events are easily evaluable – like prison breaks and long waiting lines for driver's licenses – a shift to managed agency identifies managers with policy work. Managed agency, at the same time, relieves representatives who are identifiable with broader policy aims from the pressures of accountability, particularly when those aims might be thwarted by managers' exercising their discretion.

NPM's reliance on independent agency might also allow representatives to deploy strategies of institutional reorganization if doing so separates representatives from outcomes. Indeed, in the United Kingdom, periodic "bonfires of the quangos" – reorganizations of the stock of quasi-independent agencies – reshape the independent agency landscape. For instance, in the 2011 reorganization of 403 NDPBs by the Conservative-Liberal coalition government in the United Kingdom, Bertelli and Sinclair (2018, 704) find that "ideological conflict between the new government and the mission of an independent agency" makes it more likely that an NDPB remains at arm's length. This is consistent with the logic of insulating representatives from the outcomes in independent agency, and it is possible because of the managed agency strategy of partitioning the decision-making agenda. However, we also find that those NDPBs that do lose their independence, are more likely to undergo structural change and *also* more likely to be integrated into the controlled agency of cabinet departments. Blame-avoidance strategies catalyzed by NPM are not clear cut (e.g., Lægreid 2014, 8). Institutional reorganization is an option when the political system has low commitment costs (Horn 1995) or, put differently, when both imperative (the law regarding the creation of NDPBs) and motivational commitment (ideological conflict between incumbent representatives and the aims of an NDPB) are low. Yet a version of the value reinforcement hypothesis would suggest that, in systems with higher commitment costs, representatives may not be able to act in this way because governance values will not reinforce political values. The costs here accrue because of structural features – ministerial accountability and parliamentary sovereignty, for instance – that incorporate democratic values.

Recent scholarly attention has been focused on the success of NPM reforms. Taking a comparative perspective, Hood and Dixon (2015, 128), acknowledge a general lack of systematic data fit for the task that leads to a significant problem of evaluability: "It is all but impossible to compare the cost and performance of those agencies with that of core ministerial departments over time" (133–34). They conclude that there is "relatively little evidence of difference in running costs or administrative performance between UK central government and the other comparators." Their policy-analytic conclusion stands in contrast with the behavioral findings of Hammerschmid, Van de Walle, Andrews and Mostafa (2019) from a survey of managers in twenty European countries. The study reports that managers perceive downsizing and contracting as associated with perceptions of more efficient service delivery, though the former simultaneously decreases service quality. However, the managed and independent agency elements of NPM – placing managers at arm's length from representatives, giving them flexibility in staffing and so forth – "barely influence perceptions of performance improvement" (Hammerschmid et al. 2019, 19–20). By contrast, they find that treating "service users as customers" correlates strongly with managers' positive perceptions of "overall performance" (20). Evaluating NPM reforms has yielded mixed evidence at best, and is complicated by its context dependence: how the motivation, design, and implementation of these reforms relate to national-level considerations (Lægreid, 2014). That is, it addresses the correspondence between political and governance values. Of course, representative governments can infuse different accountability and process values, and my hypothesis suggests that they will be reinforced in the governance structures of NPM as champions confront their dilemma and make inevitable trade-offs.

While many governments did adopt "benchmarking, performance-related budgeting, accruals accounting, contracting-out, public-private partnerships and so on," assuming any uniform approach to these reforms would be misleading (Homburg, Pollitt, and Van Thiel, 2007, 2). Differences in the character of reforms were especially stark between "Anglo-Saxon" countries and continental Europe, though considerable variation can be observed among European countries. Pollitt and Bouckaert (2012) suggest that these differences owed to government's varying commitments to make public administration leaner and to modernize, as in the Netherlands, or to marketize, as in Great Britain, their existing, controlled-agency structures. This renders "NPM ... a rather chameleon-like and paradoxical creature – something that springs up for different reasons in different places" (Homburg, Pollitt, and Van Thiel, 2007, 5).

In highly accountable political systems such as Australia, New Zealand, and the United Kingdom – ranked second, fifth, and first,

Value Reinforcement as a Positive Claim

respectively, in the Accountability Index (Kam, Bertelli, and Held 2020) – Pollitt observes that representatives "pursued the strategies of marketizing and privatizing faster and further than the other states" (Pollitt 2007, 17). The political systems in which NPM was most aggressively pursued are majoritarian, where the lower likelihood of coalitions allows parties in government to advance the policy agenda and to maintain centralized public administration, allowing these "governments to spread their chosen reforms more rapidly across many departments and agencies" (2007, 18).

Pro-NPM countries also do not have the legalistic frameworks associated with *Rechtsstaat*, in which "every change has to be embodied in law" and "senior civil servants are jurists, with a legal mentality" (Pollitt 2007, 18). Belgium, Finland, France, the Netherlands, Italy, Sweden, and Germany have (at least) mixed-proportional electoral formulas, subnational autonomy, and legalistic public administration. Pollitt argues that for this reason, these countries "have not been enthusiastic about the NPM recipe" (17) and "continue to place greater emphasis on the state as the irreplaceable integrative force in society" (20). While retaining controlled agency, these countries have introduced NPM ideas of professional management and a results orientation, albeit with a greater emphasis on ex post control (Pollitt and Bouckaert 2012, 119). Compared with the higher-accountability, Westminster systems of representative government, "the continental Europeans as a whole have shared a more optimistic attitude towards the future role of the state, a more constructive/less 'blaming' approach to the reform of the public services, and a less panoptic enthusiasm towards the potential private sector role within the public domain" (Pollitt 2007, 20).

Institutional Reinforcement in Britain and the Netherlands

The United Kingdom was one of the first countries to embrace NPM's mixture of managed and independent agency, making it the "vanguard standard" of the movement beginning in the 1980s, early in the premiership of Margaret Thatcher (Hood and Dixon 2015, 12). While initial ideas about the introduction of a "management ethos" – a pro-efficiency metaconsensus – in the Conservative Party government and public services were vague, driven by the general perception that "the private sector was inherently more efficient than the public sector, that the civil service was too privileged and complacent, and that the state was too big and too interventionist," a clearer and more substantiated agenda emerged in the following years (Pollitt and Bouckaert 2012, 61). The strategy was to partition the decision-making agendas of ministerial departments: "if possible[,] move all or parts of public services into the private sector; if that is not possible, introduce some kind of market-type mechanisms and competition within public services; and focus on reducing costs, improving efficiency and injecting rigorous managerial practices" (Van Thiel and Pollitt 2007, 61). These institutional reinforcement mechanisms yielded civil service staff reductions, financial and decentralized management, performance indicators for the National Health Service, new reporting standards, a wave of privatization in the utility and transport sectors, and the "Next Steps" program that created the executive agency as a governance structure (Pollitt and Bouckaert 2012, 317; Van Thiel and Pollitt 2007). A reader might reasonably see these reforms as complicating accountability because policy workers in private firms do not have accountability relationships running in a straight line to representatives. That is true for privatizations, which are independent agency's most extreme form, but this amounts to a government choice not to provide those services as a matter of policy. Representatives no longer shoulder responsibility for privatized services, which has important normative consequences that I consider in some detail in Chapter 6. The remainder of the reforms focus on an aim – efficiency – announced by representatives, and create mechanisms that enhance policy workers' accountability for that aim.

The Labour Party victory in the 1997 general election did not change the managerialist orientation all that much. Tony Blair's government pursued public-private partnerships (or privately financed initiatives) and performance measurement, while re-regulating and reorganizing the health and education sectors to strengthen accountability values (Pollitt and Bouckaert 2012). Reforms under the successive administrations – Labour, Conservative, and Lib-Con coalition – continued these initiatives. Reinforcement mechanisms included senior public positions filled with candidates coming directly from the private sector and spending on management consulting service increased substantially. Reforms to British governance structures have "have been continual, often intense, and sometimes harsh" (Pollitt and Bouckaert 2012, 318).

The course of NPM through the governance structures of the Netherlands has been quite different. While the Netherlands was one of the first nations to embrace NPM in Continental Europe, the Dutch reformers were significantly influenced by the national context, with its lower-accountability political system – ranked twenty-second of the

Value Reinforcement as a Positive Claim

twenty-eight countries on the Accountability Index (ACI) – as well as different relationship between citizens and representatives and bureaucratic culture (Pollitt and Bouckaert 2012). Dutch representative government is endorsed by citizens through multipartism and proportional representation. In elections between 1948 and 2012, the average effective number of legislative parties – the number of parties in the legislature weighted by their seat share strength (Laakso and Taagepera 1979) – was 4.97 (SD = 0.97) in the Netherlands, compared to 2.21 (SD = 0.16) in the United Kingdom. The Bipolarity Index, a measure of the extent to which these parties separate into two distinct ideological blocs was just 0.07 (SD = 0.08) on average for Dutch parties, while it was much higher on average at 0.54 (SD = 0.36) for parties in Britain (Kam, Bertelli, and Held 2020). The difference in the accountability of governments in these countries comes not just from the greater number and variability of political parties in their respective legislatures, but also from the extent to which those parties gave citizens a distinct choice over policies as discussed in Chapter 2.

The Netherlands also displayed important distinctions from the United Kingdom in terms of prereform governance structures. Dutch politics are characterized by a strong emphasis on consociationalism and a motivation toward societal and political consensus, as distinct from the government versus opposition nature of British political life. This has led to the establishment of longstanding institutions, such as advisory and consulting bodies within Dutch ministerial departments that were not present in Britain (Kickert and In´t Veld 1995). The purpose behind these structural features is "securing a peaceful cohabitation between different groups in society," and particularly in a country with "deep political, religious and societal cleavages" that can make metaconsensus on outcomes harder to leverage, though the disagreements in policy domains across the partisan landscape are familiar (Meer and Dijkstra, 2000, S. 148). Citizens in the Netherlands report higher levels of trust in public administration and government institutions than do citizens in Britain (Pollitt and Bouckaert 2012).

In the Netherlands, representatives with cabinet portfolios and the top managers who support them are identifiable and face sanction, with institutional reinforcement mechanisms that make them "responsible politically, in criminal and in civil law" (Pollitt and Bouckaert 2012, 293). In Britain, by contrast, top managers such as permanent secretaries "normally remain anonymous but have a prime duty to support and protect 'their' minister," who is highly identifiable, and do not "have any higher duty towards 'the state' ... the legislature, or the citizenry" unlike their Dutch counterparts (316). Moreover, without the institutionally "strong central power" of the British prime minister, top managers in Dutch agencies have, relatively speaking, more autonomy (293). The careers of civil servants in the Netherlands are neither political nor partisan, allowing "both business-based and academic ideas to enter public administration," and this was a crucial mechanism for the introduction of NPM in the 1980s (291). While drawing on the metaconsensus of efficiency, Dutch NPM was more concerned with modernizing controlled agency than with reducing the size of government, reinforcing political process values. For Pollitt and Bouckaert (2012, 294), the most dramatic reforms came during a center-right coalition government in 1982–1986 that cut spending, decentralized and simplified procedures, and privatized industries (2012, 68).

Beginning in 1991, the Dutch government established a slate of executive agencies. Similar to their British cousins, these independent bodies (*Zelfstandige Bestuursorganen*, ZBOs) were an influential form of managed agency, "a vision of an efficient, professionally managed organization with a stronger client orientation yet still under strategic, democratic control from the minister" and having "performance targets and indicators, set within a regularly revised operational plan" (Thiel and Pollitt 2007, 68). However, while the Dutch initiative *increased* accountability of controlled agencies to representatives, the outcome in Britain was the opposite.

Dutch parliamentarians used the structures of consociationalism when structuring the activities of the ZBOs, while in the United Kingdom "the traditional executive dominance ... meant that the House of Commons was little more than a passive recipient of news" concerning the executive agencies (Thiel and Pollitt, 2007, 69). The process of creating ZBOs was thus "a longer drawn-out, more negotiated one" than for British executive agencies under the "Next Steps" program (Thiel and Pollitt 2007, 54). In the Netherlands, the choice of creating a ZBO has consistently been that of managers in ministerial departments and can only be done when the unit that would be translated into a managed agency structure meets "an extensive range of demanding requirements." (Thiel and Pollitt, 2007, 53). Nonetheless, the accountability values in the ZBO structure are "softer" and more reliant on informal value reinforcement mechanisms than in British executive agencies, with less collection and publication of agency performance data that can be the basis of rewards or sanctions to these agencies. This makes strategies of source relocation

Value Reinforcement as a Positive Claim

less fruitful for representatives. ZBOs are perceived by scholars to lack "public accountability" and adequate financial controls, and their performance was considered by one expert to be a "blind spot" (Pollitt and Bouckaert 2012, 295).

With the first nationwide evaluation published in 1983, the United Kingdom became one of the first governments to use the performance targets of managed agency in its national health care system. In comparison, the first Dutch performance data became available in 2003, and covered fewer dimensions of policy work (Pollitt, 2007). During the 1980s, a reform package that "regulated competition between providers and mandatory national health insurance (but no performance indicators!)" failed to take hold in the Netherlands (Pollitt, 2007, 154). What ultimately succeeded in the Netherlands was a representative agency structure – though not one that enhanced pluralism – that ensured the participation of medical practitioners and hospitals as well as health policy academicians. Political values that weakened majoritarianism and the accountability of representatives were reinforced by governance values. Indeed, a proposal with considerable discretion for health care managers regarding the measurement of service quality and data collection, subject only to some baseline standards, ultimately became the 1996 Care Institutions Quality Act (Pollitt, 2007, 154). This approach had emerged from "Leidschendam" conferences "involving government agencies, national associations representing the hospitals and other institutions, professional associations and patient organizations" (154). The Dutch approach to performance indicators is "far less tightly led and controlled by the government" than the British version across the North Sea (150).

Performance indicators were not limited to the Dutch health care system. Following a period of public spending cuts in the 1980s, "in the early 1990s, results-oriented budgeting and management regained attention" with performance indicators playing a central role in the budget process beginning in 2001 (Pollitt and Bouckaert 2012, 294). Still, the importance of these indicators has become diluted over time, to an informal institutional reinforcement mechanism of "comply or explain" that gives "a degree of freedom" for managers to "explain why it is not possible or desirable to provide performance information for strategic plans and budgets, or monitoring, or reporting" (292). A performance culture has given way to one that stresses "trust-driven relationships" that reinforce the pluralism and consociationalism in the political system (294). Overall, while champions of NPM in both Britain and the

Netherlands promised efficiency and effectiveness, "the whole rhetoric and machinery of 'performance' has more 'bite' in the UK than the Netherlands" (Thiel and Pollitt, 2007, 54).

My review of this literature suggests that scholars have observed institutional value reinforcement through both formal and informal mechanisms. Political values that stress accountability result in a form of NPM wherein governance values allow for identifiability, evaluability, and sanction of policy work as well as blame-avoidance strategies by representatives. In the Netherlands, consociational political values that relax majoritarianism in favor of pluralism are reinforced by NPM reforms, as when ZBOs comply or explain their policy work to representatives interactively, weakening identifiability and the probability of sanctioning managers in those organizations.

Behavioral Reinforcement among European Managers

My attention now shifts to behavioral reinforcement. The empirical results in this section show a correlation between the accountability of governments and the attitudes of managers that is consistent with the existence of behavioral reinforcement mechanisms. This correlation illustrates the breadth of dimensions on which value reinforcement can be studied, but does not provide evidence of a causal link between political and governance values through any specific mechanism. Such analysis is encouraged in the research program I describe in the concluding chapter.

To test the value reinforcement hypothesis, I examine the relationship between accountability in national systems of representative government and the trade-offs managers perceive in the governance structures with which they are involved. Using the same survey data as Hammerschmid, Van de Walle, Andrews and Mostafa (2019), I explore implications of this institutional reinforcement mechanism quantitatively. The Coordinating for Cohesion in the Public Sector of the Future (COCOPS) project funded by the European Commission conducted a 2012 survey of senior managers in the public agencies of twenty European countries with a response rate of 27.4 percent (Hammerschmid et al. 2019, 406). Eighteen countries, listed in Table 5.3 of the appendix to this chapter, are included in the present sample. The respondents included managers in cabinet-level (41.5 percent) and subordinate (52.5 percent) administrative agencies of national governments as well as regional and state ministries in Spain and

Value Reinforcement as a Positive Claim

TABLE 5.1 *Accountability-enhancing practices*

	Democratic Value	Prediction (ACI ↑)	Mean	SD
Our goals are clearly stated.	Evaluability	+	5.53	1.37
Our goals are communicated to all staff.	Identifiability	+	5.38	1.51
We have a high number of goals.	Evaluability	–	4.93	1.53
It is easy to observe and measure our activities.	Evaluability	+	3.90	1.59
We mainly measure inputs and processes.	Evaluability	+	3.82	1.58
We mainly measure outputs and outcomes.	Evaluability	+	4.46	1.60
We face clear sanctions for not achieving our goals.	Probability of sanction	+	2.97	1.68
Politicians use indicators to monitor our performance.	Probability of sanction	+	2.82	1.53

Items are elements of the question: "To what extent do the following statements apply to your organization?" COCOPS survey of managers administered in 2012 (Hammerschmid et al. 2016). Responses range from 1 (strongly disagree) to 7 (strongly agree). Number of observations: 5,265.

Germany, where subnational autonomy is particularly important (Hammerschmid et al. 2019, 406).

Managers in the sample are all senior and policy relevant, but they are located at different levels in the hierarchies of their organizations (406): 21.8 percent at the highest level, 41.5 percent at the second level and 36.7 percent at the third level in my sample. They also represent various domains of policy work, namely, general public administration (10.2 percent); foreign affairs (4.4 percent) finance (7.6 percent); economic affairs (9.6 percent); infrastructure and transportation (7.8 percent); defense (2.7 percent); justice, public order, and safety (12.7 percent); employment services (7.8 percent); health (6.3 percent); nonhealth social protection and welfare (8.5 percent); education (8.8 percent); environmental protection (7.9 percent); and recreation, culture, and religion (5.8 percent).

My independent variable captures electoral accountability through the ACI. The variation in the ACI captures the influence of political values through the accountability identity discussed in Chapter 2 (Kam, Bertelli, and Held 2020). Specifically, it captures voters' ability to

154 *The Value Reinforcement Hypothesis*

sanction their representatives by reducing their policymaking power. As explained in the appendix to Chapter 4, higher values mean more accountability.

While there are many surveys of public managers, the COCOPS survey is nearly unique to my knowledge because it asks questions that are useful for understanding value reinforcement. Responses to two questions supply the dependent variables in my analysis, and each item records responses along a feeling thermometer from 1 (strongly disagree) to 7 (strongly agree). The first question captures managers' perceptions of accountability-enhancing practices in their organizations. Table 5.1 shows the language for each of the items and the values represented, as well as the average and standard deviations among the responses in my sample. Each statement articulates an accountability value. Clear, fewer, and observable goals promote evaluability, as does the measurement of outputs or outcomes. Clear sanctions and the use of performance information by representatives in monitoring policy work increases the probability of sanction for the senior agency managers in the sample. For this reason, as the ACI increases, the value reinforcement hypothesis would expect that agreement with these statements would all increase except for "We have a high number of goals," which, given its wording, should be negatively related to accountability in the electoral system because it makes evaluability more difficult. In this context, the behavioral reinforcement mechanism suggests that when managers experience increasing electoral accountability, their democratic belief systems work to support the accountability prevailing in the representative governments they serve.

My second dependent variable is drawn from responses to the question presented in Table 5.2. The question addresses identifiability enhancing and obviating practices when policy work faces "coordination problems" in which different units of a controlled-agency structure work together to jointly produce an output or outcome. Coordination is an important vehicle for understanding identifiability because the very idea of different managers and policy workers working together creates problems of identifiability not terribly different from those presented to citizens when their representatives serve in coalition governments, as I have argued in Chapter 2. More coordination implies *lower* identifiability. More policy workers in coordinated policy work are analogous to more parties in coalition governments. As electoral accountability measured by the ACI increases, the value reinforcement hypothesis would expect the belief systems of managers to respond to those values.

Value Reinforcement as a Positive Claim

TABLE 5.2 *Identifiability enhancing and obviating practices for coordinating policy work*

	Prediction (ACI ↑)	Mean	SD
Refer the issue upwards in the hierarchy	−	4.80	1.66
Refer the issue to political actors and bodies	−	3.67	1.83
Set up special purpose bodies (more permanent)	−	2.72	1.52
Set up a cross-cutting work/project group (ad hoc, temporary)	+	4.10	1.55
Set up a cross-cutting policy arrangement or programme	+	3.71	1.64
Decide on one lead organization	+	3.44	1.70
Consult civil society organizations or interest groups	−	2.90	1.62
Consult relevant experts (e.g., scientists or consultants)	−	3.57	1.67

Items are elements of the question: "To resolve coordination problems when working with other organizations, we typically ..." Accountability value: identifiability. COCOPS survey of managers administered in 2012 (Hammerschmid et al. 2016). Responses range from 1 (strongly disagree) to 7 (strongly agree). Number of observations: 5,265.

Representatives benefit when coordination strengthens because their strategies of blame avoidance are enhanced (see Figure 2.2). As the ACI increases, managers are less able to avoid identification by shifting issues to higher-level managers or political bodies. When considering the value trade-offs in the governance structures of Table 4.1, creating special purpose bodies like NDPBs, an independent agency structure, would obviate identifiability values and are less likely as electoral accountability rises. The same is expected for the representative agency strategies of engagement with civil society and outside experts, which likewise obviate accountability in representative government. Project groups and programs enhance identifiability (for the group) and are more likely as the ACI rises, and the same is particularly true for the option of choosing a single lead agency. Behavioral value reinforcement expects the belief systems of managers, conditioned on the existence of a coordination problem, to produce attitudes regarding coordination that reinforce the level of accountability in representative government.

To test for this relationship, I estimate ordered logistic regression models given the ordinal nature of the response sets. My models include indicator variables to control for unobserved heterogeneity across countries, policy domains, respondent positions within the organizational hierarchy, and the size of the workforce in the respondent's organization. While the COCOPS survey does not identify the name of the agency in which a manager performs policy work, I am able to isolate the effects presented below within policy domains and countries. Though less formal than agencies, the policy domain and country controls may in some ways be more realistic demarcations for shared belief systems among managers: policy workers in, say, the environmental policy domain, share similar values regardless of which agency issues their paychecks. Given the cross-sectional nature of the data, indicator variables for policy domains and countries remove the influence of particular and unobservable aspects of partisan politics, policymaking peculiarities, and aspects of national political institutions. Controlling for the hierarchical level of the response and the size of the organization captures unobserved heterogeneity within categories relating to the scope of a manager's discretion. This design, I argue, provides a reasonable strategy for identifying the relationship between electoral accountability and the accountability beliefs of managers. Additional details on the estimation are provided in the appendix to this chapter.

Results for the models regarding the accountability-enhancing practices in Table 5.1 appear graphically in Figure 5.1. While they have the appropriate sign, the coefficients capturing the effect of the ACI on multiple goals and the measurement of outputs and processes are imprecise. All other effects are consistent with value reinforcement and are substantively meaningful. *Ceteris paribus*, a one-unit increase in the ACI – roughly the difference in accountability between Spain and Canada – is associated with a 17 percent increase in the odds that a manager reports a higher response category of agreement with the statement "Our goals are clearly stated." Similarly, a unit increase in the ACI is associated with increases in odds by 13 percent for goal communication, 12 percent for goal observability and the measurement of outputs or outcomes, 15 percent for rewarding the achievement of goals, 23 percent for sanctioning the failure to meet them, and fully 27 percent in regard to representatives use of this performance information in monitoring. These patterns are overwhelmingly consistent with behavioral reinforcement. Managers' beliefs about their organizations are correlated with strategies that increase their own accountability to representatives as the accountability of representatives to citizens, captured by the ACI, increases.

Value Reinforcement as a Positive Claim

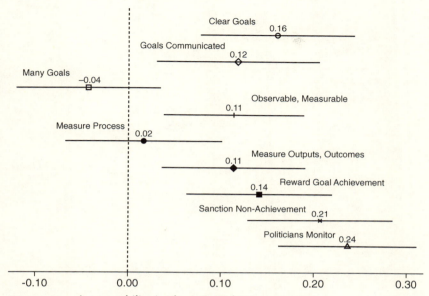

FIGURE 5.1 Accountability in elections and in governance
Ordered logistic regression coefficients represent the marginal effect of changes in the ACI (Kam, Bertelli, and Held 2020). The confidence intervals of 95 percent, which are based on bootstrapped standard errors, appear as horizontal bars.

The relationships between electoral accountability and the identifiability enhancing and obviating practices listed in Table 5.2 are shown in a similar way in Figure 5.2. This item primed managers to think about coordination, which decreases identifiability and is associated with lower identifiability and strategies of source relocation (see Figure 2.2 and Bertelli 2016). *Ceteris paribus*, a one-unit increase in the ACI is associated with a 15 percent reduction in the odds of moving to a higher response category. Analogous reductions are 19 percent and 20 percent for the reference to political principals and creating special purpose bodies, respectively. By contrast, the same one-unit rise in the ACI is associated with a 22 percent increase in the odds of selecting a higher category in response to the selection of one lead organization. Behavioral reinforcement once again corresponds to cross-national variation in electoral accountability.

Taken together, these results present a portrait of value reinforcement that also evokes the challenges for champions as they introduce governance reforms. In Figure 5.1, the significant coefficients embody the

The Value Reinforcement Hypothesis

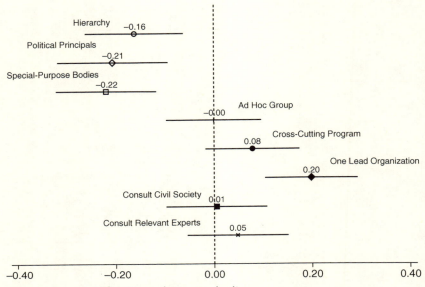

FIGURE 5.2 Identifiability and structural reliance
Ordered logistic regression coefficients represent the marginal effect of changes in the ACI (Kam, Bertelli, and Held 2020). The 95 percent confidence intervals, which are based on bootstrapped standard errors, appear as horizontal bars.

accountability enhancement of managed agency, clarifying and communicating goals, and creating measures that can be monitored and the basis of enhancement. All of these things are more likely to be on the agenda for managers in political systems where the accountability of representatives to citizens is stronger. The statistically insignificant coefficient for process measurement further supports this sketch of managed agency in that the process-obviating elements of that governance structure are not changed where electoral accountability is stronger. Representatives seeking blame avoidance, at least in this figure, are not likely to focus on the process as they do it, and this leaves process value trade-offs in the hands of managers. Strikingly, the creation of special purpose bodies, the independent agency element of NPM, is less likely as a coordinating mechanism (see Figure 5.2) where representative government is more accountable.

Managed agency seems to be the main attraction in higher-accountability European governments. Similarly, the null effects for elements of representative agency in Figure 5.2 are also telling. Higher-accountability electoral systems are not associated with building collaboratives, either ad hoc or programmatic, nor are they inclined to engage civil society and expert advice as with the Dutch case in the last section would seem to suggest. One reading of this is that champions of representative agency structures face significant challenges in high-accountability systems. Champions may prefer another reading: electoral accountability does not influence the chances that representative agency influences the democratic belief systems of managers.

A RESEARCH AGENDA FOR VALUE REINFORCEMENT

The research agenda that follows is intertwined with its normative grounding in the practice of representative government. This, I claim, is what contemporary public administration has to do. Introducing his important study of electoral institutions, the political scientist G. Bingham Powell (2000, 3) states that the book "is explicitly driven by a normative concern: the claim of democracies to be governments in which the people participate in policy making." To study the way in which elections facilitate such participation, he makes a "normative assumption that runs throughout this book ... that such citizen influence is a good thing, that elections should not only provide symbolic reassurance, but also genuinely serve as instruments of democracy" (3–4). Moreover, Powell acknowledges that the practice is behavioral and contentious, stating that "[t]he apparent consensus that elections are significant conceals deep disagreements about whether and how they serve to link citizens to policymakers" (4). The study of political institutions is, simply put, like this, and researching the value reinforcement in public administration is no different.

Research into value reinforcement might proceed in three ways: theoretical development, quantitative analysis of observational and experimental data and qualitative research.

Theory Development

Building on the relationship between normative values and structures and the value reinforcement hypothesis, a first direction for research can be to develop novel theory to explain why and how governance structures reinforce the values of the representative government by shaping the belief systems of policy workers. That is, institutional and behavioral reinforcement mechanisms could be developed to enrich the current body of theory.

160 *The Value Reinforcement Hypothesis*

Doing this would fill a void left by several leading literatures. Rational choice theories have focused on the scope and the exercise of discretion as a function of the interaction between ideology and institutions (e.g., Epstein and O'Halloran 1999; Huber and Shipan 2002). Some of this work reveals important implications of the design of governance structures (e.g., Herrera, Reuben, and Ting 2017; Ting 2002, 2003). Gailmard and Patty (2013, 2007) show that the incentives of civil service systems entice policy-motivated individuals into careers as managers. Cultural theories contend that managers' belief systems are controlled to varying degrees by rules and attachments to their organizations and by professional norms and address political control through reforms in governance structures (Hood 1995; Hood and Lodge 2006). Formal theories of corporate culture capture important aspects of coordination and cooperation (Crémer 1993; Kreps 1990), but are themselves unconnected with democracy.

While all of these theories incorporate constructs like ideology or efficiency as their arguments in one way or another, they do not distinguish them from the rudiments of representative government. New theoretical development should also account for informal dynamics in the construction of policy workers' democratic belief systems. Should it do so, it would speak to a variety of scholarly audiences from various methodological standpoints and to impact policy awareness as well as structural choices by governments.

Empirical Study

The empirical component of a value reinforcement research agenda could have three components. Figure 5.3 provides a visual guide to the role of these components in evaluating theories about institutional and behavioral mechanisms. The solid lines trace the pathway through which democratic values pass through *formal* instruments in order to shape the beliefs of policy workers. The dotted lines depict a pathway through which *informal* managerial and organizational norms act as mediators in shaping democratic belief systems.

In addition to informing theory development, the qualitative research can uncover this informal pathway, investigating, in particular, the informal mechanisms through which policy workers attribute and co-construct democratic meaning in the different governance structures discussed in Chapter 4. Advances in supervised machine-learning methods make it possible to uncover democratic values in formal texts of delegation, such

A Research Agenda for Value Reinforcement 161

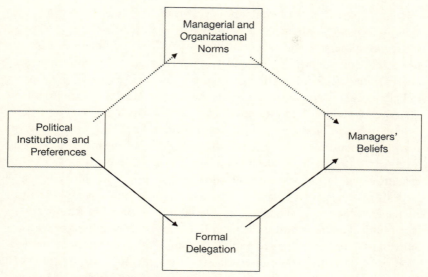

FIGURE 5.3 Researching value reinforcement mechanisms
Solid lines are pathways through which democratic values shape beliefs by means of formal rules and dotted lines depict informal mechanisms.

as legislation, and to empirically examine the connection between the preferences of representatives and the structures of their institutions, on the one hand, and the content of these enabling documents, on the other hand. Survey and laboratory experiments could be employed to understand both formal and informal mechanisms that reinforce or reshape democratic belief systems.

Qualitative research can unmask the informal mechanisms denoted in the two leftmost pathways of Figure 5.3. Two kinds of inquiries into behavioral reinforcement would be particularly useful. First, scholars can qualitatively examine how accountability and process values are achieved in the everyday work of policy workers, especially managers. What types of organizational strategies do managers create to implement and reproduce democratic belief systems? This inquiry could also examine the bottom-up creation of organizational norms and routines for the sustained reproduction of democratic values. Second, researchers could work to understand ways in which individual resistance and organizational politics can counteract the democratic values of governance structures discussed in Chapter 4. Is it possible that, despite a potentially enhancing (obviating) structure, individual policy workers develop micro-level practices to obviate (enhance) accountability or process? When are these strategies successful and when are they not? What strategies disrupt the prevailing governance structure, decouple its values, or modify representatives' intentions? Addressing these questions can uncover a wide variety of behavioral reinforcement methods that can be incorporated into mixed methods research (cf. Honig 2019; Mele and Belardinelli 2019).

For observational research, a key measurement question is how to reveal democratic value trade-offs from the formal means of delegating authority. Studies of the delegation of powers focus on the use of constraints in legislation, such as time and spending limits, public hearings, or appeals processes as a means to understand the conditions and extent of managers' discretion (Epstein and O'Halloran 1999; Franchino 2004). The political scientist and statistician L. Jason Anastasopoulos and I use a suite of machine-learning techniques that combine deep learning methodologies with more traditional classification methods to reproduce a human-coding rubric, extending it to the most recent documents (Anastasopoulos and Bertelli 2020). Such procedures could be tailored to the problem of extracting democratic values from texts. To facilitate comparative research, providing frameworks that carefully relate the same general concepts underlying accountability and process values to human coders can allow text analysis to proceed in a comparable way regardless of language differences.

Such text-based measures would allow scholars to examine the impact of political institutions and representatives' preferences on the democratic values recovered from delegation documents to test theories linking political institutions to formal rules, as illustrated by the bottom-left pathway in Figure 5.3. This work could be crucial to uncovering institutional reinforcement mechanisms. Empirical work on bureaucratic appointments and politicization considers ideology as a left-right constraint (Bertelli and Grose 2011; Lewis 2008) and clashes between career bureaucrats and appointees have long been documented (e.g., Aberbach and Rockman 1976), yet the compatibility of their democratic belief systems has not been systematically understood.

Experimental analysis can address questions of how formal *and* informal governance structures shape the individual democratic belief systems of policy workers. To address this question, illustrated via the bottom-right pathway in Figure 5.3, survey experiments on managers and laboratory experiments on student subjects could provide important first steps. Druckman and Leeper (2012), for example, show that an increasing amount of evidence suggests that results from undergraduate samples widely generalize. Conjoint experiments can present samples of managers and representatives with governance structures making trade-offs on democratic values to understand which are most highly valued by each group. Surveys could combine choice-based analysis, where respondents are given vignettes regarding alternative governance structures that vary according to the democratic values underlying them and are asked to choose which they most prefer, and rating-based analysis, which asks respondents to assign a numerical rating to each profile of attributes. Discrete choice survey experiments with between-subjects factorial designs can allow researchers to vary governance structures and democratic values to probe the extent to which democratic values can strengthen or weaken the role governance structures play in shaping policy workers' beliefs. Put differently, a conjoint analysis offers insight into the *relative* importance managers and politicians assign to different aspects of democracy (Hainmueller, Hopkins, and Yamamoto 2014). That is crucial to understanding the relationship between trade-offs in structures and practice in behavioral reinforcement.

While much can be learned about the different values reported *between* actual managers who operate in different governance structures, survey experiments such as those envisioned above pose the problem that responses are not equivalent to values. Consequently, laboratory experiments can be used to examine how the essential rules of different governance arrangements influence democratic values *within* subjects. Combining these experimental approaches can provide a powerful means for understanding the influence of governance arrangements on the democratic belief systems of managers.

Laboratory experiments might fruitfully employ hypothetical governance structures similar to the "hypothetical societies" in experiments by the social psychologists Gregory Mitchell and Philip Tetlock (2009). An experimental analog to the thought experiment common in normative political theory, this method provides several advantages. First, it permits within-subjects factorial designs that vary essential elements of those governance arrangements while allowing the researcher complete control over key socioeconomic and political aspects of the context in which those arrangements are situated. Second, it places subjects in the position of disinterested observers, where they make anonymous judgments of hypothetical arrangements and face no material consequences in doing so. This stands in important contrast to the rewards that are common in conjoint experiments that seek to assess the value subjects place on public programs, such as environmental protection (e.g., Carlsson and Martinsson 2001). Where values and complex facts interact to influence responses, as in the present context of public administration, the gap between responses and values can be pronounced (Herrmann, Tetlock, and Diascro 2001). The method of hypothetical societies can also avoid potential challenges to validity due to the familiarity that managers have with the subjects of the vignettes they consider in the survey experiments, manifest, for instance, in respondents' rejection of the facts presented (Mitchell and Tetlock 2009).

Furthermore, randomized control trials are, in an intriguing sense, already being used to test the value reinforcement hypothesis. A wide variety of studies have examined efforts to reform bureaucracies, and in doing this, they examine changes in governance structures while holding systems of representative government constant (see e.g., Finan, Olken, and Pandey 2017; Rasul and Rogger 2018). The resources and energy that have been flowing into the study of governance, particularly in developing countries – projects such as the Abdul Latif Jameel Poverty Action Lab and Innovations for Poverty Action – can be incorporated into the research agenda outlined here, both as conduit for uncovering mechanisms of value reinforcement and to uncover a metaconsensus on value reinforcement across relevant studies.

Overall, this research agenda provides an important starting point to adding the problem of value reinforcement to the control and capacity themes in the legitimating narrative of public administration. To be sure, many scholars are doing this kind of work now as is apparent from my discussion of NPM earlier in the chapter, and systematic literature reviews of how value reinforcement is being studied in a variety of areas would provide an important starting point for this agenda. In any event, I think that this research program has the potential to understand the nuanced ways in which public administration lives up to its promise of democracy administered.

CONCLUSION

The value reinforcement hypothesis has importance for the comparative study of public administration, and the case of NPM that I have considered in this chapter is instructive. Accountability in representative government shapes the flavor of NPM that countries adopt. In countries where representatives are highly accountable to citizens, managed agency appears to dominate independent agency in NPM reforms. And the value

Conclusion

trade-offs that favor accountability in managed agency are reflected in the belief systems of managers, suggesting that this facet of NPM is more accountability-enhancing. While the evidence I have assembled in this chapter illustrates how institutional and behavioral reinforcement mechanisms might reveal themselves, the research agenda for value reinforcement offers a broader program for testing the hypothesis.

It is surely possible that the value reinforcement hypothesis could be generated by a variety of positive theories, and those theories would be able to predict a set of archetypical equilibria that relate governance values to political values. I strongly encourage this theoretical work. However, in the rest of this book, I want to argue that, like accountability or representation, the value reinforcement hypothesis has a normative basis, and it is one that that addresses the fundamental problem of public administration. For value reinforcement to stand its ground – along with control and capability – as a means of legitimating public administration, the behavior the hypothesis predicts must occur when policy workers behave responsibly. In Chapter 6, I will argue value reinforcement is, indeed, a part of responsible policy work in states with representative governments.

Appendix: Data, Methods, and Detailed Results

A list of the countries and the number of respondents for each that are included in the models summarized by Figures 5.1 and 5.2 appears in Table 5.3. Sampled managers in high- and low-accountability representative governments are roughly equivalent; the average number of respondents for countries below the mean ACI is 294, while it is 289 above the mean ACI.

TABLE 5.3 *Country coverage and ACI*

COCOPS survey of managers administered in 2012 (Hammerschmid et al. 2016).

Country	ACI	Observations	Percent of Sample
United Kingdom	10.38	182	3.46
Germany	2.52	403	7.65
France	1.82	495	9.40
Spain	3.41	251	4.77
Italy	0.88	158	3.00
Estonia	1.29	278	5.28
Norway	1.86	297	5.64
Netherlands	1.64	189	3.59
Hungary	2.23	231	4.39
Austria	1.81	448	8.51
Portugal	3.68	278	5.28
Ireland	2.08	363	6.89
Sweden	1.95	500	9.50
Denmark	2.16	140	2.66
Finland	4.86	679	12.90
Iceland	1.96	185	3.51
Poland	1.32	132	2.51
Belgium	3.06	56	1.06
Total		5,265	100

TABLE 5.4 *Accountability in elections and in governance*

	(1) Clear	(2) Communicated	(3) Many	(4) Measurable	(5) Processes	(6) Outcomes	(7) Rewards	(8) Sanctions	(9) Monitoring
ACI	0.160*** (0.042)	0.118*** (0.045)	-0.043 (0.040)	0.114*** (0.039)	0.017 (0.043)	0.113*** (0.039)	0.141*** (0.040)	0.207*** (0.040)	0.237*** (0.038)
Number of employees in organization (reference category: less than 50)									
50–99	-0.322** (0.132)	-0.259* (0.134)	0.210 (0.133)	-0.321** (0.136)	0.282* (0.145)	-0.149 (0.142)	0.010 (0.133)	-0.140 (0.135)	-0.142 (0.131)
100–499	-0.389*** (0.100)	-0.530*** (0.113)	0.382*** (0.109)	-0.398*** (0.115)	0.270** (0.113)	-0.187 (0.119)	0.151 (0.104)	-0.118 (0.109)	0.078 (0.110)
500–999	-0.367*** (0.112)	-0.608*** (0.129)	0.448*** (0.115)	-0.456*** (0.121)	0.406*** (0.121)	-0.109 (0.128)	0.193* (0.114)	-0.053 (0.120)	0.204* (0.117)
1,000–5,000	-0.429*** (0.116)	-0.619*** (0.120)	0.466*** (0.117)	-0.337*** (0.124)	0.530*** (0.123)	-0.169 (0.125)	0.101 (0.110)	-0.001 (0.120)	0.373*** (0.118)
5,000+	-0.021 (0.126)	-0.222* (0.126)	0.782*** (0.122)	-0.241* (0.132)	0.550*** (0.127)	0.166 (0.132)	0.446*** (0.114)	0.335*** (0.126)	0.873*** (0.119)
Organization type (reference category: state or regional)									
	0.586***	0.511***	0.145**	0.665***	0.238***	0.548***	0.294***	0.183***	0.677***

(continued)

TABLE 5.4 *(continued)*

	(1) Clear	(2) Communicated	(3) Many	(4) Measurable	(5) Processes	(6) Outcomes	(7) Rewards	(8) Sanctions	(9) Monitoring
Central ministry	(0.061)	(0.064)	(0.063)	(0.062)	(0.063)	(0.064)	(0.064)	(0.064)	(0.063)
Central agency	−0.178 (0.144)	−0.399** (0.155)	0.176 (0.151)	0.049 (0.148)	0.483*** (0.162)	−0.134 (0.165)	−0.792*** (0.151)	−0.422*** (0.162)	0.346** (0.154)
Position in the organizational hierarchy (reference category: third level)									
Top level	−0.359*** (0.070)	−0.358*** (0.074)	0.128* (0.070)	−0.315*** (0.068)	−0.063 (0.071)	−0.371*** (0.071)	−0.084 (0.066)	−0.292*** (0.072)	0.027 (0.075)
Second level	−0.615*** (0.078)	−0.579*** (0.081)	0.017 (0.077)	−0.490*** (0.076)	−0.138* (0.077)	−0.447*** (0.076)	−0.352*** (0.077)	−0.415*** (0.075)	−0.066 (0.076)
Cutpoints									
τ_1	−4.391*** (0.414)	−4.571*** (0.444)	−3.425*** (0.407)	−2.967*** (0.386)	−2.266*** (0.431)	−2.884*** (0.402)	−0.264 (0.405)	−0.598 (0.412)	0.473 (0.383)
τ_2	−3.149*** (0.404)	−3.346*** (0.440)	−2.050*** (0.404)	−1.363*** (0.383)	−0.729* (0.424)	−1.394*** (0.398)	0.946** (0.403)	0.915** (0.412)	1.558*** (0.383)
τ_3	−2.269*** (0.399)	−2.543*** (0.435)	−1.057*** (0.406)	−0.403 (0.384)	0.166 (0.423)	−0.540 (0.396)	1.656*** (0.403)	1.874*** (0.414)	2.188*** (0.382)

τ_4	-1.349***	-1.741***	-0.058	0.563	1.121***	0.319	2.530***	2.891***	2.928***
	(0.398)	(0.434)	(0.406)	(0.383)	(0.425)	(0.396)	(0.402)	(0.411)	(0.383)
τ_5	-0.161	-0.645	0.964**	1.637***	2.112***	1.398***	3.510***	3.698***	3.830***
	(0.398)	(0.432)	(0.406)	(0.382)	(0.426)	(0.395)	(0.402)	(0.412)	(0.383)
τ_6	1.318***	0.779*	2.226***	2.954***	3.595***	2.999***	4.872***	4.894***	4.990***
	(0.404)	(0.431)	(0.404)	(0.382)	(0.430)	(0.395)	(0.413)	(0.412)	(0.387)
Country indicators	Yes	Yes	Yes	Yes	Yes	Yes	Yes	Yes	Yes
Sector indicators	Yes	Yes	Yes	Yes	Yes	Yes	Yes	Yes	Yes
N	5,265	5,244	5,211	5,226	5,173	5,193	5,203	5,234	5,212
BIC	16,378.045	16,978.277	18,366.971	19,078.355	19,161.548	18,789.310	18,170.926	17,478.482	19,102.204

Ordered logistic regression models with bootstrapped standard errors (500 replications) in parentheses. Dependent variables are items in Table 5.1. Significance: * $p < 0.10$, ** $p < 0.05$, *** $p < 0.01$.

TABLE 5.5 Identifiability and structural reliance

	(1) Upwards	(2) Politicians	(3) Special Purpose	(4) Cross-Cut Group	(5) Cross-Cut Program	(6) One Lead	(7) Civil Society	(8) Experts
ACI	-0.162*** (0.051)	-0.206*** (0.057)	-0.219*** (0.052)	-0.001 (0.049)	0.078 (0.049)	0.198*** (0.048)	0.005 (0.052)	0.048 (0.052)

Number of employees in organization (reference category: fewer than 50)

	(1) Upwards	(2) Politicians	(3) Special Purpose	(4) Cross-Cut Group	(5) Cross-Cut Program	(6) One Lead	(7) Civil Society	(8) Experts
50–99	-0.047 (0.147)	0.209 (0.143)	0.362** (0.143)	0.334** (0.144)	0.147 (0.158)	0.014 (0.146)	0.060 (0.149)	-0.020 (0.149)
100–499	-0.007 (0.116)	0.357*** (0.121)	0.658*** (0.110)	0.432*** (0.119)	0.257** (0.122)	0.120 (0.113)	0.295** (0.121)	0.170 (0.125)
500–999	0.075 (0.125)	0.387*** (0.134)	0.753*** (0.118)	0.520*** (0.130)	0.302** (0.132)	0.254** (0.123)	0.142 (0.129)	0.143 (0.134)
1,000–5,000	0.093 (0.125)	0.365*** (0.133)	0.879*** (0.120)	0.579*** (0.131)	0.438*** (0.130)	0.257** (0.128)	0.301** (0.132)	0.240* (0.138)
5,000+	-0.010 (0.129)	0.497*** (0.136)	0.944*** (0.126)	0.600*** (0.138)	0.578*** (0.130)	0.234* (0.138)	0.422*** (0.130)	0.327** (0.141)

Organization type (reference category: state or regional)

	(1) Upwards	(2) Politicians	(3) Special Purpose	(4) Cross-Cut Group	(5) Cross-Cut Program	(6) One Lead	(7) Civil Society	(8) Experts
	-0.277***	-1.044***	-0.067	-0.175***	-0.230***	-0.336***	-0.185***	0.042

Central ministry	(0.071)	(0.069)	(0.066)	(0.064)	(0.069)	(0.067)	(0.067)	(0.065)
Central agency	−0.152	0.271*	0.285*	0.260*	0.158	0.014	0.256	0.030
	(0.165)	(0.162)	(0.156)	(0.150)	(0.163)	(0.186)	(0.161)	(0.151)

Position in the organizational hierarchy (reference category: third level)

Top level	0.382***	0.106	0.067	−0.224***	−0.338***	−0.205***	−0.067	−0.031
	(0.075)	(0.075)	(0.078)	(0.080)	(0.077)	(0.075)	(0.075)	(0.074)
Second level	0.444***	0.050	0.049	−0.288***	−0.420***	−0.218**	−0.116	−0.004
	(0.079)	(0.082)	(0.084)	(0.086)	(0.083)	(0.086)	(0.082)	(0.078)

Cutpoints

τ_1	−3.719***	−3.411***	−2.291***	−2.847***	−2.104***	−0.721*	−1.274***	−1.460***
	(0.424)	(0.403)	(0.423)	(0.461)	(0.386)	(0.412)	(0.452)	(0.414)
τ_2	−2.550***	−2.234***	−1.035**	−1.767***	−0.913**	0.418	−0.032	−0.314
	(0.418)	(0.402)	(0.424)	(0.456)	(0.383)	(0.415)	(0.451)	(0.411)
τ_3	−1.929***	−1.606***	−0.279	−0.978**	−0.153	1.119***	0.661	0.385
	(0.418)	(0.401)	(0.425)	(0.451)	(0.384)	(0.413)	(0.453)	(0.412)
τ_4	−1.055**	−0.831**	0.696*	0.092	0.890**	2.087***	1.559***	1.273***
	(0.416)	(0.402)	(0.423)	(0.449)	(0.383)	(0.414)	(0.451)	(0.412)

(continued)

TABLE 5.5 *(continued)*

	(1) Upwards	(2) Politicians	(3) Special Purpose	(4) Cross-Cut Group	(5) Cross-Cut Program	(6) One Lead	(7) Civil Society	(8) Experts
τ_5	−0.056	0.143	1.796***	1.431***	2.081***	3.068***	2.552***	2.445***
	(0.415)	(0.400)	(0.426)	(0.450)	(0.385)	(0.415)	(0.451)	(0.414)
τ_6	1.397***	1.479***	3.114***	3.120***	3.769***	4.522***	4.006***	4.076***
	(0.416)	(0.403)	(0.438)	(0.464)	(0.386)	(0.417)	(0.467)	(0.428)
Country indicators	Yes	Yes	Yes	Yes	Yes	Yes	Yes	Yes
Sector indicators	Yes	Yes	Yes	Yes	Yes	Yes	Yes	Yes
N	4,617	4,562	4,490	4,573	4,495	4,488	4,480	4,528
BIC	16,510.658	17,009.792	15,299.397	16,419.767	16,255.980	16,556.783	15,745.727	16,754.282

Ordered logistic regression models with bootstrapped standard errors (500 replications) in parentheses. Dependent variables are items in Table 5.1. Significance: * $p < 0.10$, ** $p < 0.05$, *** $p < 0.01$.

Appendix: Data, Methods, and Detailed Results

Tables 5.4 and 5.5 present fuller results of the ordered logistic models summarized in Figures 5.1 and 5.2. As noted in the text of this chapter, the models take the following form for the response, R, of manager i in country j and organization k:

$$R_{ijk} = \alpha + \beta_1 ACI_j + \beta_2 E_k + \beta_3 T_k + \beta_4 L_i + \beta_5 D_k + \beta_5 C_j + \varepsilon$$

Each model controls for the staff size of the organization to address the possibility that larger organizations have different organizational characteristics – and managers' attitudes about them – than do their smaller counterparts. The COCOPS survey captures this through a series of indicators of ranges of employees, E. Indicator variables for the level of the respondent in the hierarchy, L, the type of organization, T, and its policy domain, D; and country, C are also included in the specifications. Because the ACI is a variable estimated with uncertainty by Kam, Bertelli, and Held (2020), the models report bootstrapped standard errors based on 500 replications.

6

The Complementarity Principle

The project of public administration effortlessly embodies Kurt Lewin's (1951, 169) maxim "[t]here's nothing so practical as a good theory." Champions are theorists, and their theories – governance structures – must engage the practice of policy work. At the same time, champions cannot ignore the realities of government, the institutions that shape the roles, incentives and values of representatives (see e.g., Bertelli and Riccucci 2020). The project of public administration is to integrate policy work into representative government *in theory* and to ensure that the behavior of policy workers supports each theory of such integration *in practice*. And because the champion's dilemma means that any such theory will make trade-offs that shape democracy, there cannot be one narrative about democracy that justifies all the value trade-offs described in Chapter 4. This project of integrating theory and practice unites champions in their disagreements with one another. As a consequence, practical *and* theoretical debates are essential in our field. This book, if nothing else, is a guide to understanding these disagreements.

What is more, champions are not policy analysts. Champions do not just analyze data through the lens of "the fundamental goals, priorities, and political constraints" of representatives, or use empirical findings "to change the conventions policymakers abide by" or "to reorder the goals and priorities of the practical policy world," to the extent that they do these things at all (Weiss 1977, 544). Nor should they. In his classic debate in the pages of *Public Administration Review* with Nobel laureate Herbert Simon, Robert Dahl (1947, 3 emphasis added) makes the case for the champion's role plainly: "[t]he student of public administration cannot avoid a concern with ends. What he ought to avoid is the *failure*

The Complementarity Principle 175

to make explicit the ends or values that form the groundwork of his doctrine." He continues: "to refuse to recognize that the study of public administration must be founded on some clarification of ends is to perpetuate the gobbledygook of science in the area of moral purposes." What champions contribute, the governance structures I have been discussing, *challenge* democracy, and provide claims about how we might resolve the champion's dilemma in a way that respects the goal of democracy administered.

The fundamental problem of public administration is not one of control over managers nor of their capability, but of their responsibility. To be responsible, policy workers must use their discretion to serve public aims. These aims are expressed and articulated formally through the mechanisms of representative government – elections, representation, legislation, oversight, the rule of law. To be responsible, policy workers must use the capabilities they have – and those they can get – as well as their judgments and informal actions to serve public aims as effectively as possible within the limits of the law. The last four sentences present the normative theory of public administration in representative government on which this book is built. In this chapter, I provide a normative argument about how value reinforcement ought to be done so that it might work alongside control and capability to transform public administration into democracy administered.

Such an argument requires a theory of the state, and I begin by arguing that a particular conception of the modern state, arguably born from the political thought of Thomas Hobbes, is the one that has shaped the traditional narrative of public administration with its control and capability themes. This view sees the state as having tremendous authority over citizens, and the legitimation of that power plays an essential role in understanding what responsible policy work looks like. To make this claim, I begin by briefly describing the Hobbesian state and two mechanisms for legitimating it. One of these, the mechanism of representation, lies at the heart of this book and underlies foundational arguments about the legitimacy of public administration. Armed with these ideas of the state and of responsibility, I can consider responsible policy work within the basic governance structures described in Chapter 4. This analysis admits a general claim about responsible value reinforcement that I call the complementarity principle. If champions respect what responsible value reinforcement means for policy workers by embracing the complementarity principle, they can address the champion's dilemma in a way that takes the fundamental problem of public administration in hand.

THE STATE AND RESPONSIBLE POLICY WORK

The intellectual historian Quentin Skinner (1989, 90) observes that Hobbes's *De Cive* advances the modern notion that citizens owe a duty not to the person of a ruler, but to the state itself. The goal of the Hobbesian state is to preserve an order that allows humanity to survive. The state aims for "the achievement of stability and security – of domestic tranquility," which "is a *sine qua non* of political society." This aim was shared by conceptions of the polity expressed in Plato, Aristotle and Augustine (Steinberger 2005, 49). The Hobbesian state is created "when a multitude of men do agree and covenant ... every one, as well he that voted for it as he that voted against it," to authorize "the actions and judgments of" a leader or "assembly of men ... in the same manner as if they were his own, to the end to live peaceably amongst themselves, and be protected against other men" (Hobbes 2014 [1651], 136). The properties of the modern state that must be considered in any theory of responsible policy work are its awesome power over citizens, its separateness from them, and citizens' need to see its powers as being legitimately exercised. To be sure, those who serve in the official positions are citizens also. Yet in their capacity as policy workers, they become a part of this separated state because their actions are on behalf of those citizens who authorize them (Runciman 2009). I will argue that the design of public administration has historically meant to legitimate the actions of policy workers in light of a powerful state that exists separately from citizens. It is the separation between the state and citizens that compels the normative goal of transforming the power exercised by public administration into democracy administered.

To understand the power of the state, I find it reasonable to begin with Skinner's (1989, 117) claim that the Hobbesian state, is not "seen as the powers of citizens under another guise," but, rather, as "a distinct form of power." Hobbes writes that even if a state were created by covenant as outlined in the last paragraph, "that right which every man had before to use his faculties to his own advantages is now wholly translated on some certain man or council for the common benefit" (Skinner 1989, 117, quoting Hobbes 1983 [1642], 105). This translation makes the state *separate* from the people with "'its own rights and properties, insomuch as neither any one citizen, nor all of them together' can now be accounted its equivalent" (Skinner 1989, 117, quoting Hobbes 1983 [1642], 89).

Citizens are equal in being subject to this state that they have created, "though they shine some more, some less" from the vantage of the state,

The State and Responsible Policy Work

"they shine no more than stars in the presence of the sun" (Hobbes 2014 [1651], 143). Hobbes acknowledges that there is great danger for citizens, who believe themselves to be "obnoxious to the lusts and irregular passions of him or them that have so unlimited a power in their hands" (143). Citizens, individually and collectively, cannot really know when or if the state will use its might against them. While this uncertainty seems to create a very bad bargain for citizens, Hobbes is in for the long game, writing that his state avoids "civil war; or that dissolute condition of masterless men" (144). He is aware that citizens are prone to the view that "every little payment appeareth a great grievance" rather than the perspicacity "to see afar off the miseries that hang over them, and cannot without such payments be avoided" (144). Contemporary public administration might conflate this with negativity bias, in which citizens emphasize the mistakes of policy work – the policy events of Chapter 2 – and not a quotidian record of satisfactory performance (e.g., Hood 2010). Yet I think the appropriate lesson for policy work is not the skepticism of citizens, but the need for legitimacy *because* the state is comprehensively powerful. The normative basis for negativity bias, in other words, is more important to champions than more positive evidence about it.

Legitimating State Power

The citizens of modern states need more than foresight to accept such a powerful concentration of authority over their lives. The state ought to be made to restrain itself to allay citizens' justifiable fears.

One way to think of this is that the state must *tolerate* certain things that citizens do. This is different from claiming that certain things are not within the functional capacity of the state. Max Weber (1970 [1918]) contends that an argument that, say, regulating religious beliefs is simply not a function of the state is less powerful than a capability claim that the state does not have the right tools to regulate those beliefs. Weber's argument is, in the words of the political theorist Jeremy Waldron (1988, 64), that "[a] state by definition is an organization which uses means of type M. But means of type M are ill-fitted for producing ends of type E. They never produce E-type effects (but perhaps at best mockeries or travesties of them). Therefore it is irrational to use M-type means in order to produce (genuine) E-type effects." Waldron (1988) argues that this is essentially the logic of John Locke's extrication of religious beliefs from the authority of the state in *A Letter on Toleration* in 1689.

The means of the state are not suited to integrating religion into what citizens regard as a good life.

Toleration for some political theorists is a matter of ensuring that the state maintains neutrality in regard to how citizens conceive of a life worth living because this allows the state to uphold individual liberties (e.g., Ackerman 1980). For others, "the state must embrace and pursue a substantial theory of the good, because this is the best way to ensure a healthy society and sound politics" (Sandel 1982; Steinberger 2005, 177). The political theorist Peter Steinberger (2005, 178) sees the state as "composed of propositions about how things in the world really are and about how to achieve the good health of society" and this implies that "the neutral state is neither good nor bad; it is impossible." This is surely a provocative statement for some students of public administration to read, what with "neutral competence" being a textbook claim about what policy work ought to embody: "A neutral efficient civil service was viewed as not merely desirable; it was essential to democracy itself" (Mosher 1968, 202). Crucially, however, traditional arguments about neutrality in policy work are not about the ends of the state, but, rather, about the means. The distinction between means and ends lies at the heart of the Friedrich-Finer debate that I discussed in Chapter 4, and underpins the ideal of separating politics from administration (Bertelli and Lynn 2006, 38; see also Frederickson 1980). That is, one policy worker can implement first a left-leaning policy that creates a program and then a right-leaning policy that eliminates it, and while neither policy is neutral, the policy worker must be committed – through capacity and control – to carry out both.

Another mechanism for legitimating policy work is *representation*. On this view, policy work is done by the state on behalf of citizens. For Hobbes, representing citizens as though they were one person is what gives rise to the state itself, which from the perspective of the citizen "makes representation a form of transformation: it is by being represented that the state is born" (Brito Viera and Runciman 2008, 26). For John Locke, representation depended on consent, which takes us closer to the ideas of representative government in which my argument in this book has been grounded. Legislative authority is "only a Fiduciary power to act for certain ends, there remains still in the People a Supream Power *to remove or alter* the Legislative, when they find the Legislative act contrary to the trust reposed in them" (Locke 1988 [1689], 367, emphasis added). The sanctioning view of accountability thus plays a crucial role. The Lockean executive is parliamentary in nature, "has also a share in the

The State and Responsible Policy Work

Legislative," yet "is visibly subordinate and accountable to" [parliament] (368). The policy workers in his state, those "[m]inisterial and subordinate Powers ... have no manner of authority any of them, beyond what is, by positive Grant, and Commission, delegated to them, and are all of them accountable to some other Power in the Commonwealth" (369). Similarly, Hobbes theorized about the highest level of civil government, not the cast of managers and other policy workers that are the subject of this book (Skinner 1989, 90). Nonetheless, the crucial point for responsible policy work is that in thinking about how the state is justified to citizens, representation and accountability for what is done in the name of citizens are inextricably connected. This connection gives significance to the accountability and process values of Chapters 2 and 3.

Representative government can, of course, have different legitimating narratives. For instance, Locke through the American revolutionaries gave *political elites* – particularly in the arguments of the Federalists that elite decision-making is incentivized to avoid capture by factional interests under the constitution – a privileged position in the United States (Brito Viera and Runciman 2008, 38; see also Bertelli and Lynn 2006). The American constitutional debate of 1787 was indeed divided on the idea of representation. The Federalists' *forward-looking* view was that representatives who stand for a constituency in a national legislature must have the disposition to transcend factionalism by promising "to follow the constituents' instructions or expressed desires" or "to further the constituency's long-run interests and the interests of the nation as a whole" (Mansbridge 2003, 516). Conversely, the Anti-Federalists' idea was *backward-looking*, representatives should have similar characteristics to those citizens they represent (Brito Viera and Runciman 2008, 40). In regard to the state, then, the forward-looking view leads to the legitimation strategy of accountability to representatives as in controlled and managed agency structures, while the backward-looking view clears a place for the citizen involvement of representative agency structures.

American Public Administration and the State

Laurence Lynn and I have argued that the Madisonian view of the state, shared in this aspect by Sieyès (Brito Viera and Runciman 2008, 44), is one in which policy work supports forward-looking representation by elites (representatives) with their electoral connection to citizens. Forward-looking representation makes *accountability* "the entire purpose of public management as an institution" in controlled-agency structures,

180   *The Complementarity Principle*

rendering it synonymous with "responsibility" in the canonical literature of American public administration before 1945 (Bertelli and Lynn 2006, 146). I will argue in this brief section that, in the United States, structures of controlled agency were legitimated through the idea of responsibility and in reference to a powerful state that shares important characteristics with the Hobbesian one. Such a justification is not limited to public administration in the United States, of course, but the field's multinational literature has been influenced substantially by this context.

In the early twentieth century, American progressives looked to reform governments through legitimate forms of public administration. Consider the city management movement, which aimed to place appointed, non-partisan, and professional managers in charge of the administration of towns and cities across the United States. The authority such city managers would exercise was delegated by politicians, and city managers do their policy work with an understanding that "city hall" is where "representatives of interest groups meet to resolve their conflicts" (Schiesl 1977, 188). The resulting controlled-agency structure involved specific powers granted to city managers in city charters. It was intended to undermine the political strong-arming of party bosses that had become a hallmark of urban politics (Bertelli and Lynn 2006, 20). Managers in controlled-agency structures were seen as experts who could enhance evaluability "with facts so citizens could be efficient in performing their role of providing consent" to their representative governments (Bertelli and Lynn 2006, 21; Cleveland 1913; Dahlberg 1966). Accountability would be served when evaluability increased citizens' capacity to consent to policy work done in their name (Bertelli 2016; Bertelli and Van Ryzin 2020).

The reorganization of public administration in the next few decades likewise embraced the idea of consent, but it implicitly recognized the notion that accountability is what ought to legitimate policy work. The political scientist John Mabry Mathews wrote that, in state governments, increasing executive power to expand policy work was acceptable "if it is accompanied with commensurate responsibility," and the burden of responsibility "will be enforced in part through the simplified machinery and the greater publicity in which the work of the administration will be conducted" (Mathews 1917, 397). What controlled agency must incorporate is "the means whereby the acts of governmental agents may be made known to the people" linking "government and citizenship" (Cleveland 1913, 454). Evaluability was meant to serve citizens' consent to a state that was growing in authority. Identifiability was

The State and Responsible Policy Work

simultaneously considered an important premise for accountability. The political scientist Leonard White (1933, 174) noted in regard to business organization that the president was "now in effective control of administrative policy and operation" and this meant the end of agencies "independent and uncoordinated position." That is, the president was the identifiable locus of federal policy work in the New Deal.

Was the American state really all that Hobbesian? For the political scientist Frank Goodnow (1900), it surely was. He writes that the state has a useful "abstract" conception as an "organism," and he is explicit in saying that this is due to Hobbes (8). Further, "the action of the state" in this conception "consists either in operations necessary to the *expression* of its will, or in operations necessary to the *execution* of that will" (9, emphasis added). Unlike Friedrich (1940), Goodnow sees a clear temporal order according to which "the will of the state" is "formulated before political action" and "must be executed after it is formulated" (9). Crucially, "[a]ll of the actions of the state" are done "with the object, either of facilitating the expression of this will or of aiding in its execution" (9). This means that Goodnow does not share the Lockean view of policy workers as lacking authority and of being mechanically accountable to representatives. By contrast, he believed they were an essential part of that state: "administrative hierarchies have profound influence on the course of legislative policy" and the "complexity of political conditions makes it practically impossible for the same governmental organ to be intrusted in equal degree" with both politics and administration (Goodnow 1900, 84). For at least one similar reason as Max Weber (1964 [1921]), Goodnow did not see politicians as making good policy workers.

Goodnow's view was not exceptional among political scientists in the United States before World War II. Remarking on an expanding New Deal state, Marshall Dimock (1933, 26) claimed that "any view should be discouraged which tends to regard public administration as a detached, self-sufficient entity" from the state and its representative government. He felt that policy work should be done by "a civil service cultured and self-sufficient enough to act with sense and vigor, and yet so intimately connected with the popular thought *by means of elections and constant public council*" (Dimock 1933, 40, emphasis added). E. Pendleton Herring (1936, 21) agreed, suggesting "making guardianship part of the duty of officials" and that its object was the representation of citizens' views: "Opinion is like water. Administrators must dig for it." John Gaus (1936, 43) argued similarly that a collaboration with citizens groups would emerge from "the attitude of the civil servant as an individual toward his work and his profession." Legitimation of a more complex administrative state may be seen as hinting at representative agency structures, but it certainly conceived representation as a legitimating strategy in controlled agency. Understanding citizens' opinion was not a matter of managers doing polling, but of their interaction with groups of citizens about policy work. And that interaction would lead to representation of citizens by policy workers.

Politics and administration are inextricably part of the state. Once one sees the state through this lens, the postwar claim to discovering the impossibility of separating politics and administration is, at best, obvious. The maligned dichotomy is a feature of a Hobbesian conception of the state shared by these early thinkers in the American tradition: a state that is strong *and* separate from citizens, but which requires their *consent*. The importance of transparency or publicity about how policy work is done and the citizens' opinion about it was part and parcel of a deep understanding that the power of this kind of state, which could only be understood as including policy workers, was vast, and it could be turned against citizens.

What was decidedly less Hobbesian was the belief of these champions that consent could be given over time, and that the public's wishes might be directly communicated to policy workers rather than through the laws made by representatives. Dimock (1936, 40) connected effective policy work to trust by citizens in its principles, which was not just a function of efficiency, but, rather "dependent upon their consistency with and contribution to those democratic values which the community [of policy workers] is determined to preserve at all costs." While Harvey Walker (1937, 99) was adamant that policy workers "cannot be permitted to construe laws in their own way," he was aware that to respect consent, governance structures would have to change as policy work became more complex: "more intricate and ingenious devices must be constructed than are available today if popular control over administrative officers is to be asserted and maintained" (9). Importantly, he went so far as to differentiate policy work from the controlled-agency structure in which it is done: "The absence of such control permits the administration to degenerate into a bureaucracy" (9). A direct linkage between citizens and policy workers, which was alive in this New Deal–era thinking, has continued influence. This connection is routinely emphasized by champions of managed agency and its outcome orientation, as well as those advocating the role of citizen participation in representative agency.

The State and Responsible Policy Work

Governance Structures and Representation

The historical view of the last section sees the controlled agency of prewar American public administration as a mechanism for forward-looking representation. It emphasizes accountability, seeks to be transparent enough in its processes to make policy workers identifiable, and to render their work evaluable by citizens. Yet it also allows for feedback from citizens outside the electoral calendar, and in a form that does not flow through the ballot box. What it did not consider was the broader obviation of accountability and process values in the governance structures discussed in Chapter 4 as alternatives to controlled agency. How does representation feature in those governance structures? Asking this question returns attention to Figure 4.1 and reveals an important distinction between structures that obviate accountability values and those that obviate process values.

In his influential book *The Administrative State*, the public administration scholar Dwight Waldo (1948, 74) argues that prewar "[s]tudents of administration all profess democracy. Substantively, they regard it as striving toward the ideals which they themselves seek." In this sense, Waldo sees the goal of public administration as democracy administered as I do. This is because, in representative governments, democracy is the first value, and representation can only serve it (Brito Viera and Runciman 2008, 59). Representation legitimates the state. I disagree with Waldo's view that these scholars "have tended to regard it as external or at least incidental to their field of inquiry: administration" (Waldo 1948, 74; see also Bertelli and Lynn 2003, 2006). In obviating accountability values, champions, including those prewar champions of controlled-agency structures, wrestle with the difficulty of restraining policy work from *evading* the institutions of representative government in order to understand citizens' preferences. Champions must understand the risk of compromising democracy administered by allowing policy workers to privilege a direct channel of information about citizens' wants over one that flows through representatives. The trade-offs among actor- and procedure-relative values described in Chapter 4 illuminate champions' theories of representation given a powerful state.

Managed agency, like controlled agency, embraces forward-looking representation, and privileges accountability values accordingly. The difference, as I discussed in Chapter 4, is that accountability in managed agency attaches to outcomes rather than to procedures. In either controlled or managed agency, actor-relative values are central to legitimating policy work because legitimacy requires a respect for representative government, which, in turn, preserves democratic values. The onus is on policy workers and the predominant role of accountability is retrospective and accords with the sanctioning view.

Procedure-relative values are central to a different legitimating strategy for representative government most readily apparent in varieties of representative agency. For instance, champions of representative bureaucracy embrace backward-looking representation, seeking a better match between the socioeconomic characteristics of policy workers and the citizens. The public administration scholar Frederick Mosher (1968, 17) argued that a "passive" kind of representation that descriptively compared such characteristics between populations of citizens and policy workers could not be a sufficient condition for his view of democracy administered, but its value came through an "open service." Public administration in representative government takes "[a] third step away from direct democracy" by choosing policy workers "on bases of stated criteria" (Mosher 1968, 5). The democratically relevant content of a passive representative bureaucracy is not the policy work it performs, but "the fact that the incumbent employees are there at all." Both the successes and failures of passive representation are made transparent by simply identifying policy workers and their characteristics. This information, when made available to citizens, enhances evaluability.

The selection of mini-publics and organized interests in participatory and collaborative structures are also backward-looking to the characteristics of citizens and interests *pro tempore*, and they may have to change the cast of participants over time as the complexion of the represented group of citizens changes. A focus on stakeholders, or "those groups without whose support the organization would cease to exist" (Freeman and Reed 1983, 89), and the various techniques managers use to identify them and to foster their participation (e.g., Bryson 2004) limit the scope of representation.

Independent agency views representation differently still. The political theorist Chiara Cordelli (2020) makes an important Kantian argument about privatization, an extreme form of independent agency, concluding that it is incongruous with democracy. She bases her claim on two premises for achieving democracy administered. First, the discretion policy workers enjoy must be validly authorized by representatives. Second, this discretion must translate into policy work that represents citizens, that is, it is done "in the name of all" citizens (Cordelli 2020, 124). To perform policy work in the name of all citizens, a "bureaucratic

The State and Responsible Policy Work 185

ethos" that is Friedrichian and reminiscent of the political scientist Emmette Redford's (1969) "inner check" must be established. Doing policy work, Cordelli claims, "must carry out (and, in the process, help reconstitute) the shared will of the people throughout the process of administration" (Cordelli 2020, 125). This requires that policy workers "do not impose their unilateral judgment on citizens" and that they avoid actions that exceed their legitimately delegated authority (125). Third, the foregoing requirements are served only by "a tight procedural integration between the bureaucratic and the democratic from the top to the bottom, and from the bottom to the top" allowing policy work to be "omnilateral, in the sense of genuinely representative, power and as an instantiation of an omnilateral, because shared, will" of and with citizens (125).

Privatization, Cordelli contends, fails all three conditions. It permits some discretionary actions that may not be legitimately authorized by citizens, as when a private railway operator makes choices about the scope of policy work in ending service to certain communities. Private managers can operate outside, or even against the all-citizen-regarding ethos of public service when making choices, for instance, that are compelled by profit-seeking. Finally, unilateral private actions like restricting rail service to improve profit margins sever the connection between policy workers and representatives, and thus, to the people.

While there are plenty of arguments in the public administration literature that private policy work is not democracy administered, I find Cordelli's among the most principled. By comparison, Janet Denhardt and Robert Denhardt (2007, 76) argue that the problem for private policy work owes to its situation within competitive markets where the "need to talk about or act upon the 'public interest' largely disappears" because its champions believe that "individual choices in a market-like arena are superior to collective action based on shared values." Their argument would benefit from Cordelli's focus on the disjuncture between policy work and citizens due to the unilateral choices of competing firms, but, instead, they blame the superiority of "self-interest" as a desiratum on "[p]ublic choice theorists" who surely have an argument about how individual interests are aggregated in nonmarket arenas – I discussed it in Chapter 3 – that necessitates much more nuance in the argument. In Chapter 4, I argued that treating citizens as customers can reshape the relationship between citizens and representatives. The needs of *all* citizens are not aggregated, only those having a relationship that might be considered that of a customer with policy workers, and only their interests as customers inform policy work. The risks to democracy administered from

186   *The Complementarity Principle*

private policy work, in my view, accrue from its ability to change the nature of representation by limiting which citizens are represented and what the content of that representation can be.

While privatization is extreme, the foregoing discussion does shed light on how independent agency views representation. Representation is forward-looking in independent agency, and as under managed agency, it privileges on actor-centric values and outcomes. But accountability values are obviated in these structures, and to be legitimate, independent agency must not exclusively focus on the interests of stakeholders because, if it does, it cannot represent citizens more generally. Policy workers must consider the range of citizens' interests relevant to the policy work in question. And independent agency structures must not allow policy workers – including, and especially, managers when making strategic choices about the scope, quantity, and quality of policy work – to engage in actions that exceed what representatives authorized when enabling them. Crucially, as Cordelli (2020) cautions, it cannot sever the connection with citizens and leave the idea of representation ill-defined at best in the process.

The Idea of Responsible Policy Work

This chapter has thus far provided the materials for me to build a normative argument about how responsibility ought to work in the governance structures of Chapter 4. I do this, first, by situating value reinforcement into what constitutes responsible policy work in a modern state and thus into the fundamental problem of public administration. I begin from the premise that the state is *not* neutral as to the policies it undertakes or the accountability and process values that it upholds. Whether accountability and process value trade-offs champions make in designing governance structures are the consequence of means-ends incompatibilities, a communitarian theory of the good, or the impossibility of neutrality is immaterial to my present argument. What matters is that there *are* trade-offs. The state, in my argument, has incredibly broad authority over citizens, but its representative government can commit to accountability and process value trade-offs by passing laws that implement specific governance structures or which give managers the discretion to choose them. Put simply, the state is sovereign, but capable of credible self-restraint.

Credible commitments to self-restraint should be familiar to the reader as they are central to control arguments in the positive political theory of

The State and Responsible Policy Work 187

bureaucracy discussed in Chapter 4. The political economists Douglass North and Barry Weingast (1989, 803) contend that "[r]ules the sovereign can readily revise differ significantly in their implications for performance from exactly the same rules when not subject to revision" Consider regulations on which businesses rely. Easily revised regulations diminish "the expected returns from investment" for business because it cannot rely on them when making strategic choices. Representatives and policy workers exercising state authority have two pathways to stabilizing their expectations about the rules they make: "One is by setting a precedent of 'responsible behavior,' appearing to be committed to a set of rules that he or she will consistently enforce. The second is by being constrained to obey a set of rules that do not permit leeway for violating commitments. We have very seldom observed the former" (804). Yet responsible behavior – Cordelli's (2020) bureaucratic ethos, Redford's (1969) inner check and Friedrich's (1940) community preferences – is essential to the legitimacy of policy work.

Responsibility is tied to the Hobbesian notion of representation – representing citizens as though they were one person brings about the state itself – and how policy workers facilitate representation is, I contend, the key to their responsibility. In Chapter 3, I explained how representation by *representatives* was shown to be legitimate if it can be endorsed by the public through elections that are capable of holding incumbents accountable in retrospect. In Chapter 4, I discussed Max Weber's belief that representatives could not serve as policy workers. The crucial distinction – and Weber's thesis for legitimate controlled agency – was that policy workers, "the modern 'servant of the State' and all those bearers of power who resemble him in this respect," exercise state authority "by virtue of 'legality,'" which "rests on a predisposition to fulfil one's statutory obligations obediently" (Weber 1970 [1918], 312). Policy workers play a distinct role in representation, and it is the rule of law that makes this role legitimate. Once created, the state has tremendous power over citizens, policy workers exercise this power on behalf of citizens (representation), and citizens accept their use of this power as legitimate when it is done in fulfillment of policy workers' legal obligations.

The idea of conditional representation from Chapter 4 allows representatives more freedom to maneuver than policy workers. Representatives may take the actions that citizens would want if they knew what representatives know about the political economy (Bertelli and John 2013). While not a kind of Burkean "virtual representation" in which elites avoid factionalism and the temptation of localized interests

188   *The Complementarity Principle*

by acting as trustees of citizens' national interests (Burke 1912 [1790]), conditional representation is forward-looking and allows for campaign promises to be broken and for a narrative to be presented to citizens that such action was in their long-term or collective interest, which citizens are free to reject in the next election. Whether this freedom to maneuver extends to policy workers depends on an application of Weberian legal authority. Independent agency provides the most illustrative example. Representatives can, for instance, create an independent regulatory agency overseeing banks that invest personal funds for retirement because they believe that if the public knew how much market volatility was possible, they would want stronger regulation of that sector. Yet managers in the agency they create can exercise only such discretion that they are granted in the law representatives enacted to create the agency. That enabling law may allow the flexibility to "manage for results" rather than to follow strict procedures in gathering information about the banks they regulate and how compliance is achieved, and that might amount to a restriction of investment options. One might even see this as conditional representation by managers if citizens expressed a desire for more choice in retirement investment options, but did not know as much about market volatility as the managers in the new agency. The crucial difference is that managers' leeway for conditional representation must be permitted by the law. Conditional representation by representatives is possible because of the nature of representative government. Policy workers enjoy the same privilege only when it is founded in the legal authority representatives give them.

The *responsible* use of discretion is connected to conditional representation and is the core concept of the fundamental problem of public administration. Laurence Lynn and I (Bertelli and Lynn 2003, 2006) argue that responsible policy work is constituted of balancing competing interests, of exercising judgment, of rationally connecting the means of policy work to its aims, and, above all, of accountability to representatives, and through them, to citizens. Balancing interests is rooted in the process value of pluralism. Judgment allows the policy worker latitude for conditional representation of citizens within legal limits and fulfills the capability element of the traditional narrative of public administration. Rationality gives legitimacy to the state through a Weberian capability argument: if a policy worker with a given complement of legal discretion can use only a set of means that is unlikely to produce "good" outcomes – against criteria such as justice or fairness – then the policy worker ought not to act at all. Accountability respects the role of representatives in

Responsible Value Reinforcement

representative government, but it restrains policy workers from actions beyond their legal discretion and thereby maintains the rule of law. Rationality and accountability adhere to the control element of the traditional view of public administration. Seen as a whole, our argument is that responsible discretion allows elites – managers and other policy workers – to make representative government work *better*.

Still one element remains before policy work can become democracy administered: value reinforcement. To appreciate its role, I work through a scenario in the next section that explores value reinforcement in each of the basic governance structures – controlled, managed, representative and independent agency. This analysis leads to the complementary principle, which summarizes what I argue to be the role of value reinforcement in *responsible* policy work.

RESPONSIBLE VALUE REINFORCEMENT

How should policy workers reinforce values? To address this question, I find it useful to think through the following case, which illustrates how each of the governance structures described in Chapter 4 allows policy workers to reinforce values and to uncover a baseline standard for responsible value reinforcement.

Administering the Vote. Taylor is a directly elected executive in a country with a representative government and universal suffrage. Taylor lawfully promulgates an immediately effective, unilateral executive order requiring all citizens to present valid identification cards at their polling places in order to access a ballot. Rory leads the elections agency, which has broad authority to administer all elections. Quinn heads the transportation agency, which has broad authority for issuing national identification cards.

A fundamental characteristic of policy workers, particularly managers, is their discretionary authority. This authority is restrained by the rule of law to maintain accountability values and the possibility of a self-restraining state. For this reason, managers may not use their discretionary authority *ultra vires*, or beyond that which they are granted by representatives. While how it operates is a source of debate, the prohibition of *ultra vires* policy work is central to Anglo-American administrative law (cf. Elliott 1999; Merrill 2010; Oliver 1987). Civilian legal systems have an equivalent concept. In European Union law, the principle of conferral in Article 5(2) of the Treaty on European Union states that "[p]ublic authorities must have a legal basis and be justified on the grounds laid down by law." This means that policy workers cannot "act *ultra vires* and have to comply with the procedural rules spelt out" in their enabling laws (Hoffman 2017, 208). In Italy, the principle of legality, which is derived from the principle of separation of power and various constitutional provisions – establishes that policy workers in the public administration "can only do what the law provides for and in the way it indicates" (Ferrari 2008, 101, 102). As a consequence, managers are likewise obligated to implement lawful mandates. Administrative law has two basic functions in this regard to *ultra vires* action: "(1) to redress harm to individuals inflicted by government in the pursuit of government objectives, and (2) for positive control of government agencies by branches of government with sovereign authority in lawmaking" (Bertelli 2005, 133). Thus, we can expect managers both to have the capability and the duty to exercise discretion when implementing lawful mandates and to anticipate sanctions for *ultra vires* policy work.

The rule of law, in this way, binds Rory and Quinn to implement Taylor's order so long as they do not exceed their discretionary authority when doing so. I will argue that they have an individual *responsibility* to use their discretionary authority, separately or collectively, to implement Taylor's order so long as doing so does not constitute *ultra vires* action. Different governance structures afford them different levels of flexibility in doing this policy work, and the bounds of their discretionary authority help in understanding the character of their responsibility to reinforce values.

Taylor's order relaxes the process value of pluralism by restricting universal suffrage, and this runs counter to the values in the system of representative government that Taylor serves. By the time of the 2016 general election, at least nine American states had identification requirements, and this has led to a robust empirical effort to understand their impact on turnout (Highton 2017, 152). Nonetheless, I want to emphasize that Administering the Vote is *not* about this American context, but about a more general potential influence that Taylor's order may have on citizen participation in elections. Requiring identification in order to vote can reduce turnout among citizens who would vote, but do not have appropriate identification and lack motivation, interest, or capacity to get it before Election Day (Highton 2017, 156). The executive order would weaken pluralism, for instance, if it is possible to identify two groups of citizens, A and B, that are "similar with respect to their ID [identification] holding and turnout rates" but citizens in one group are "more likely to be asked for ID and therefore to be kept from voting if

Responsible Value Reinforcement

they do not have or have forgotten their ID" than their compatriots in the other (157). Managers can influence this decision in a number of ways, for instance, by providing information or easing the burden of acquiring valid identification "when requirements are new and even those who have the required identification, or could obtain it, are unaware of the new rules" (Vercellotti and Andersen 2009, 117). For present purposes, the mechanism of *group exclusion* and the countervailing mechanisms of *legal information* and *convenient procurement* are far from the only ones in evidence, but I think they are sufficient for my current purpose.

Controlled Agency A. This case is the same as Administering the Vote, but Rory subsequently institutes an information campaign about the new requirement. Quinn changes procedures so that valid identification cards are easier and faster to get.

My claim has been that managers ought to use their discretionary authority, individually and collectively, to implement lawful orders, and they must do so without engaging in *ultra vires* policy work. Assume that the controlled-agency framework in which Rory and Quinn operate gives them the formal discretionary authority to engage in the information campaign and procedural modifications, respectively. That is, their efforts are not *ultra vires*. I hypothesize that managers are obligated to reinforce values when using their discretionary authority. The sole value in question for present purposes is pluralism, which is relaxed by Taylor's order. The actions taken by Rory and Quinn are meant to increase participation in the next election through the legal information and convenient procurement mechanisms.

I think it is reasonable to conclude that Quinn and Rory have met their obligations to reinforce pluralism when implementing Taylor's order. Two things are important to observe in this regard. First, it may be that Taylor really meant to restrain pluralism, say, to gain electoral advantage by suppressing turnout among citizens unlikely to have appropriate identification cards. While this may have been Taylor's intent, the obligation of Rory and Quinn to reinforce values is unaffected by it. Citing practice in many countries, a reader would be quite right to observe that courts could enter and reframe the obligation, rendering the value-reinforcement requirement unlawful. This is certainly correct, and what it would do is determine the actions of Rory and Quinn to have been *ultra vires*, overturning them ex post – a matter of control, not value reinforcement. The default principle for the latter, I claim, should be for policy workers to reinforce values. Were citizens to punish Taylor at the polls because the court emphasized the intent behind the order, their action would be consistent with the sanctioning view of accountability in Chapter 2. Taylor's responsibility for the lawful order is to the citizens in all of these scenarios. Second, Controlled Agency A involved Rory and Quinn taking consistent actions that reinforce pluralism. My argument is that they have *individual* duties to do so, but they are not required to collaborate in doing so. Managers can collaborate to the extent that their discretionary authority allows, but it is their discretion and judgment that allows for collaboration. Of course, as in the case of the nonfiscal transfers discussed in Chapter 5 (see also Bertelli, Clouser McCann, and Travaglini 2019), such collaboration may be required by law, and then managers would be obliged to collaborate because failing to do so would be unlawful and *ultra vires*. A legislative requirement of collaboration would constitute a commitment to the incorporation of collaborative policy work, and Rory and Quinn would be irresponsible should they not do so.

Controlled Agency B. This case is the same as Controlled Agency A, but Rory does not institute the information campaign and Quinn changes no procedures. Consequently, election officials only accept identification cards issued by the transportation agency on Election Day and many citizens, disproportionately the working poor, are turned away from the polls for having expired identification cards or none on their persons.

In this scenario, I have added a premise of *nonneutral inaction*: discretionary inaction influences values just as consequentially as discretionary action does. My hypothesis is that managers ought to use discretionary inaction to reinforce values. Taylor's order obviates pluralism and Quinn and Rory are obliged to use discretionary action and inaction to reinforce pluralism without performing policy work *ultra vires*. I think that Rory and Quinn both failed in their obligation to reinforce pluralism because they had the discretion to take actions that could work through the legal information and convenient procurement mechanisms, just as they did in Controlled Agency A. While their failure to do so may have contributed to weakening pluralism, I do not think that this *outcome* alters their obligations. It is reasonable to expect that managers in the positions of Rory and Quinn should expect that not providing information or making access to identification cards straightforward *might* lead to voters being turned away on Election Day, as they were in this scenario.

The question, for me, turns on a capability claim. If the elections and transportation agencies had the capability to engage in the actions they took in Controlled Agency A, their obligation to reinforce values was not met when they took no action. If they had no such capacity, or if doing so involved *ultra vires* policy work, they would have no corresponding obligation to act. Yet even dramatically under-resourced units could take some action through the legal information and convenient procurement mechanisms.

It is also important to consider that the mutual inaction of managers in this scenario is not required. Their obligation to reinforce values is hypothesized to be individual, and it does not depend on consequences. So, Quinn might have acted to enhance both legal information and convenient procurement campaigns if that were within the discretion afforded to the transportation agency. Quinn, in so doing, would have met the obligation to reinforce pluralism while Rory would not.

Managed Agency A. This case is the same as Administering the Vote, but Rory subsequently creates a new, easy-to-acquire identification card, IVOTED, specifically for implementing Taylor's order and sends an application to acquire an IVOTED card to all citizens in the country. Quinn creates all necessary exceptions for IVOTED so that the new scheme cannot be contested as not following transportation agency procedures. IVOTED cards and identification cards issued by the transportation agency are accepted on Election Day.

This scenario works from a new premise, namely, that managers are only accountable to representatives for outcomes and have broad discretion over procedures. The hypothesis here is that managers have a duty to reinforce values as long as outcomes meet those intended by representatives. The outcome that Taylor's order mandates is identification at the polls. The managed agency premise gives Quinn and Rory the discretion to create and to administer the new IVOTED card as well as the authority to work separately and collectively to achieve the outcome mandated by Taylor's order. Under these circumstances, I contend that Quinn and Rory met their dual duties to reinforce pluralism and to be accountable for outcomes to Taylor.

Managed Agency B. This case is the same as Managed Agency A except that Quinn rejects the IVOTED scheme and a turf war ensues until after the election. Consequently, election officials only accept identification cards issued by the transportation agency on Election Day.

Managed agency provides the discretion to collaborate, which controlled agency may or may not have done. Because this discretion exists, collaboration would not be *ultra vires*. If Rory could reasonably anticipate that IVOTED would fail in the absence of Quinn's action to make exceptions to transportation department procedures, it would also be

The Complementarity Principle

incumbent upon Rory to engage Quinn in a joint solution. Likewise, if Quinn could reasonably expect that protecting turf in advance of the election could reduce the pluralism of voices that can access the ballot box, rejecting IVOTED out of hand would be irresponsible.

What is critical to recognize is that managed agency heightened both discretion and the responsibility to reinforce pluralism while achieving the outcome that was mandated by Taylor's order, checking a valid identification card on Election Day. Indeed, innovations such as IVOTED are an advantage of letting managers manage, but such innovations create a corresponding responsibility to reinforce values.

Representative Agency A. This case is the same as Administering the Vote, but Rory invites Quinn and a nonrandomly selected mini-public of citizens to deliberate toward a consensus action. Quinn does not challenge the nonrandom selection, proposes the IVOTED card, and consensus quickly emerges around it. IVOTED cards and identification cards issued by the transportation agency are accepted on Election Day.

As before, I begin with the claim that managers have a duty to reinforce values when using their discretionary authority. Representative agency adds an additional premise for understanding responsible behavior, namely, that managers must directly consult the public when implementing lawful orders and have broad discretion over consultation procedures.

A crucial choice in Representative Agency A is Rory's selection of a procedure for deliberation. Rory's discretion might have come from explicit statutory language, which might even have required both Quinn's participation and a nonrandom selection mechanism. The scenario would thus begin to collapse to controlled agency, though the conduct of the deliberation and both managers' participation during it would be subject to questions of responsibility. Rory might also have broader discretion over procedure – including both Quinn's inclusion and the public selection mechanism – because of managed agency. The source of discretion matters only insofar as it places collaboration and representation into the hands of managers, creating a responsibility over them that includes value reinforcement.

My hypothesis is that managers have a duty to reinforce values in choosing consultation procedures as long as their choices do not constitute *ultra vires* action. Taylor's order weakens pluralism, and if Rory and Quinn have the discretion to create procedures that can reinforce pluralism, they have the obligation to do so. By making selection less pluralistic due to its nonrandom nature, Rory would have failed this duty to reinforce pluralism if it could be reasonably expected that a procedure that would invite more pluralistic participation could have been implemented given the capabilities of the elections agency. If random selection were feasible on the appropriate scale to enhance pluralism, Rory's choice was irresponsible. Quinn's participation in the deliberation was responsible both because it is reasonable to expect that IVOTED would reinforce pluralism through the legal information mechanism and because Quinn could reasonably expect that IVOTED would require Rory's efforts to ensure that IVOTED cards would be accepted at the polls. That Quinn agreed to participate in this deliberation, though Rory did not select a more pluralistic selection mechanism from the feasible alternatives, does not render participation irresponsible.

Representative Agency B. This case is the same as Representative Agency A except that Rory makes the choice to randomly select a mini-public from all citizens and the resulting citizens' assembly, after deliberation, rejects Quinn's IVOTED procedure, which was supported by Rory. Rory subsequently institutes an information campaign about the new requirement. Quinn changes procedures so that valid identification cards are easier and faster to get. Consequently, election officials only accept identification cards issued by the transportation agency on Election Day.

My hypothesis now is that managers have the same duty to reinforce values as in the prior scenario. Taylor's order weakened pluralism. I think that both Rory and Quinn have acted responsibly. Rory selected the mini-public randomly. Quinn participated and proposed IVOTED, which could be reasonably expected to enhance pluralism through the legal information and convenient procurement mechanisms. Importantly, I do not believe that the rejection of IVOTED by a representative group of citizens absolves either manager of their responsibility to reinforce values. They maintained responsibility by taking discretionary actions that can be reasonably expected to enhance pluralism.

Independent Agency A. This case is the same as Administering the Vote, but Rory contracts with Dewberry, a high-tech company, and Dewberry proposes IVOTED. Quinn then uses the election agency's contracting authority with Dewberry to make appropriate changes to the procedures of the transportation agency so that it can issue IVOTED cards. IVOTED cards and identification cards issued by the transportation agency are accepted on Election Day.

This scenario shifts authority for the procedural innovations of Managed Agencies A and B to an independent actor, Dewberry. Independent agency gives managers broad discretion over processes and outcomes as long as they do not violate the rule of law, eliciting a hypothesis that managers have a duty to reinforce values when choosing both outcomes and procedures. Taylor's order is lawful and Dewberry may propose any process that does not violate the order or constitute *ultra vires* action. An answer to the question of what constitutes *ultra vires* action must center on the authority that Rory and Quinn have. These managers may accept and implement any proposal from Dewberry that does not violate the order. Assuming that IVOTED is within the discretion of the elections agency, Rory and Quinn both met their obligations to reinforce pluralism. Dewberry did as well because IVOTED can reasonably be expected to enhance pluralism, as I have argued above.

Independent Agency B. This case is the same as Independent Agency A except that Quinn uses the transportation agency's contracting authority to hire Syllabary, Dewberry's chief competitor to implement IVOTED, which Quinn supports in principle. Syllabary proposes no changes to transportation agency procedures citing serious data security issues. Quinn finds the advice persuasive and does not implement IVOTED. Rory subsequently institutes an information campaign about the new requirement. Aided by Syllabary, Quinn changes procedures so that valid identification cards are easier and faster to get. Election officials only accept identification cards issued by the transportation agency on Election Day.

Both managers now hire independent agents and accept their advice, which leads to the abandonment of IVOTED, which could reasonably have brought a more pluralistic electorate to the polls. Dewberry and Syllabary may propose anything that does not constitute *ultra vires* action for the agencies with which they have contracted. Crucially, Rory had no discretion to change Quinn's decision; it was an internal management choice at the transportation agency. Quinn had to balance the interests of data security against enhancing pluralism and acted on what appears to be a determination that making existing identification easy to acquire was more appropriate. Quinn acted responsibly by reinforcing pluralism, as did Rory, who took action reasonably anticipated to work through the legal information mechanism. Dewberry acted responsibly because its situation is unchanged from Independent Agency A. Syllabary, too, was responsible for the same reason as was Quinn. However, had Syllabary not aided Quinn's effort to enhance pluralism through the convenient procurement mechanism with no other changes, it would not have acted responsibly.

THE COMPLEMENTARITY PRINCIPLE

The foregoing scenarios have implications for the fundamental problem of public administration because the reinforcing acts of Rory, Quinn,

Dewberry, and Syllabary *represent* the aims of citizens, or they do not. Citizens' aims can be better understood when the value of pluralism operates in elections. Rory, Quinn, Dewberry, and Syllabary have the discretion to reshape democracy. I think that three criteria govern for their responsibility. First, a policy worker, when performing policy work, has an individual duty to reinforce political values through governance values. In this way, value reinforcement forms part of a Fredrichian ethos of responsibility. Second, policy workers cannot perform *ultra vires* policy work, even if it reinforces values. Third, policy workers must act to reinforce values if they have the capability to use means that are likely, in fact, to reinforce the values in question. The second and third criteria are consistent with Weberian legal authority and respect representative government. Furthermore, I contend that champions ought to respect these obligations of individual policy workers when designing governance structures for the very simple reason that if they do not, policy workers will be incentivized toward irresponsible policy work and these champions will not address the fundamental problem of administration.

Meeting the responsible value-reinforcement criteria in the design and discharge of policy work has different meaning and urgency across political jurisdictions. In some countries, representative government is working well, and it is making citizens feel that they live in a self-governing society. In others, such sentiment cannot be further from the truth. Responses to the question "How democratic do you think [your country] is overall?" analyzed in Chapter 3 are, on average, almost four times higher in Denmark (2.4 on a ten-point scale) than in Bulgaria (8.2). For this reason, value reinforcement might tend toward controlled or managed agency in Denmark, preserving the values of representative government. By contrast, structures of representative and independent agency in Bulgaria can be value reinforcing if they complement political values with governance values that are consistent with what representative government aims to provide, but is not now providing, to its citizens.

At their most general level, the responsible value-reinforcement criteria can be summarized by a *complementarity principle*: governance values ought to complement political values. When designing governance structures, abiding by this principle resolves the champion's dilemma in a contextually appropriate way that addresses the fundamental problem of public administration. Reinforcement mechanisms that satisfy the complementarity principle promote responsible public administration because they serve *their* representative governments. Complementarity enhances the self-restraining nature of *their* powerful states. Of course, as I noted in Chapter 2, the link between representatives and citizens can leave much to be desired in practice, and can involve corruption or clientelism. At the policy worker level, Quinn and Rory provided an example of reinforcing pluralism even when it contravenes the intended purposes of representatives such as Taylor, who may well have wanted to reduce voter turnout. For champions, reinforcing complementary values can be done while mitigating *practices*, like corruption, that make such values harder to implement in a particular context.

Critiques of representative government abound in this era, and the complementarity principle likewise will have its detractors. Within the scholarly field of public administration, one of the most enduring – and, I think, problematically enduring challenges (see Bertelli and Lynn, 2006; Lynn 2001) to value complementarity is that of Dwight Waldo because it takes direct aim at representative government. Building on the argument in Mary Parker Follett's *The New State* (1918) that likewise informs Ansell's (2011) theory of representative agency in Chapter 5, Waldo (1952, 92) calls the institutions of representative democracy "mechanical counterfeits" and argues that "[t]he essence of democracy lies not in these, but in the development of common, shared purposes in organizations in which all participate." This is not complementarity, but, rather, substitutability. Waldo allows the governance values of representative agency – the "common, shared purposes" – to *replace* the political values behind the deliberations and voting of citizens in elections and of representatives in lawmaking. The complementarity principle is at odds with Waldo's belief that "both private and public administration were in an important and far-reaching sense false to the ideal of democracy" (87). This conceit, which damns controlled and managed agency in their accountability-enhancing ambitions is due to the impossibility of a politics-administration dichotomy: "They were false by reason of their insistence that democracy, however good and desirable, is nevertheless something peripheral to administration" (87). Surely when Rory and Quinn reinforced pluralism without taking *ultra vires* action in Administering the Vote, they were not "false" to the representative government they serve, and they did so within controlled and managed agency structures.

From where I stand, Ansell (2011) offers a far more encouraging way to champion representative agency in a way that respects the complementarity principle. My reading of his argument is that the policy work he seeks to ground normatively is not simply living in the pages of John Dewey (1927) and Mary Parker Follett (1918), but in legislation, formulated in the institutions of representative government, that mandates

The Complementarity Principle

forms of representative agency. Ansell offers a path toward understanding what to do when representatives *choose* representative agency. The point of collaborative governance is to seek supermajority support, all the while appreciating that majorities may become a necessary resort. The strategies for collaboration that Ansell (2011) presents are particularly instructive. A strategy within representative agency to "focus stakeholders on concrete problems and to shift their attention and energies away from doctrinaire position-taking" can relax collective rationality by partitioning the agenda, but also complement accountability by focusing "fruitful conflict" on the group mandate from representatives, rather than encouraging *ultra vires* activity (181). Likewise, representative agency procedures that are able to "to reconstruct and reframe the terms of debate" can avoid incompletely theorized agreements by "shifting to a more abstract level of deliberation or ... focusing on particulars" in a way that allows an evaluable decision to be made, strengthening accountability to representatives (182). This kind of theoretical work can support democracy administered when scholars keep the complementary principle in mind.

The political philosopher Pierre Rosanvallon (2011), through an insightful historical and normative analysis, reaches an important normative pillar on which independent agency might stand in representative government. His focus is on legitimating the practice of an *"art* of governing" that "means increasingly to pay close attention to individual situations and deal with particular cases" (Rosanvallon 2011, 180, emphasis original). Citizens' efforts "to make the actions of government more democratic" insist "that greater attention be paid to social diversity so that no one is sacrificed on the altar of abstract principle" (185). For enlightenment thinkers, "liberty depended on the generality of the law: generality of origin (a product of parliamentary representation), generality of form (impersonality of the law), and generality of administration (the state)" (181). We now have "a new definition of generality as a radical form of immersion in concrete social facts and a determination to comprehend society's irreducible diversity and complexity" (185). This "generality of attention to particularity" (185) requires "close attention to the infinite variety of singularities that exist in the real world," and "can do no more than suggest a regulatory horizon" or "political method characteristic of the art of government" rather than "a policy in itself" (186; compare Ochoa Espejo 2011). Because this method is "autonomous and distinct" from the institutional application of rules (Rosanvallon 2011, 186), "the agencies of indirect democracy are important actors" because "the majoritarian logic is relatively less important" (221). As a consequence, "[o]versight bodies, regulatory agencies, and constitutional courts thus define a new democratic horizon" (221).

Rosanvallon's argument provides a principled rationale for obviating accountability and process values through independent agency. It also supports the process obviation (particularly in regard to majoritarianism) of managed agency. His arguments satisfy the complementarity principle because they imbue independent agency with the values of representative democracy. The "structure and function" of independent agency must be "transparent"; its "activities should be explained in public documents and widely debated"; policy events and other problems in policy work "should also be discussed publicly"; and "[c]itizen access should be facilitated" (103). The value trade-offs of independent agency cannot be the same for all systems of representative government because transparency and public debate do not work the same way across systems. This implies, in my reading, an application of the complementarity principle. What matters is "whether they are representative in character, whether society can exert control over them, and whether they meet standards of establishment and accountability," and these are political values that can be reinforced by governance values (87).

This argument for value reinforcement through independent agency shares the spirit of the sociologist Philip Selznick's (1957) claim about institutionalized organizations, which come to serve public purposes. In that sense, it also relates to the public policy scholar Mark Moore's (1995, 29) claim that managers' goal in policy work is to create "public value," which does not simply accrue from doing things that people find valuable. He adds the additional criterion of achieving outcomes that are worth the opportunity cost citizens bear to produce them. Yet it stands in contrast, I think, to the "market accountability" that underpins privatization and replaces the accountability of representative government with citizen-as-customer satisfaction and choice (e.g., Borowiak 2011, 135–36). The problem, once again, is that citizens must become something else. My claim is that champions must reach complementarity in a principled way that does not reconstruct what it means to be a citizen (see Bevir 2010). If a privatized industry can meet Rosanvallon's criteria for transparency and public debate and satisfy the complementarity principle, I do not see it as a threat to representative government. But the fact that citizens participate in markets as consumers does not make it benign.

I want to encourage scholars in a variety of literatures to take the complementarity principle more seriously than they have to date. The literature on bureaucratic reputation provides an illustration of where

Conclusion

more work can be done. Scholars argue with evidence that managers cultivate reputations that allow them to increase their ability to contribute the governance arrangements they inhabit (e.g., Carpenter 2010; Carpenter 2001). But when they take a normative turn, champions of this reputation-sourced authority make epistemic arguments that managers working in agencies with "good" reputations (e.g., Carpenter and Krause 2015), or who invite the participation of expert communities and citizens (e.g., Moffitt 2014) produce "correct" policies that managers can employ to overcome the "perverse" preferences of representatives (Miller and Whitford 2016). They seem to justify independent or representative agency through results rather than through the adherence of policy workers to the complementarity principle, and privilege capability over control in the traditional narrative of public administration. Madalina Busuioc and I contend that these claims do not integrate well with representative government (Bertelli and Busuioc 2020). They can weaken ex ante control over policy work through the claims-making (Saward 2006) and strategies of managers while they cultivate reputations with representatives and groups of citizen stakeholders. A reputational mechanism for independence can also undermine ex post oversight over policy work. The very stakeholders that supply the agency with its autonomy can assist it in resisting oversight. This obviates both accountability and process values with only an epistemic claim that citizens are getting "good" policy. That may be an instance of conditional representation, but it could well be *ultra vires* and, worse, may undermine representative government. The impact of policy workers' reputation on representative government can hinge on value reinforcement, and in particular, on managers' use of reinforcement mechanisms that satisfy the complementarity principle. Ansell (2011) and Rosanvallon (2011) provide some tactics for arguing the conditions under which complementarity can be achieved. At present, it is ambiguous how reputation might help this form of independent agency to support democracy administered.

CONCLUSION

In Chapter 5, I introduced the idea of value complementarity between systems of representative government and the governance structures that serve them, provided some evidence that it can be observed in practice, and suggested a strategy for studying it further. In this chapter, I have made an argument about why such value complementarity improves representative government.

202   *The Complementarity Principle*

I encourage scholars of public administration, and champions especially, to treat the complementarity principle seriously.

One important starting point for doing this is to appreciate that, like accountability or representation, the complementarity principle cannot be divorced from its normative basis. For instance, it cannot be properly considered the manifestation of a culture of policy work (Hood 2000). While the *ultra vires* restriction might reflect "grid" and the contexts of the representative governments for which governance structures are designed and where policy work is done might reveal "group," the normative basis for complementarity would be left to one side. More generally, cultural and other positive theories can help to establish behavioral and institutional mechanisms underlying the value-reinforcement hypothesis of Chapter 5, but they do not reach the normative claim in the complementarity principle. Being transparent about the normative basis of the claims we advance and investigate is what the project of public administration demands. Considering value complementarities can make the study of public administration, I think, more comparative and more relevant to communities of practice as well as to politics.

The complementarity principle provides an analytic foundation for what I have argued is a third component of the traditional narrative of public administration, working together with control and capability. While various arguments for upholding values in public administration have been influential in public administration, the complementarity principle provides a basis for the incorporation of a variety of democratic values, not specific categories of them. To take one example, the public administration scholar H. George Frederickson (1980, 31) understands that policy work is a "vehicle for implementing the values or preferences of individuals, groups, social classes, or whole societies," and in that sense a vehicle for representation. Yet like Rawls (1971) from which he draws, Frederickson ultimately sees this representation more as "a device, but never a principle" of appropriate policy work (Brito Viera and Runciman 2008, 59). The consequence is that, rather than the particular values of representative government in a context, Frederickson's "new" public administration would compel policy workers "to be deeply concerned for the social consequences" of policy work, that a policy worker "will very likely be an advocate" who must "develop and defend criteria and measures of equity and to understand the impact of public services on the dignity and well-being of citizens" (46). But what accountability and process values are traded away in favor of equity and dignity? And do policy workers have the authority to "develop and defend" without

Conclusion 203

acting *ultra vires*? The complementarity principle and the criteria for responsible value reinforcement developed in this chapter can help to provide an analytic foundation for addressing these questions in a way that clarifies the obligations of responsible policy work and clarifies what is, in fact, being championed.

The complementarity principle can also provide the foundation for champions' claims about how to represent citizens' interests. In their call for a "New Public Service," Denhardt and Denhardt (2007, 77) contend that policy workers "have a central and important role in helping citizens to articulate the public interest" and must develop strategies to do this because "shared values and collective citizen interests should guide the behavior and decision making." I have argued that, like Rory and Quinn, they can only do such things if they reinforce the values of the representative governments they serve and if they have the legal authority to do so. The New Public Service that policy workers "must work to ensure that citizens are given a voice in every stage of governance" is, write Denhardt and Denhardt, "not to say that the outcomes of the political process are wrong, or that public administrators should substitute their own judgments for policies with which they disagree" (78). Yet if taking actions that give citizens a voice are *ultra vires*, the New Public Service fails to come to terms with the complementarity principle and the fundamental problem of public administration.

7

Further Problems for Democracy Administered

This book has looked to the values of representative government in order to move beyond two problems traditionally considered when legitimating policy work. The first concerns the control of managers by representatives who themselves have an accountability link to citizens. The second concerns the capability that policy workers have for the effective conduct of policy work. This book raises a third problem in which representatives transmit the democratic values and trade-offs of a system of government to policy workers, thereby shaping the democratic belief systems of the latter group. Because the champion's dilemma requires a trade-off among values, governance structures may reinforce the values of representative democracy, but need not necessarily do this. If they do, the combination of control, capability, and value reinforcement can facilitate democracy administered.

The normative argument for value reinforcement is that the values of representative government ought to be fortified by governance structures and the belief systems of policy workers within them. This contributes – with control and capability – to the legitimacy of policy work in a powerful state that is separate from its citizens. It is not simply a matter of representatives drafting delegating legislation particularly well. Managers and other policy workers must act responsibly, using their discretion and capabilities to fulfill the aims of the public, as expressed through the institutions of representative government (Bertelli and Lynn 2003, 2006). Responsibility thus has a behavioral bent because the extent to which policy workers – and managers, in particular – behave in this way is contingent on their democratic belief systems, and these are, in turn, shaped in important ways by champions when they design governance structures. That is why the complementary principle should guide these efforts. Some structures enhance the accountability values of Chapter 2 and others obviate those values. Some enhance the process values of Chapter 3, while still others obviate them. Choices about which values to privilege and which to relax are what creates the champion's dilemma. Chapter 4 defined and illustrated four basic structures that represent different approaches to the champion's dilemma, each with different consequences for representative government.

The value reinforcement hypothesis should be subjected to varieties of empirical examination. Chapter 5 provided two illustrative examinations of the correlation between political and governance values. Correlation, of course, does not imply causation, and the institutional and behavioral reinforcement mechanisms that might underlie these correlations can be carefully considered. The research agenda in Chapter 5 provides an initial sketch of how this kind of inquiry might be taken up.

Chapter 6 built the normative foundation on which I think correlations between governance and political values rest. As long as their action is not *ultra vires*, or contrary to law, policy workers ought to reinforce the democratic values in their systems of representative government. The reason why is that doing so helps to legitimate policy work as a form of representation: policy work is done on behalf of citizens, and recognizing this integrates policy workers and the state, which itself is born from representation. Champions must not advocate structural choices that compromise the legitimating that representation has for policy work, and they can only craft structures capable of producing democracy administered from values that complement those of the representative governments toward which they direct their proposals. One structure thus cannot fit all political jurisdictions because their representative governments make different trade-offs in the accountability and process values of Chapters 2 and 3. But attending to value complementarity helps to facilitate representation, to legitimate the state of which policy workers are a part, to address the fundamental problem of public administration, and to nurture democracy administered.

While the scope of this book is broad, it certainly leaves many important institutions and practices in contemporary policy work undiscussed. I conclude by looking briefly at what I think are four important omissions with an eye toward how they might be considered in light of my argument. My aim in doing this is not to provide detailed analysis, but, rather, to identify ways to continue a conversation about value reinforcement.

My first observation regards the rapidly evolving practice and scholarship on hybrid organizations (see Skelcher and Smith 2015). In practical terms, the champion's dilemma and the complementarity principle read collectively mean that champions must be flexible about governance structures. Put differently, when they call for governance structures that do not reinforce values through institutional or behavioral means, they are in for a fight with representatives and citizens about the legitimacy of those governance structures. Hybrid governance structures can be an important response to these conflicts about trade-offs, but they can also lead to messy institutions that are inconsistent across jurisdictions. This has important implications for the comparative study of governance structures, particularly when value reinforcement is considered, because institutions, and as I have argued, must be context-specific. Hybrid structures make the importance of clarifying value trade-offs through the framework in Chapter 4 and the challenge posed by the champion's dilemma particularly plain.

A second important consequence of the value conflicts that ensue between champions, on the one hand, and between representatives and citizens on the other hand, is that they reveal situations in which champions have *not* addressed the fundamental problem of public administration. This is due to failures of complementarity and it essentially reflects disagreement between political realities and policy work about the nature of responsibility. Not adhering to the complementarity principle can cause pathologies for practice that are important to study. Consider a collaboration between managers and an agenda-setting consulting firm. That is, the decision-making agenda in the managers' policy domain is shaped by the policy work this consultancy does. Collaborating on policy work in this way fits the needs of a political system and is consistent with a statutory mandate. Envision, now, a champion of representative agency, who is frustrated with the "undemocratic" influence of the consultancy and suggests a solution that does not go over very well with representatives or managers. This is not simply a matter of control and capacity, say, of the over-accountability of managers to representatives or of human and financial resource limitations that require capacity to be contracted out to consultants. Without considering complementarity between governance and political values, it would be difficult for the champion to understand *why* things are going wrong.

A concrete example of institutions where the fundamental problem of public administration has not been satisfactorily addressed is the international organization, which has an outsized influence in the question of

Further Problems for Democracy Administered

democracy administered in most of the world's nations (Bertelli et al. 2020). Control of these organizations lies one step away from national representatives in the best cases – developed country donors to international development banks, for example. Most countries cannot rely on international organizations to reinforce *their* values through the governance structures they champion. By contrast, champions transmit their collective values, which may be the values of the privileged donor countries, through the governance structures and policy workers in international organizations. Scholars of these organizations, such as Dan Honig (2018), confront the capability problem more directly and seek to study the effectiveness of governance structures put in place by international organizations. The *aims* of this effectiveness suffer from the control difficulties I just discussed: they are defined, to put it most generously, by the international organization advocating them rather than by the citizens on whose behalf policy work is being done. Honig's capability-based response is to empower the judgment of managers from these organizations "on the ground" in the countries where citizens are being served, not just over the means of policy work, but also over its ends. Intriguingly, managers become the actors who can reinforce the values of citizens directly, with their representatives playing a minor role, or none at all. How might this policy work approach democracy administered? Value reinforcement by these managers might be considered to have the same kind of responsibility as did Rory and Quinn in Chapter 6. Like their responsibility to reinforce pluralism even though Taylor might not be pleased with the outcome, Honig's managers in Liberia and South Africa might be obligated to reinforce the political values of those representative governments and represent the aims of their citizens when they stand in conflict with those of the managers' executive boards in London or Washington.

Even in contexts where control and capability are much clearer, the fundamental problem of public administration eludes scholars aiming to make policy work more democratic.

Consider the efforts of legal scholars in regard to notice-and-comment rulemaking in the United States. Champions of a representative agency structure to make rulemaking more democratic encourage something like the collaborative governance arrangements I have discussed (cf. Arkush 2013; Ansell 2011; Bertelli, Clouser McCann, and Travaglini 2019). Representative agency in this context is meant to diminish the influence of organized interest groups (e.g., Seifter 2016) which "lack the resources to participate in *all* relevant agency actions and, as a result, they and their

208   *Further Problems for Democracy Administered*

financial supporters must choose the matters in which to engage" (Arkush 2013, 1481; Stewart 1975). Frug (1990, 568) offers the caveat that "the role of interest groups has been limited to the giving of advice, and government decisions have remained the responsibility of government employees." Still, advising plays its intended role only when "the group represents the membership it purports to speak for" (Seifter, 2016, 1327), a condition resting on a control-based argument: "A group that does not have or engage with a membership cannot reliably convey those sorts of constituency-based insights" (1306). Cuéllar (2005) empirically observes that comments from the laypersons constitute most of the comments agencies receive and raise relevant concerns, but are also less sophisticated, specialized, and technical than are those from interest groups which become more influential over managers decisions, even when their views are quite different from those of impacted citizens. As a response, Frug (1990, 569) champions a simplistic version of representative agency: boards of directors "consisting of a majority of representatives of the public and a minority of representatives of the agency's employees." Yet he shows little regard for the character of the selection mechanism of these public representatives. Arkush (2016, 1492) cautions that champions "may over-assume the interest of ordinary citizens in the administrative process" as well as their "resource constraints" including "financial resources but also education and free time." Frug (1990, 584) sees such critiques as concealing a distrust of democracy: "Meetings will go on forever; no decisions will ever be made. Anyway, people want to have experts make decisions for them." What is missing in all this is a transparent confrontation of the champion's dilemma and a reflection on American representative government that would allow the complementarity principle to be considered.

A third observation concerns the rise of antidemocratic sentiment across the world. While it is tempting to think of this in connection with the rise of populist parties, that would incompletely present the challenge for the characters in this book. Moreover, there are many unsatisfying ways to conceive populism – like ironic proposals from political economists that populism means a penchant for "short-term protection" (Guiso et al. 2017, 3) when the myopia of politicians is their defining feature in many of political-economic theories. The problem is more one of "unpolitical democracy" in which the pulling and hauling of the processes of democratic politics has just become unappealing to citizens, champions, and even representatives and political theorists (Urbinati 2010). In this environment of proposing alternatives to what seems an unacceptable

Further Problems for Democracy Administered

status quo, process-accountability trade-offs and complementarity cannot be more important.

Being a student of public administration, I am inclined toward the hopeful position in which democracy can accommodate "both conflict and consensus" if "the distinction between the two is clear and each is linked to specific institutions" like the governance structures of Chapter 4 (Rosanvallon 2011, 224). Nonetheless, when "institutional forbearance" is low (Levitsky and Ziblatt 2018), it is even more important to take care when championing structures that require representatives to build norms that defer to policy workers who can reinforce the values of representative government. When champions implicitly reject the complementarity principle in this environment, they open up the opportunity for representative government to be exploited. At a minimum, our current environment requires champions to be crystalline in their transparency about the value trade-offs they are considering. It also crucially requires policy workers to reinforce values responsibly. Given the political climate, this may mean taking advantage of opportunities to reinforce values when they are palatable for other reasons. In the example of the *questore* at the beginning of Chapter 1, my hypothetical manager delayed the demonstration because of the importance of pluralism in her democratic belief system. Yet an orthogonal consideration of preventing violence may be easier for representatives and many citizens to grasp, and the scenario presents the opportunity for both narratives to be presented, or to comingle. This kind of principled representation seems a vital source of democracy administered in our era. It also demonstrates the extent to which the normative analysis in Chapter 6 is an incomplete effort. Specifically, "Administering the Vote" cannot be quickly extended to capture the influence of such conflicting narratives on how policy workers ought to act when reinforcing values. I urge scholars to take up extensions like these to develop a fuller theory of responsible value reinforcement.

Finally, I believe that understanding the ways in which value reinforcement operates can help us to be better citizens. The champion's dilemma and the fundamental problem of public administration can help us to see how a complex array of organizations can help us to self-govern because they reinforce the values of our form of self-government. Normative claims from the New Public Administration (Frederickson 1980) to the Minnowbrook (Marini 1971) and Blacksburg (Wamsley and Wolf 1996) "manifestos" provide arguments for managers to embracing a sense of independence from representatives in their policy work. In this book, my claim has been that legitimacy is lacking when the actions encouraged by these champions cannot comport with the complementarity principle.

If managers do not have belief systems that reinforce values, they can make decisions on the basis of all kinds of things that contradict the representative governments they serve. While they might not always think this is a bad thing, it is always something that citizens have to understand and appreciate for themselves. Citizens need to understand that their public administrations are *meant* to achieve democracy administered, and can do so through a mix of control, capability, and value reinforcement. It is important for all of us to think carefully about this. If we don't, all of these scholarly references to "democratic" policy work are just so many wasted words.

Bibliography

Aberbach, Joel D., and Bert A. Rockman. 1976. "Clashing Beliefs within the Executive Branch: The Nixon Administration Bureaucracy." *American Political Science Review* 70(2): 456–68. doi: 10.2307/1959650.

Achen, C. H., and L. M. Bartels. 2017. *Democracy for Realists: Why Elections Do Not Produce Responsive Government*. Princeton, NJ: Princeton University Press. doi: 10.2307/j.ctvc7770q.

Ackerman, Bruce A. 1998. *We the People: Transformations*, Vol. 2 of *We the People*. Cambridge, MA: Belknap Press of Harvard University Press.

1980. *Social Justice in the Liberal State*. New Haven, CT: Yale University Press.

Adelhardt, Christine, and Stella Peters. 2019. "BAMF-'Skandal' wird immer kleiner." *Das Erste – Panorama – Sendungen – 2019*. https://daserste.ndr.de/panorama/archiv/2019/BAMF-Skandal-wird-immer-kleiner,bamf204.html (April 4, 2020).

AGI Cronaca. 2019. "Cosa Prevede Il Decreto Sicurezza per Il Caso Sea Watch." *AGI Cronaca*. www.agi.it/cronaca/sea_watch_decreto_sicurezza-5728455/news/2019-06-26/ (April 12, 2020).

Anastasopoulos, L. Jason, and Anthony M. Bertelli. 2020. "Understanding Delegation through Machine Learning: A Method and Application to the European Union." *American Political Science Review* 114(1): 291–301. doi: 10.1017/S0003055419000522.

Ansell, Christopher. 2011. *Pragmatist Democracy: Evolutionary Learning as Public Philosophy*. New York: Oxford University Press. doi: 10.1093/acprof:oso/9780199772438.001.0001.

APSA Committee on Political Parties. 1950. *Toward a More Responsible Two-Party System: A Report of the Committee on Political Parties*, Vol. 44(3) Part 2 of the Supplement. New York: Rinehart.

Arkush, David J. 2013. "Direct Republicanism in the Administrative Process." *George Washington Law Review* 81(5): 1458–1528.

Bibliography

Arts Council England. 1996. *The Arts Council of England – 2nd Annual Report and Accounts 1995/96.* London: Arts Council England. www.artscouncil .org.uk/sites/default/files/download-file/The%20Arts%20Council%20of%20 England%20Annual%20Report%201995-96.pdf (April 4, 2020).

2015. *Arts Council England: Grant-in-Aid and Lottery Distribution Annual Report and Accounts 2014/15.* London: Arts Council England. www .artscouncil.org.uk/arts-council-england-grant-aid-and-lottery-distribution-annual-report-and-accounts-201415 (April 4, 2020).

2018. "How We Invest Public Money Where the Money Goes." www .artscouncil.org.uk/about-us/how-we-invest-public-money (March 21, 2020).

2019. "About Us." www.artscouncil.org.uk/about-us-0 (March 21, 2020).

Attianese, Carla. 2019. "Sea Watch, Chiesto l'intervento Della Corte Europea Dei Diritti Umani." *Democratica.* www.democratica.com/focus/sea-watch-migranti-corte-diritti-umani (April 12, 2020).

Austen-Smith, David, and Jeffrey S. Banks. 1996. "Information Aggregation, Rationality, and the Condorcet Jury Theorem." *American Political Science Review* 90(1): 34–45. doi: 10.2307/2082796.

Avellaneda, Claudia, and Ricardo Corrêa Gomes. 2017. "Mayoral Quality and Municipal Performance in Brazilian Local Governments." *Organizações & Sociedade* 24(83): 555–79. doi: 10.1590/1984-9240831.

Bach, Tobias. 2012. "16-Germany" in *Government Agencies Practices and Lessons from 30 Countries,* eds. Koen Verhoest, Sandra van Thiel, Geert Bouckaert and Per Lægreid, 166–78. Basingstoke, Hampshire: Palgrave Macmillian. doi: 10.1057/9780230359512.

Baldassarri, Delia. 2013. *The Simple Art of Voting: The Cognitive Shortcuts of Italian Voters.* New York: Oxford University Press. doi: 10.1093/acprof:oso/ 9780199828241.001.0001.

Barnard, Chester Irving. 1938. *The Functions of the Executive.* Cambridge, MA: Harvard University Press.

Barro, Robert J. 1973. "The Control of Politicians: An Economic Model." *Public Choice* 14(1): 19–42. doi: 10.1007/BF01718440.

BBC. 2010. "Entertainment & Arts: Arts Council's Budget Cut by 30%." *BBC News.* www.bbc.com/news/entertainment-arts-11582070 (March 21, 2020).

Bendor, Jonathan, and Adam Mierowitz. 2004. "Spatial Models of Delegation." *American Political Science Review* 98(2): 293–310. doi: 10.1017/ S0003055404001157.

Bertelli, Anthony M. 2005. "Law and Public Administration" in *Oxford Handbook of Public Management.* eds. Ewan Ferlie, Laurence E. Lynn, Jr., and Christopher Pollitt, 133–55. New York: Oxford University Press. doi:10.1093/oxfordhb/9780199226443.003.0007.

2008. "Credible Governance? Transparency, Political Control, the Personal Vote and British Quangos." *Political Studies* 56(4): 807–29. doi: 10.1111/ j.1467-9248.2007.00713.x.

2012. *The Political Economy of Public Sector Governance.* Cambridge, UK: Cambridge University Press. doi: 10.1017/CBO9781139018982.

2016. "Who Are the Policy Workers, and What Are They Doing? Citizen's Heuristics and Democratic Accountability in Complex Governance." *Public*

Performance & Management Review 40(2): 208–34. doi: 10.1080/15309576.2016.1180306.

Bertelli, Anthony M., and J. Andrew Sinclair. 2015. "Mass Administrative Reorganization, Media Attention, and the Paradox of Information." *Public Administration Review* 75 (6): 855–66. doi: 10.1111/puar.12396.

2018. "Democratic Accountability and the Politics of Mass Administrative Reorganization." *British Journal of Political Science* 48(3): 691–711. doi: 10.1017/S0007123416000077.

Bertelli, Anthony M., J. Andrew Sinclair, and Haram Lee. 2015. "Media Attention and the Demise of Agency Independence: Evidence from a Mass Administrative Reorganization in Britain." *Public Administration* 93(4): 1168–83. doi: 10.1111/padm.12190.

Bertelli, Anthony M., and Christian Robert Grose. 2011. The Lengthened Shadow of Another Institution: Ideal Point Estimates for the Executive Branch and Congress. *American Journal of Political Science* 55(4): 767–81. doi: 10.1111/j.1540-5907.2011.00527.x.

2013. *Public Policy Investment: Priority-Setting and Conditional Representation in British Statecraft.* New York: Oxford University Press. doi: 10.1093/acprof:oso/9780199663972.001.0001.

Bertelli, Anthony M., and Gregg G. Van Ryzin. 2020. "Citizens' Heuristics and Political Accountability in Complex Governance: An Experimental Test." *Research & Politics* 7(3): 1–5.

Bertelli, Anthony M., Jennifer M. Connolly, Dyana P. Mason, and Lilian C. Conover. 2014. "Politics, Management, and the Allocation of Arts Funding: Evidence from Public Support for the Arts in the UK." *International Journal of Cultural Policy* 20(3): 341–59. doi: 10.1080/10286632.2013.786057.

Bertelli, Anthony M., and Laurence E. Lynn. 2003. "Managerial Responsibility." *Public Administration Review* 63 (3): 259–68. doi: 10.1111/1540-6210.00288.

2006. "Public Management in the Shadow of the Constitution." *Administration and Society* 38(1): 31–57. doi: 10.1177/0095399705284201.

2006. *Madison's Managers: Public Administration and the Constitution.* Baltimore, MD: Johns Hopkins University Press.

Bertelli, Anthony M., and E. Madalina Busuioc. 2020. "Reputation-Sourced Authority and the Prospect of Unchecked Bureaucratic Power." *Public Administration Review.* doi: https://doi.org/10.1111/puar.13281

Bertelli, Anthony M., and Norma M. Riccucci. 2020. "What Is Behavioral Public Administration Good For?" *Public Administration Review.* Forthcoming.

Bertelli, Anthony M., Pamela J. Clouser McCann, and Giulia Leila Travaglini. 2019. "Delegation, Collaborative Governance, and Nondistributive Policy: The Curious Case of Joint Partnerships in American Federalism." *Journal of Politics* 81(1): 377–84. doi: 10.1086/700724.

Bertelli, Anthony M., and Peter John. 2013. "Public Policy Investment: Risk and Return in British Politics." *British Journal of Political Science* 43(04): 741–73. doi: 10.1017/S0007123412000567.

Bevir, Mark. 2010. *Democratic Governance.* Princeton, NJ: Princeton University Press.

Bibliography

Bianchi, Francesco, Thilo Kind, and Howard Kung. 2019. "Threats to Central Bank Independence: High-Frequency Evidence with Twitter." *SSRN Electronic Journal*. doi: 10.2139/ssrn.3454246.

Black, Duncan. 1976. "Partial Justification of the Borda Count." *Public Choice* 28(1): 1–15. doi: 10.1007/BF01718454.

Bohman, J. 1998. "Survey Article: The Coming of Age of Deliberative Democracy." *Journal of Political Philosophy* 6(4): 400–25. doi: 10.1111/1467-9760.00061.

Boix, Carles. 2007. "Emergence of Parties and Party Systems" in *The Oxford Handbook of Comparative Politics*, eds. Carles Boix and Susan Stokes, 499–521. New York: Oxford University Press. doi: 10.1093/oxfordhb/9780199566020.003.0021.

Bormann, Nils-Christian, and Matt Golder. 2013. "Democratic Electoral Systems around the World, 1946–2011." *Electoral Studies* 32(2): 360–69. doi: 10.1016/j.electstud.2013.01.005.

Borowiak, Craig. 2011. *Accountability and Democracy. The Pitfalls and Promise of Popular Control*. New York: Oxford University Press. doi: 10.1093/acprof:oso/9780199778256.001.0001.

Bovaird, Tony. 2012. "Participatory Budgeting in the City of Recife, Brazil – The World's Most Participative Public Agency?" www.govint.org/good-practice/case-studies/participatory-budgeting-in-the-city-of-recife-brazil-the-worldas-most-participative-public-agency/ (visited September 3, 2020).

Bovens, Mark. 2007. "Analysing and Assessing Accountability: A Conceptual Framework." *European Law Journal* 13(4): 447–68.

1998. *The Quest for Responsibility: Accountability and Citizenship in Complex Organizations*. Cambridge, UK: Cambridge University Press.

Brazil, Federative Republic of. 2019. "How the Government Works – Learn about the Structure of the Brazilian State." www.brazil.gov.br/government/how-the-government-works (April 4, 2020).

Brennan, Geoffrey, and Alan P. Hamlin. 2000. *Democratic Devices and Desires*. Cambridge, UK: Cambridge University Press. doi: 10.2307/2586218.

Brito Vieira, Mónica, and David Runciman. 2008. *Representation*. Cambridge, UK: Polity Press.

Bryson, John M. 2004. "What to Do When Stakeholders Matter: Stakeholder Identification and Analysis Techniques." *Public Management Review*, 6(1): 21–53.

Bryson, John M., Barbara C. Crosby, and Laura Bloomberg. 2014. "Public Value Governance: Moving beyond Traditional Public Administration and the New Public Management." *Public Administration Review* 74(4): 445–56. doi: 10.1111/puar.12238.

Bryson, John M., Kathryn S. Quick, Carissa Schively Slotterback, and Barbara C. Crosby. 2013. "Designing Public Participation Processes." *Public Administration Review* 73(1): 23–34.

Burgess, Simon, Carol Propper, Marisa Ratto, and Emma Tominey. 2017. "Incentives in the Public Sector: Evidence from a Government Agency." *Economic Journal* 127(605): F117-F141. doi: 10.1111/ecoj.12422.

Burke, Edmund. 1912 [1790]. *Reflections on the French Revolution* Cambridge, UK: Cambridge University Press.

Bibliography

Busby, Ethan C., James N. Druckman, and Alexandria Fredendall. 2016. "The Political Relevance of Irrelevant Events." *The Journal of Politics* 79(1): 346–50. doi: 10.1086/688585.

Carlsson, Fredrik, and Peter Martinsson. 2001. "Do Hypothetical and Actual Marginal Willingness to Pay Differ in Choice Experiments?" *Journal of Environmental Economics and Management* 41(2): 179–92. doi: 10.1006/jeem.2000.1138.

Carman, Joanne G. 2009. "Nonprofits, Funders, and Evaluation: Accountability in Action." *American Review of Public Administration* 39(4): 374–90. doi: 10.1177/0275074008320190.

Carpenter, Daniel P. 2000. "State Building through Reputation Building: Coalitions of Esteem and Program Innovation in the National Postal System, 1883–1913." *Studies in American Political Development* 14(2): 121–55. doi: 10.1017/S0898588X00003382.

2001. *The Forging of Bureaucratic Autonomy: Reputations, Networks, and Policy Innovation in Executive Agencies, 1862-1928*. Princeton, NJ: Princeton University Press.

2010. *Reputation and Power: Organizational Image and Pharmaceutical Regulation at the FDA*. Princeton, NJ: Princeton University Press.

Carpenter, D., and G. A. Krause. 2015. "Transactional Authority and Bureaucratic Politics." *Journal of Public Administration Research and Theory* 25(1): 5–25. doi: 10.1093/jopart/muu012.

Cheibub, José Antonio. 2006. "Presidentialism, Electoral Identifiability, and Budget Balances in Democratic Systems." *American Political Science Review* 100(3): 353–68. doi: 10.1017/S0003055406062223X.

Christiano, Thomas. 1996. *The Rule of the Many*. New York: Routledge. doi: 10.4324/9780429495861.

Cleveland, Frederick A. 1913. *Organized Democracy: An Introduction to the Study of American Politics*. New York: Longmans, Green, and Company.

Congleton, R. 1982. "A Model of Asymmetric Bureaucratic Inertia and Bias." *Public Choice* 39(3): 421–25. doi: 10.1007/BF00118798.

Converse, Philip E. 2006. "The Nature of Belief Systems in Mass Publics (1964)." *Critical Review* 18(1): 1–74. doi: 10.1080/08913810608443650.

Cordelli, Chiara. 2020. *The Privatized State*. Princeton, NJ: Princeton University Press.

Cox, Gary. 1997. *Making Votes Count: Strategic Coordination in the World's Electoral Systems (Political Economy of Institutions and Decisions)*. Cambridge, UK and New York: Cambridge University Press. doi: 10.1017/CBO9781139174954.

Crémer, Jacques. 1993. "Corporate Culture and Shared Knowledge." *Industrial and Corporate Change* 2(3): 351–86. doi: 10.1093/icc/2.3.351.

Cuéllar, Mariano-Florentino. 2005. "Rethinking Regulatory Democracy." *Administrative Law Review* 57(2): 411–99.

Curry, Dion, and Steven Van de Walle. 2018. "A Bibliometrics Approach to Understanding Conceptual Breadth, Depth and Development: The Case of New Public Management." *Political Studies Review* 16(2): 113–24. doi: 10.1177/1478929916644869.

Bibliography

Dahl, Robert A. 1947. "The Science of Public Administration: Three Problems." *Public Administration Review* 7(1): 1–11. doi: 10.2307/972349.

1956. *A Preface to Democratic Theory*. Chicago: University of Chicago Press.

1971. *Polyarchy; Participation and Opposition*. New Haven, CT: Yale University Press.

1989. *Democracy and Its Critics*. New Haven, CT: Yale University Press.

Dahlberg, Jane. 1966. *The New York Bureau of Municipal Research: Pioneer in Government Administration*. New York: New York University Press.

Datla, Kirti, and Richard L. Revesz. 2013. "Deconstructing Independent Agencies (and Executive Agencies)." *Cornell Law Review* 98(4): 769–843. http://scholarship.law.cornell.edu/clr/vol98/iss4/1 (April 12, 2020).

De Sio, Lorenzo, Davide Angelucci, Roberto D'Alimonte, Vincenzo Emanuele, Nicola Maggini, Aldo Paparo. 2019. Issue Competition Comparative Project (ICCP). GESIS Data Archive, Cologne (ZA7499 Data file Version 1.0.0). doi: 10.4232/1.13374.

Denhardt, Janet V., and Robert B. Denhardt. 2007. *The New Public Service: Serving, Not Steering*. New York: Taylor & Francis.

Desilver, Drew. 2019. "Despite Global Concerns about Democracy, More than Half of Countries Are Democratic." *Pew Research Center*. www.pewresearch.org/fact-tank/2019/05/14/more-than-half-of-countries-are-democratic/ (April 12, 2020).

Deutsche Welle. 2019. "Italy Allows 10 Migrants to Leave German Sea-Watch Ship." www.dw.com/en/italy-allows-10-migrants-to-leave-german-sea-watch-ship/a-49223421 (April 12, 2020).

Dewey, John. 1927. *The Public and Its Problems*. New York: Holt.

Di Maggio, Marco, and Manuela Perrone. 2019. "The Political Culture of the Movimento Cinque Stelle, from Foundation to the Reins of Government." *Journal of Modern Italian Studies* 24(3): 468–82. doi: 10.1080/1354571X.2019.1605729.

Dicke, Lisa A., and J. Steven Ott. 1999. "Public Agency Accountability in Human Services Contracting." *Public Productivity & Management Review* 22(4): 502–16. doi: 10.2307/3380933.

Dorf, Michael C., and Charles F. Sabel. 1998. "A Constitution of Democratic Experimentalism." *Columbia Law Review* 98(2): 267–473. doi: 10.2307/1123411.

Druckman, James N., and Thomas J. Leeper. 2012. "Learning More from Political Communication Experiments: Pretreatment and Its Effects." *American Journal of Political Science* 56(4): 875–96. doi: 10.1111/j.1540-5907.2012.00582.x.

Dugher, Michael. 2018. "Arts Council Funding to Opera Is Unfair – Pop Needs Support Too." *The Guardian*. www.theguardian.com/music/2018/apr/12/arts-council-music-funding-unfair-opera-pop (March 30, 2020).

Dummer, Niklas, Martin Klingst, and Caterina Lobenstein. 2018. "Bamf Aktenberge Und Urlaubssperren." *Die Zeit* No. 25/2018. www.zeit.de/2018/25/bamf-behoerde-fluechtlinge-asylverfahren-versagen-fehler (April 4, 2020).

Dummett, Michael. 1998. "The Borda Count and Agenda Manipulation." *Social Choice and Welfare* 15(2): 289–96. doi: 10.1007/s003550050105.

Bibliography

Durose, Catherine, Jonathan Justice, and Chris Skelcher. 2015. "Governing at Arm's Length: Eroding or Enhancing Democracy?" *Policy and Politics* 43(1): 137–53. doi: 10.1332/030557314X14029325020059.

Duverger, Maurice. 1962. *Political Parties*. New York: Wiley.

Eckstein, Harry. 1966. *Division and Cohesion in Democracy: A Study of Norway*. Princeton, NJ: Princeton University Press.

1971. *Political Performance*. Beverly Hills, CA: Sage.

Elliott, Mark. 1999. "The Ultra Vires Doctrine in a Constitutional Setting: Still the Central Principle of Administrative Law." *Cambridge Law Journal* 58(1): 129–58.

Ellison, Robin. 2018. "The Regulators" in *Red Tape: Managing Excess in Law, Regulation and the Courts*. Cambridge, UK: Cambridge University Press.

Emerson, Peter. 2013. "The Original Borda Count and Partial Voting." *Social Choice and Welfare* 40(2): 353–58. doi: 10.1007/s00355-011-0603-9.

Epstein, David, and Sharyn O'Halloran. 1999. *Delegating Powers: A Transaction Cost Politics Approach to Policy Making under Separate Powers*. Cambridge, UK: Cambridge University Press. doi: 10.1017/CBO9780511609312.

Estlund, David M. 2008. *Democratic Authority: A Philosophical Framework*. Princeton, NJ: Princeton University Press. doi: 10.2307/j.ctt7t8jx.

Federal Republic of Germany, Office for Migration and Refugees (BAMF). 2016. *The Federal Office and Its Tasks – Centre of Excellence for Asylum, Migration and Integration*. Bonn: Bundesamt für Migration und Flüchtlinge.

2017. *Geschäftsordnung für das Bundesamt für Migration und Flüchtlinge*. Bonn: Bundesamt für Migration und Flüchtlinge.

Federative Republic of Brazil. 2019. "How the Government Works – Learn about the Structure of the Brazilian State." www.brazil.gov.br/government/howthe-government-works (April 4, 2020).

Feldman, Martha S., and Anne M. Khademian. 2000. "Managing for Inclusion: Balancing Control and Participation." *International Public Management Journal* 3(2): 149–67. doi: 10.1016/S1096-7494(01)00035-6.

Fernandez, Raquel, and Dani Rodrik. 1991. "Resistance to Reform: Status Quo Bias in the Presence of Individual-Specific Uncertainty." *The American Economic Review* 81(5): 1146–55. doi: 10.1257/0002828041464425.

Fernández-Albertos, José. 2015. "The Politics of Central Bank Independence." *Annual Review of Political Science* 18(1): 217–37. doi: 10.1146/annurev-polisci-071112-221121.

Ferrari, Ettore. 2019. "Salvini Vuole Vietare l'ingresso Della Sea Watch 3 in Acque Italiane." *Il Post*. www.ilpost.it/2019/06/15/salvini-divieto-sea-watch-3/ (April 12, 2020).

Finan, Federico, Benjamin A. Olken, Rohini Pande. 2017. "The Personnel Economics of the Developing State" in *Handbook of Field Experiments*, eds. Abhijit Banerjee and Esther Duflo. Amsterdam: Elsevier.

Finer, Herman J. 1941. "Administrative Responsibility in Democratic Government." *Public Administration Review* 1(4): 335–50. www.jstor.org/stable/972907 (April 12, 2020).

Bibliography

Fiorina, Morris P. 1978. "Economic Retrospective Voting in American National Elections: A Micro-Analysis." *American Journal of Political Science* 22(2): 426–43. doi: 10.2307/2110623.

Fishkin, James S. 2011. *When the People Speak: Deliberative Democracy and Public Consultation.* New York: Oxford University Press. doi: 10.1093/acprof:osobl/9780199604432.001.0001.

"Flüchtlingsamt: Weise stellt sich gegen interne Kritik." 2015. *Süddeutsche Zeitung.* www.sueddeutsche.de/politik/fluechtlingsamt-weise-stellt-sich-gegen-interne-kritik-1.2736790 (April 4, 2020).

Follett, Mary Parker. 1918. *The New State: Group Organization the Solution of Popular Government.* London: Longmans, Green and Co.

Fox, Justin, and Stuart V. Jordan. 2011. "Delegation and Accountability." *Journal of Politics* 73(3): 831–44. doi: 10.1017/s0022381611000491.

Fraenkel, Jon, and Bernard Grofman. 2014. "The Borda Count and Its Real-World Alternatives: Comparing Scoring Rules in Nauru and Slovenia." *Australian Journal of Political Science* 49(2): 186–205. doi: 10.1080/10361146.2014.900530.

Franchino, Fabio. 2004. "Delegating Powers in the European Community." *British Journal of Political Science* 34(2): 269–93. doi: 10.1017/S0007123404000055.

Fréchette, Guillaume R., John H. Kagel, and Massimo Morelli. 2005. "Gamson's Law versus Non-Cooperative Bargaining Theory." *Games and Economic Behavior* 51(2): 365–90. doi: 10.1016/j.geb.2004.11.003.

Fredrickson H. George. 1980. *New Public Administration.* Tuscaloosa: University of Alabama Press.

Friedrich, Carl J. 1940. "Public Policy and the Nature of Administrative Responsibility" in *Public Policy*, eds. Carl Joachim Friedrich and E. S. Manson, 3–24. Cambridge, MA: Harvard University Press.

Frug, Gerald. 1990. "Administrative Democracy." *University of Toronto Law Journal* 40(3): 559–86.

Fung, Archon. 2006. "Varieties of Participation in Complex Governance." *Public Administration Review* 66 (s1): 66–75. doi: 10.1111/j.1540-6210.2006.00667.x.

2015. "Putting the Public Back into Governance: The Challenges of Citizen Participation and Its Future." *Public Administration Review* 75(4): 513–22. doi: 10.1111/puar.12361.

Gailmard, Sean. 2009. "Discretion Rather than Rules: Choice of Instruments to Control Bureaucratic Policy Making." *Political Analysis* 17(1): 25–44. doi: 10.1093/pan/mpn011.

Gailmard, Sean, and John W. Patty. 2007. "Slackers and Zealots: Civil Service, Policy Discretion, and Bureaucratic Expertise." *American Journal of Political Science* 51(4): 873–89. doi: 10.1111/j.1540-5907.2007.00286.x.

2013. *Learning while Governing: Expertise and Accountability in the Executive Branch.* Chicago: University of Chicago Press.

Gamson, William A. 1961. "A Theory of Coalition Formation." *American Sociological Review* 26(3): 373–82. doi: 10.2307/2090664.

Bibliography

Gasper, John T., and Andrew Reeves. 2011. "Make It Rain? Retrospection and the Attentive Electorate in the Context of Natural Disasters." *American Journal of Political Science* 55(2): 1–16. doi: 10.1111/j.1540-5907.2010.00503.x.

Gersen, Jacob E., and Matthew C. Stephenson. 2014. "Over-Accountability." *Journal of Legal Analysis* 6(2): 185–243. doi: 10.1093/jla/lau008

Gibbard, Allan. 1973. "Manipulation of Voting Schemes: A General Result." *Econometrica* 41(4): 587–601. doi: 10.2307/1914083.

Gigerenzer, Gerd, Peter M. Todd, and ABC Research Group. 1999. *Simple Heuristics That Make Us Smart.* New York: Oxford University Press.

Gilardi, Fabrizio. 2002. "Policy Credibility and Delegation of Regulatory Competencies to Independent Agencies: A Comparative Empirical Consideration." *Journal of European Public Policy* 9(6): 873–93. doi: 10.1080/13501760220000046409.

2005. "The Formal Independence of Regulators: A Comparison of 17 Countries and 7 Sectors." *Swiss Political Science Review* 11(4): 139–67. doi: 10.1002/j.1662-6370.2005.tb00374.x.

Goldfrank, Benjamin. 2007. "The Politics of Deepening Local Democracy: Decentralization, Party Institutionalization, and Participation." *Comparative Politics* 39(2): 147–68.

Gombrich, Ernst Hans Josef. 2006. "Preface" in *The Story of Art*, 7–18. London: Phaidon.

Gómez, Braulio, Sonia Alonso, and Laura Cabeza. 2018. Regional Manifestos Project Dataset (Version 11/2018). Available from www.regionalmanifestosproject.com (April 12, 2020).

Goodnow, Frank J. 1900. *Politics and Administration: A Study in Government.* New York: Macmillan.

Granberg, Donald, and Soren Holmberg. 1990. "The Intention-Behavior Relationship among U.S. and Swedish Voters." *Social Psychology Quarterly* 53(1): 44–54. doi: 10.2307/2786868.

Grunau, Andrea. 2018. "Fakten Und Fragen Zum Fall Franco A." *Deutsche Welle.* www.dw.com/de/fakten-und-fragen-zum-fall-franco-a/a-43511651 (April 4, 2020).

Guiso, Luigi, Helios Herrera, Massimo Morelli, and Tommaso Sonno. 2017. *Demand and Supply of Populism.* Working Paper n. 610. London: Centre for Economic Policy Research. ftp://ftp.igier.unibocconi.it/wp/2017/610.pdf (visited April 14, 2020).

Hainmueller, Jens, Daniel J. Hopkins, and Teppei Yamamoto. 2014. "Causal Inference in Conjoint Analysis: Understanding Multidimensional Choices via Stated Preference Experiments." *Political Analysis* 22(1): 1–30. doi: 10.1093/pan/mpt024.

Hammerschmid, Gerhard, Steven Van de Walle, Rhys Andrews, and Ahmed Mohammed Sayed Mostafa. 2019. "New Public Management Reforms in Europe and Their Effects: Findings from a 20-Country Top Executive Survey." *International Review of Administrative Sciences* 85(3): 399–418. doi: 10.1177/0020852317751632.

Hammerschmid, Gerhard, Steven Van de Walle, Rhys Andrews, and Philippe Bezes. 2016. *Public Administration Reforms in Europe: The View from the*

Top. Cheltenham, UK: Edward Elgar Publishing, Inc. doi: 10.4337/9781783475407.

Hammond, Thomas H., and Paul A. Thomas. 1989. "The Impossibility of a Neutral Hierarchy." *Journal of Law, Economics, and Organization* 5(1): 155–84. doi: 10.1093/oxfordjournals.jleo.a036962.

Hanretty, Chris, and Christel Koop. 2012. "Measuring the Formal Independence of Regulatory Agencies." *Journal of European Public Policy* 19(2): 198–216. doi: 10.1080/13501763.2011.607357.

Healy, Andrew J., Neil Malhotra, and Cecilia Hyunjung Mo. 2010. "Irrelevant Events Affect Voters' Evaluations of Government Performance." *Proceedings of the National Academy of Sciences* 107(29): 12804–9. doi: 10.1073/pnas.1007420107.

Her Majesty's Prison & Probation Service. 2019. *HM Prison and Probation Service Annual Report and Accounts 2018–19*. London: Her Majesty's Prison & Probation Service & The House of Commons. https://assets .publishing.service.gov.uk/government/uploads/system/uploads/attachment_ data/file/818788/HMPPS_Annual_Report_and_Accounts_2018-19__web_ .pdf (April 12, 2020).

2019. *HMPPS Organisation Chart 2019*. Her Majesty's Prison & Probation Service. https://assets.publishing.service.gov.uk/government/uploads/system/ uploads/attachment_data/file/796982/HMPPS-OrganisationChart-2019-smaller.pdf (April 4, 2020).

Herrera, Helios, Ernesto Reuben, and Michael M. Ting. 2017. "Turf Wars." *Journal of Public Economics* 152: 143–53. doi: 10.1016/j.jpubeco.2017.06.002.

Herrmann, Gunnar. 2018. "Chronologie Der Bamf-Probleme: Vier Jahre Ärger Und Kein Ende." *Süddeutsche Zeitung*. www.sueddeutsche.de/politik/bamf-skandal-chronologie-1.4002426-0#seite-2 (April 4, 2020).

Herrmann, Michael Simon Munzert, and Peter Selb. 2016. "Determining the Effect of Strategic Voting on Election Results" *Journal of the Royal Statistical Society Series A* 179(2): 583–605.

Herrmann, R. K., P. E. Tetlock, and M. N. Diascro. 2001. "How Americans Think about Trade: Reconciling Conflicts among Money, Power, and Principles." *International Studies Quarterly* 45(2): 191–218. doi: 10.1111/0020-8833.00188.

Hibbing, John R., and Elizabeth. Theiss-Morse. 2002. *Stealth Democracy: Americans' Beliefs about How Government Should Work*. Cambridge, UK: Cambridge University Press. doi: 10.1017/CBO9780511613722.

Higgins, Charlotte. 2011. "Arts Council Told to Sell Off Masterpieces in Damning Report by MPs." *The Guardian*. www.theguardian.com/culture/2011/mar/28/arts-council-report-select-committee (April 4, 2020)

Highton, Benjamin. 2017. "Voter Identification Laws and Turnout in the United States." *Annual Review of Political Science* 20(1): 149–67.

Hobbes, Thomas. 2014 [1651]. *Leviathan*. Ware, UK: Wordsworth Editions Limited.

1983 [1642]. *De Cive: The English Version*. H. Warrender, ed. Oxford, UK: Clarendon Press.

Bibliography

Hofmann, Herwig C. H. 2017 "General Principles of EU Law and EU Administrative Law" in *European Union Law*, eds. Catherine Barnard and Steve Peers, 198–226. Oxford, UK: Oxford University Press.

Homburg, Vincent, Christopher Pollitt and Sandra van Thiel. 2007. "Introduction" in *New Public Management in Europe Adaptation and Alternatives*, eds. Sandra van Thiel, Vincent Homburg, and Christopher Pollitt, 1–9. New York: Palgrave Macmillian.

Honig, Dan. 2018. *Navigation by Judgment: Why and When Top-Down Management of Foreign Aid Doesn't Work*. New York: Oxford University Press.

2019. "Case Study Design and Analysis as a Complementary Empirical Strategy to Econometric Analysis in the Study of Public Agencies: Deploying Mutually Supportive Mixed Methods." *Journal of Public Administration Research and Theory*, 29(2): 299–317. doi: 10.1093/jopart/muy049.

Hood, Christopher. 1991. "A Public Management for All Seasons?" *Public Administration* 69(1): 3–19. doi: 10.1111/j.1467-9299.1991.tb00779.x.

1995. "Control over Bureaucracy: Cultural Theory and Institutional Variety." *Journal of Public Policy* 15(3): 207–30. doi: 10.1017/S0143814X00010023.

2000. *The Art of the State: Culture, Rhetoric, and Public Management*. Oxford, UK: Oxford University Press.

2010. *The Blame Game: Spin, Bureaucracy, and Self-Preservation in Government*. Princeton, NJ: Princeton University Press.

Hood, Christopher, and Martin Lodge. 2006. *The Politics of Public Service Bargains*. Oxford, UK: Oxford University Press.

Hood, Christopher, and Ruth Dixon. 2015a. "Performance Data Breaks: Breaking the Mould and Burying the Evidence" in *A Government That Worked Better and Cost Less? Evaluating Three Decades of Reform and Change in UK Central Government*, 44–64. Oxford, UK: Oxford University Press. doi: 10.1093/acprof:oso/9780199687022.001.0001.

2015b. "Did Government Cost Less? Running Costs and Paybill" in *A Government That Worked Better and Cost Less? Evaluating Three Decades of Reform and Change in UK Central Government*, 65–85. Oxford, UK: Oxford University Press. doi: 10.1093/acprof:oso/9780199687022.001.0001.

2015c. "Yesterday's Tomorrows Revisited—the Route to Better and Cheaper Public Services" in *A Government That Worked Better and Cost Less? Evaluating Three Decades of Reform and Change in UK Central Government*, 1–19. Oxford, UK: Oxford University Press. doi: 10.1093/acprof:oso/9780199687022.001.0001.

Horn, Murray J. 1995. *The Political Economy of Public Administration: Institutional Choice in the Public Sector*. Cambridge, UK: Cambridge University Press. www.loc.gov/catdir/samples/cam031/94044897.html.

House of Commons: Culture, Media, and Sport Committee. 2011. *Funding of the Arts and Heritage – Third Report of Session 2010–11 (Volume I–III)*. London: House of Commons. https://publications.parliament.uk/pa/cm201011/cmselect/cmcumeds/464/464i.pdf (March 20, 2020)

House of Commons Justice Committee. 2012. *The Budget and Structure of the Ministry of Justice Second Report of Session 2012–13 Volume I.* London: House of Commons Justice Committee. https://publications.parliament.uk/pa/cm201213/cmselect/cmjust/97/97.pdf (April 4, 2020).

Huber, John D., and Charles R. Shipan. 2002. *Deliberate Discretion: The Institutional Foundations of Bureaucratic Autonomy.* Cambridge, UK: Cambridge University Press. doi: 10.1017/CBO9780511804915.

Huber, John D., and Nolan McCarty. 2004. "Bureaucratic Capacity, Delegation, and Political Reform." *American Political Science Review* 98(3): 481–94. doi: 10.1017/S0003055404001297.

Il Sole 24 Ore. 2019. "Migranti, Juncker a Conte: Pronti a Gestire Cellule Di Crisi Ma Gli Sbarchi Non Sono Competenza Ue." *Il Sole 24 Ore.* www.ilsole24ore.com/art/migranti-juncker-conte-pronti-gestire-cellule-crisi-ma-sbarchi-non-sono-competenza-ue-AEthOqPF (April 12, 2020)

James, Aaron. 2013. "Why Practices?" *Raison Politiques* 51(1): 43–62.

2017. "Investor Rights as Nonsense—on Stilts" in *Just Financial Markets? Finance in a Just Society,* ed. Lisa Herzog, 205–28. New York: Oxford University Press. doi: 10.1093/oso/9780198755661.001.0001.

James, Michael Rabinder. 2015. "Two Concepts of Constituency." *Journal of Politics* 77(2): 381–93. doi: 10.1086/679494.

James, Oliver. 2003a. "Executive Agencies and Joined-up Government in the UK" in *Unbundled Government: A Critical Analysis of the Global Trend to Agencies, Quangos and Contractualisation,* eds. Christopher Pollitt and Colin Talbot, 75–93.. London: Routledge. doi: 10.4324/9780203507148.

2003b. *The Executive Agency Revolution in Whitehall Public Interest versus Bureau-Shaping Perspectives.* Hampshire, UK: Palgrave Macmillan. doi: 10.1057/9781403943989.

James, Oliver, Alice Moseley, Nicolai Petrovsky, and George Boyne. 2012. "6 – United Kingdom" in *Government Agencies Practices and Lessons from 30 Countries,* eds. Koen Verhoest, Sandra van Thiel, Geert Bouckaert and Per Lægreid, 57–68. Basingstoke, Hampshire, UK: Palgrave Macmillian,

James, Oliver, Sebastian Jilke, Carolyn Petersen, and Steven Van de Walle. 2016. "Citizens' Blame of Politicians for Public Service Failure: Experimental Evidence about Blame Reduction through Delegation and Contracting." *Public Administration Review* 76(1): 83–93. doi: doi.org/10.1111/puar.12471.

Jefferson, Thomas. 1975. "Notes on the State of Virginia" in *The Portable Thomas Jefferson,* ed. Merrill D. Peterson, 23–232. New York: Penguin.

Jenkins, Kate, Karen Caines and Andrew Jackson. 1988. *Improving Management in Government: The Next Steps: Report to the Prime Minister.* London: HMSO, Efficiency Unit. www.civilservant.org.uk/library/1988_improving_management_in_government_the%20_next_steps.pdf (April 12, 2020).

Jordana, Jacint, Xavier Fernández-i-Marín, and Andrea C. Bianculli. 2018. "Agency Proliferation and the Globalization of the Regulatory State: Introducing a Data Set on the Institutional Features of Regulatory

Bibliography

Agencies." *Regulation and Governance* 12(4): 524–40. doi: 10.1111/rego.12189.

Kam, Christopher, Anthony Michael Bertelli, and Alexander Held. 2020. "The Electoral System, the Party System, and Accountability in Parliamentary Government." *American Political Science Review,* forthcoming.

Kang, Michael S. 2002. "Democratizing Direct Democracy: Restoring Voter Competence through Heuristic Cues and Disclosure Plus." *UCLA Law Review* 50 (5): 1141–88.

Katzenberger, Paul. 2018. "'Anne Will' zur Bamf-Affäre: Warum nur schwieg Herr Mayer von der CSU?" *Süddeutsche Zeitung.* www.sueddeutsche.de/medien/anne-will-zur-bamf-affaere-warum-nur-schwieg-herr-mayer-von-der-csu-1.3993176 (April 4, 2020).

Kaufman, Herbert. 1956. "Emerging Conflicts in the Doctrines of Public Administration." *American Political Science Review* 50(4): 1057–73. doi: 10.2307/1951335.

Kawai, Kei, and Yasutora Watanabe. 2013. "Inferring Strategic Voting." *American Economic Review* 103(2): 624–62.

Keefer, Philip, and David Stasavaga. 2003. "The Limits of Delegation: Veto Players, Central Bank Independence, and the Credibility of Monetary Policy." *American Political Science Review* 97(3): 407–23. doi: 10.1017/S0003055403000777.

Kickert, Walter, and K. In't Veld. 1995. "National Government, Governance and Administration" in *Public Policy and Administration Sciences in the Netherlands,* eds. Walter J. M. Kickert and Frans A. van Vught, 45–62. New York: Prentice Hall.

Kinder, Donald R., and D. Roderick Kiewiet. 1981. "Sociotropic Politics: The American Case." *British Journal of Political Science* 11(2): 129–61. doi: 10.1017/S0007123400002544

Kingdon, John W. 1984 [1995]. *Agendas, Alternatives, and Public Policies,* 2nd ed. Boston, MA: Little, Brown and Company.

Knight, Ben. 2019. "Migrant Rescue Vessel Sea-Watch 3: What You Need to Know." *Deutsche Welle.* www.dw.com/en/migrant-rescue-vessel-sea-watch-3-what-you-need-to-know/a-49433631 (April 12, 2020).

Kollman, Ken 1998. *Outside Lobbying: Public Opinion and Interest Group Strategies.* Princeton, NJ: Princeton University Press.

Krehbiel, Keith. 1991. *Information and Legislative Organization.* Ann Arbor: University of Michigan Press.

Kreps, David M. 1990. "Corporate Culture and Economic Theory" in *Perspectives on Positive Political Theory,* eds. James E Alt and Kenneth A Shepsle, 90–144. Cambridge, UK: Cambridge University Press.

La Repubblica. 2019a. "Caso Sea Watch, Chiesto Intervento Della Corte Di Strasburgo. Commissione Ue: 'Stati Trovino Soluzione.'" *La Repubblica.* www.repubblica.it/cronaca/2019/06/24/news/sea_watch_corte_strasburgo-229509821/ (April 12, 2020).

2019b. "Sea Watch, Salvini Se La Prende Con l'Olanda: 'Siete Responsabili Di Quello Che Potrà Accadere.'" *La Repubblica.* www.repubblica.it/cronaca/2019/06/23/news/alarm_phone_migranti-229441062/ (April 12, 2020).

Bibliography

Laakso, Markku, and Rein Taagepera. 1979. "'Effective' Number of Parties: A Measure with Application to West Europe." *Comparative Political Studies* 12 (1): 3–27. doi: 10.1177/001041407901200101.

Lacey, Stephen. 2004. "The British Theatre and Commerce, 1979–2000" in *The Cambridge History of British Theatre*, Volume 3, ed. Baz Kershaw, 442–43. Cambridge, UK: Cambridge University Press.

Lægreid, Per. 2014. "Accountability and New Public Management" in *The Oxford Handbook of Public Accountability*, eds. Mark Boven, Robert E. Goodin, and Thomas Schillemans, 324–38. New York: Oxford University Press.

Lafont, Cristina. 2019. *Democracy without Shortcuts: A Participatory Conception of Deliberative Democracy*. Oxford, UK: Oxford University Press. doi: 10.1093/oso/9780198848189.001.0001.

2015. "Deliberation, Participation, and Democratic Legitimacy: Should Deliberative Mini-Publics Shape Public Policy?" *Journal of Political Philosophy* 23(1): 40–63. doi: 10.1111/jopp.12031.

Landemore, Hélène. 2013. *Democratic Reason: Politics, Collective Intelligence, and the Rule of the Many*. Princeton, NJ: Princeton University Press.

Landemore, Hélène, and Scott E. Page. 2015. "Deliberation and Disagreement: Problem Solving, Prediction, and Positive Dissensus." *Politics, Philosophy & Economics* 14(3): 229–54. doi:10.1177/1470594X14544284.

Leeuw, F. 1998. "The Dutch Perspective: Trends in Performance Measurement." Presented at the International Evaluation Conference, Vancouver, lst–5th November.

León, Sandra. 2011. "Who Is Responsible for What? Clarity of Responsibilities in Multilevel States: The Case of Spain." *European Journal of Political Research* 50(1): 80–109. doi: 10.1111/j.1475-6765.2010.01921.x.

Lever, Annabelle, and Andrei Poama. 2018. "Introduction" in *Routledge Handbook of Ethics and Public Policy*, eds. Annabelle Lever and Andrei Poama, 1–10. London: Routledge.

Levitsky, Steven, and Daniel Ziblatt. 2018. *How Democracies Die*. New York: Broadway Books.

Lewin, Kurt. 1951. "Problems of Research in Social Psychology" in *Field Theory in Social Science: Selected Theoretical Papers*, ed. D Cartwright, 155–69. New York: Harper & Row.

Lewis, David E. 2008. *The Politics of Presidential Appointments: Political Control and Bureaucratic Performance*. Princeton, NJ: Princeton University Press. doi:10.2307/j.ctt7rnqz.

Lijphart, Arend. 1984. *Democracies: Patterns of Majoritarian and Consensus Government in Twenty-One Countries*. New Haven, CT: Yale University Press.

List, Christian. 2011. "The Logical Space of Democracy" *Philosophy & Public Affairs* 39(1): 262–97. doi: 10.1111/j.1088-4963.2011.01206.x.

List, Christian, and Philip Pettit. 2011. *Group Agency: The Possibility, Design, and Status of Corporate Agents*. Oxford, UK: Oxford University Press.

Long, J. Scott. 1997. *Regression Models for Categorical and Limited Dependent Variables*. Advanced Quantitative Techniques in the Social Sciences, Volume 7. Thousand Oaks, CA: SAGE.

Bibliography

Lowi, Theodore J. 1979. *The End of Liberalism: The Second Republic of the United States*, 2nd ed. New York: W. W. Norton & Company. doi: 10.2307/1955703.

Lublin, David. 2015. *Minority Rules: Electoral Systems, Decentralization, and Ethnoregional Party Success*. New York: Oxford University Press. doi: 10.1093/acprof:oso/9780199948826.001.0001.

Lupia, Arthur. 1994. "Shortcuts versus Encyclopedias: Information and Voting Behavior in California Insurance Reform Elections." *American Political Science Review* 88(1): 63–76. doi: 10.2307/2944882

Lynn., Laurence E., Jr. 2001. "The Myth of the Bureaucratic Paradigm: What Traditional Public Administration Really Stood For." *Public Administration Review* 61(2): 144–60. doi: 10.1111/0033-3352.00016.

Lynn, Laurence E., Carolyn J. Heinrich, and Carolyn J Hill. 2001. *Improving Governance: A New Logic for Empirical Research*. Washington, DC: Georgetown University Press.

Lückoff, Janina. 2018. "BAMF-Ausschuss sieht gravierende Qualitätsdefizite." *Bayrischer Rundfunk*. www.br.de/nachrichten/das-wichtigste/bamf-ausschuss-sieht-gravierende-qualitaetsdefizite,QuP4DCs (April 4, 2020).

Mackie, Gerry. 2003. *Democracy Defended*. Cambridg, UK: Cambridge University Press. doi: 10.1017/CBO9780511490293.

MacKuen, Michael B., Robert S. Erikson, and James A. Stimson. 1989. "Macropartisanship." *American Political Science Review* 83(4): 1125–42. doi: 10.2307/1961661.

Manin, Bernard. 1997. *The Principles of Representative Government*. Cambridge, UK: Cambridge University Press. doi: 10.1017/CBO9780511659935.

Mansbridge, Jane. 2003. "Rethinking Representation." *American Political Science Review* 97(4): 515–28. doi: 10.1017/S0003055403000856.

2009. "A Selection Model of Political Representation." *Journal of Political Philosophy* 17(4): 369–89. doi: 10.1111/j.1467-9760.2009.00337.x

Marini, Frank, ed. 1971. *Toward a New Public Administration: The Minnowbrook Perspective*. Scranton, PA: Chandler Publishing Company.

Mathews, John Mabry. 1917. *Principles of American State Administration*. New York: D. Appleton.

Mayr, Markus. 2017. "Flüchtlinge: Großes Fehlersuchen." *Süddeutsche Zeitung*. www.sueddeutsche.de/politik/fluechtlinge-grosses-fehlersuchen-1.3529624 (April 4, 2020).

McCubbins, Matthew D., Roger G. Noll, and Barry R. Weingast. 1989. "Structure and Process, Politics and Policy: Administrative Arrangements and the Political Control of Agencies." *Virginia Law Review* 75(2): 431–82. doi: 10.2307/1073179.

McCubbins, Matthew D., and T. Schwartz. 1984. "Congressional Oversight Overlooked: Police Patrols versus Fire Alarms." *American Journal of Political Science* 28(1): 165–79. doi: 10.2307/2110792.

McGraw, Kathleen M. 1990. "Avoiding Blame: An Experimental Investigation of Political Excuses and Justifications." *British Journal of Political Science* 20(1): 119–31.

1991. "Managing Blame: An Experimental Test of the Effects of Political Accounts." *American Political Science Review* 85(4): 1133–57.

Bibliography

Meer, Frits M. van der, and Gerrit Dijkstra. 2000. "The Development and Current Features of the Dutch Civil Service System" in *Civil Service Systems in Western Europe*, ed. Hans A.G.M. Bekke and Frits van der Meer, 148–79. Cheltenham, UK: Edward Elgar Publishing Limited.

Mele, Valentina and Paolo Belardinelli. 2019. "Mixed Methods in Public Administration Research: Selecting, Sequencing, and Connecting." *Journal of Public Administration Research and Theory* 29(2): 334–47. doi: 10.1093/jopart/muyo46.

Merrill, Thomas W. 2010. "Delegation and Judicial Review" *Harvard Journal of Law & Public Policy* 33(1): 73–85.

Milanovic, Branko. 2019. *Capitalism, Alone: The Future of the System That Rules the World*. Cambridge, MA: Harvard University Press.

Miller, Gary J. and Andrew B. Whitford. 2016. *Above Politics: Bureaucratic Discretion and Credible Commitment*. New York: Cambridge University Press. doi: 10.1017/CBO9781139017688.

Millett, John D. 1954. *Management in the Public Service*. New York: McGraw Hill.

Mills, Heather. 1995. "Prison Drama Ends in Political Farce." *The Independent*. www.independent.co.uk/news/prison-drama-ends-in-political-farce-1578591.html (April 4, 2020).

Mitchell, Gregory, and Philip E. Tetlock. 2009. "Disentangling Reasons and Rationalizations: Exploring Perceived Fairness in Hypothetical Societies" in *Social and Psychological Bases of Ideology and System Justification*, eds. John T. Host, Aaaron C. Kay and Hulda Thorisdottir, 126–57. New York: Oxford University Press. doi: 10.1093/acprof:oso/9780195320916.001.0001.

Moffitt, Susan L. 2014. *Making Policy Public: Participatory Bureaucracy in American Democracy*. New York: Cambridge University Press. doi: 10.1017/CBO9781107588141.

Moore, Mark H. 1995. *Creating Public Value: Strategic Management in Government*. Cambridge, MA: Harvard University Press.

Morelli, Massimo. 1999. "Demand Competition and Policy Compromise in Legislative Bargaining." *American Political Science Review* 93(04): 809–20. doi: 10.2307/2586114.

Mortensen, Peter B. 2013. "Public Sector Reform and Blame Avoidance Effects." *Journal of Public Policy* 33(2): 229–53. doi: 10.1017/S0143814X13000032.

Mosher, Frederick C. 1968. *Democracy and the Public Service*. New York: Oxford University Press.

Moynihan, Donald. 2007. "Citizen Participation in Budgeting: Prospects for Developing Countries" in *Public Sector Governance and Accountability Series: Participatory Budgeting*, eds. Anwar Shah. Washington, DC: World Bank, 55–90. https://elibrary.worldbank.org/doi/abs/10.1596/978-0-8213-6923-4 (April 4, 2020).

Nabatchi, Tina. 2010. "Addressing the Citizenship and Democratic Deficits: The Potential of Deliberative Democracy for Public Administration." *The American Review of Public Administration* 40(4): 376–99. doi: 10.1177/0275074009356467.

Bibliography

Niedzwiecki, Sara. 2016. "Social Policies, Attribution of Responsibility, and Political Alignments: A Subnational Analysis of Argentina and Brazil." *Comparative Political Studies* 49(4): 457–98. doi: 10.1177/0010414015612392.

Nino, Carlos Santiago. 1996. *The Constitution of Deliberative Democracy*. New Haven: Yale University Press.

North, Douglass C. 1993. "Institutions and Credible Commitment." *Journal of Institutional and Theoretical Economics (JITE) / Zeitschrift für die gesamte Staatswissenschaft* 149(1): 11–23.

North, Douglass C., and Barry R. Weingast. 1989. "Constitutions and Commitment: The Evolution of Institutions Governing Public Choice in Seventeenth-Century England." *Journal of Economic History* 49(4): 803–32.

Ochoa Espejo, Paulina. 2011. *The Time of Popular Sovereignty: Process and the Democratic State*. University Park Pennsylvania State University Press.

OECD, UCLG. 2016. *Latin America: Brazil – Federal Country*. OECD and United Cities and Local Government. www.oecd.org/regional/regional-policy/profile-Brazil.pdf (April 4, 2020).

Oliver, Dawn. 1987. "Is the 'Ultra Vires' Rule the Basis of Judicial Review?" *Public Law* 4(1987): 543–69.

Oltermann, Philip. 2017. "German Coalition Talks Collapse after Deadlock on Migration and Energy." *The Guardian*. www.theguardian.com/world/2017/nov/19/german-coalition-talks-close-to-collapse-angela-merkel (April 12, 2020).

2018. "Merkel Secures Fourth Term in Power after SPD Backs Coalition Deal." *The Guardian*. www.theguardian.com/world/2018/mar/04/germany-social-democrats-spd-vote-in-favour-of-coalition-angela-merkel (April 12, 2020)

Osborne, David, and Ted Gaebler. 1992. *Reinventing Government: How the Entrepreneurial Spirit Is Transforming the Public Sector*. Reading, MA: Addison-Wesley Pub. Co. www.loc.gov/catdir/enhancements/fy0830/91031307-b.html.

Ott, J. Steven and Lisa Dicke. 2001. "Challenges Facing Public Sector Management in an Era of Downsizing, Devolution, Dispersion and Empowerment—and Accountability?" *Public Organization Review* 1: 321–39. doi: 10.1023/A:1012232829168.

Page, Stephen B., Melissa M. Stone, John M. Bryson, and Barbara C. Crosby. 2018. "Coping with Value Conflicts in Interorganizational Collaborations." *Perspectives on Public Management and Governance* 1(4): 239–55.

Papadopoulos, Yannis. 2010. "Accountability and Multi-level Governance: More Accountability, Less Democracy?" *West European Politics* 33(5): 1030–49. doi: 10.1080/01402382.2010.486126.

Patty, John W. and Elizabeth Maggie Penn. 2014. *Social Choice and Legitimacy: The Possibilities of Impossibility*. New York: Cambridge University Press.

Pennock, J. Roland. 1952. "Responsiveness, Responsibility, and Majority Rule." *American Political Science Review* 46: 790–807. doi: 10.2307/1952285

Persson, T., G. Roland, and G. Tabellini. 1997. "Separation of Powers and Political Accountability." *The Quarterly Journal of Economics* 112(4): 1163–202. doi: 10.1162/003355300555457.

Bibliography

Pettit, Philip. 2009. "Varieties of Public Representation" in *Political Representation*, eds. Ian Shapiro, Susan C. Stokes, *Elisabeth Jean Wood, and Alexander S Kirshner*, 61–89. New York: Cambridge University Press.

Pickford, James. 2017. "Arts Council Cuts Funding for Four Biggest Recipients – Grants to Royal Opera House, Southbank Centre, National Theatre and RSC Will Fall." *The Financial Times*. www.ft.com/content/56f832d8-5b3e-11e7-b553-e2df1b0c3220 (March 20, 2020).

Pires, Thiago Magalhães. "Sources of Sub-National Constitutional Law – Brazil." *International Encyclopaedia for Constitutional Law*, eds. André Alen and David Haljan, 37–64. Alphen aan den Rijn: Kluwer Law International.

Pitkin, Hanna F. 1967. *The Concept of Representation*. Berkeley: University of California Press.

Poguntke, Thomas, and Lucy Kinski. 2018. "Germany: Political Development and Data for 2017." *European Journal of Political Research Political Data Yearbook* 57(1): 108–20. doi: 10.1111/2047-8852.12195.

Pollitt, Christopher. 1993. *Managerialism and the Public Services: Cuts or Cultural Change in the 1990s?* Oxford, UK: Blackwell Business.

2007a. "Convergence or Divergence: What Has Been Happening in Europe?" in *New Public Management in Europe Adaptation and Alternatives*, eds. Sandra van Thiel, Vincent Homburg, and Christopher Pollitt, 10–25. New York: Palgrave Macmillian.

2007b. "Hospital Performance Indicators: How and Why Neighbors Facing Similar Problems Go Different Ways- Building Explanations of Hospital Performance Indicator Systems in England and the Netherlands" in *New Public Management in Europe Adaptation and Alternatives*, eds. Sandra van Thiel, Vincent Homburg, and Christopher Pollitt, 149–64. New York: Palgrave Macmillian.

Pollitt, Christopher, and Geert Bouckaert. 2004. *Public Management Reform: A Comparative Analysis*. 2nd ed. Oxford, UK: Oxford University Press. www.loc.gov/catdir/toc/fy051/2004556488.html.

2011. *Public Management Reform: A Comparative Analysis – Into the Age of Austerity*. Oxford, UK: Oxford University Press.

2012. *Public Management Reform – A Comparative Analysis – New Public Management, Governance, and the Neo-Weberian State*. Oxford, UK: Oxford University Press.

Pötzsch, Horst. 2009. "Verwaltung des Bundes" in *Dossier Deutsche Demokratie*, eds. Martin Hetterich and Stephan Trinius, 108–10. Bonn: Bundeszentrale für politische Bildung (bpb).

Powell, G. Bingham. 2000. *Elections as Instruments of Democracy: Majoritarian and Proportional Visions*. New Haven, CT: Yale University Press.

Propper, C. 2003. "The Use and Usefulness of Performance Measures in the Public Sector." *Oxford Review of Economic Policy* 19(2): 250–67. doi: 0.1093/oxrep/19.2.250.

Przeworski, Adam, Susan C. Stokes, and Bernard Manin. 1999. "Elections and Representation" in *Democracy, Accountability, and Representation*, 29–54. New York: Cambridge University Press. doi: 10.1017/CBO9781139175104.

Bibliography

Rasul, Imran, and Daniel Rogger. 2018. "Management of Bureaucrats and Public Service Delivery: Evidence from the Nigerian Civil Service." *Economic Journal* 128(608): 413–46.

Rawls, John. 1971. *A Theory of Justice*. Cambridge, MA: The Belknap Press of Harvard University Press.

Redford, Emmette S. 1969. *Democracy in the Administrative State*. New York: Oxford University Press.

Rehfeld, Andrew. 2005. *The Concept of Constituency: Political Representation, Democratic Legitimacy, and Institutional Design*. New York: Cambridge University Press.

Riccucci, Norma M., Gregg G. Van Ryzin, and Cecilia F. Lavena. 2014. "Representative Bureaucracy in Policing: Does It Increase Perceived Legitimacy?" *Journal of Public Administration Research and Theory* 24 (3): 537–51. doi: 10.1093/jopart/muu006.

Riccucci, Norma M., and Marcia K. Meyers. 2004. "Linking Passive and Active Representation: The Case of Frontline Workers in Welfare Agencies." *Journal of Public Administration Research and Theory* 14(4): 585–97. doi: 10.1093/jopart/muho38.

Riding, Alan. 1995. "Lottery's Art Grants Stir Furor in Britain." *New York Times*. www.nytimes.com/1995/08/07/arts/lottery-s-art-grants-stir-furor-in-britain.html (April 4, 2020)

Riker, William H. 1982. *Liberalism against Populism: A Confrontation between the Theory of Democracy and the Theory of Social Choice*. New York: W.H. Freeman.

Robinson, Scott E., and Kenneth J. Meier. 2006. "Path Dependence and Organizational Behavior: Bureaucracy and Social Promotion." *American Review of Public Administration* 36(3): 241–60. doi: 10.1177/0275074006288299.

Romzek, Barbara S., and Jocelyn M. Johnston. 2005. "State Social Services Contracting: Exploring the Determinants of Effective Contract Accountability." *Public Administration Review* 65(4): 436–49. doi: 10.1111/j.1540-6210.2005.00470.x.

Romzek, Barbara S., and Melvin J. Dubnick. 1987. "Accountability in the Public Sector: Lessons from the Challenger Tragedy." *Public Administration Review* 47(3): 227–38. doi: 10.2307/975901.

Rosanvallon, Pierre. 2011. *Democratic Legitimacy: Impartiality, Reflexivity, Proximity*. Princeton, NJ: Princeton University Press.

Rourke, Francis E. 1992. "Responsiveness and Neutral Competence in American Bureaucracy." *Public Administration Review* 52(6): 539. www.jstor.org/stable/977164?origin=crossref (July 30, 2019).

Runciman, David. 2009. "Hobbes's Theory of Representation: Anti-Democratic or Proto-Democratic" in *Political Representation*. eds. Ian Shapiro, Susan C. Stokes, Elisabeth Jean Wood, and Alexander S. Kirshner, 15–34. New York: Cambridge University Press.

Saffon, Maria Paula, and Nadia Urbinati. 2013. "Procedural Democracy, the Bulwark of Equal Liberty." *Political Theory* 41(3): 441–81. doi: 10.2307/977164.

Samuels, David, and Richard Snyder. 2001. "The Value of a Vote: Malapportionment in Comparative Perspective." *British Journal of Political Science* 31(4): 651–71. doi: 0.1017/S0007123401000254.

Sandel, Michael J. 1982. *Liberalism and the Limits of Justice*. New York: Cambridge University Press.

2012. *What Money Can't Buy: The Moral Limits of Markets*. New York: Farrar, Straus and Giroux.

Sangiovanni, Andrea. 2016. "How Practices Matter." *Journal of Political Philosophy* 24(1): 3–23. doi: 10.1111/jopp.12056.

Sartori, Giovanni. 1976. *Parties and Party Systems: A Framework for Analysis*. New York: Cambridge University Press.

Satterthwaite, Mark Allen. 1975. "Strategy-Proofness and Arrow's Conditions: Existence and Correspondence Theorems for Voting Procedures and Social Welfare Functions." *Journal of Economic Theory* 10(2): 187–217. doi: 10.1016/0022-0531(75)90050-2.

Satz, Debra. 2010. *Why Some Things Should Not Be for Sale: The Moral Limits of Markets*. New York: Oxford University Press.

Savas, E. S. 1977. "Policy Analysis for Local Government: Public vs. Private Refuse Collection." *Policy Analysis* 3(1): 49–74.

Saward, Michael. 2006. "The Representative Claim" in *Contemporary Political Theory*. 5(3): 297–318.

Scenaripolitici. 2019. "Mese: giugno 2019" https://scenaripolitici.com/2019/06/ (visited August, 1 2019).

Schelling, Thomas C. 1978. *Micromotives and Macrobehavior*. New York: WW Norton & Company.

Schiesl, Martin. 1977. *The Politics of Efficiency: Municipal Administration and Reform in America, 1800–1920*. Berkeley: University of California Press.

Schuppert, Gunnar Folke. 2010. "Siebter Aufzug: Metamorphosen Des Staates" in *Staat Als Prozess, Eine Staatstheoretische Skizze in Sieben Aufzügen*, 137–63. Frankfurt am Main: Campus Verlag.

Schwartzberg, Melissa. 2014. *Counting the Many: The Origins and Limits of Supermajority Rule*. New York: Cambridge University Press.

2015. "Epistemic Democracy and Its Challenges." *Annual Review of Political Science* 18(2015): 187–203.

Seifter, Miriam. 2016. "Second-Order Participation in Administrative Law". *UCLA Law Review* 63(5): 1300–64.

Selin, Jennifer L. 2015. "What Makes an Agency Independent?" *American Journal of Political Science* 59(4): 971–87. doi: 10.1111/ajps.12161.

Selznick, Philip. 1957. *Leadership in Administration: A Sociological Interpretation*. Berkeley: University of California Press.

Sen, Amartya. 1970. "The Impossibility of a Paretian Liberal." *Journal of Political Economy* 78(1): 152–7.

Senate of the Republic. 1947. *Constitution of the Italian Republic*. Rome: Senate Service for Official Reports and Communication.

Shah, Anwar. 2007. "Overview" in *Public Sector Governance and Accountability Series: Participatory Budgeting*, eds. Anwar Shah. Washington, DC: World

Bank, 1–18. https://elibrary.worldbank.org/doi/abs/10.1596/978-0-8213-6923-4 (April 4, 2020).

Shepsle, Kenneth A. 1985. "Prospects for Formal Models of Legislatures." *Legislative Studies Quarterly* 10 (1): 5. doi: 10.2307/440112.

1991. "Discretion, Institutions, and the Problem of Government Commitment" in *Social Theory for a Changing Society*, eds. Pierre Bordieu and James Coleman, 245–65. Boulder, CO: Westview Press.

Simon, Herbert A., Donald W. Smithburg, and Victor A. Thompson. 1950. *Public Administration*. New York: Knopf.

Skelcher, Chris, and Steven Rathgeb Smith. 2015. "Theorizing Hybridity: Institutional Logics, Complex Organizations, and Actor Identities: The Case of Nonprofits." *Public Administration* 93(2): 433–48. doi: 10.1111/padm.12105.

Skinner, Quentin. 1989. "The State" in *Political Innovation and Conceptual Change*. eds. Terence Ball, James Farr, and Russell L. Hanson, 90–131. New York: Cambridge University Press.

Soroka, Stuart N., and Christopher Wlezien. 2009. *Degrees of Democracy: Politics, Public Opinion, and Policy*. Cambridge: Cambridge University Press. doi: 10.1017/CBO9780511804908.

Space Weather Coordination Act of 2019, Committee on Science, Space and Technology, H. Rep. 115–1129, 115th Cong. (2019). www.congress.gov/congressional-report/115th-congress/house-report/1129/1?s=3&r=2 (October 14, 2019).

Steinberger, Peter J., 2005. *The Idea of the State*. New York: Cambridge University Press.

Steiner, Claudia. 2016. "Weise gibt Doppelspitze komplett ab." *Bayrischer Rundfunk*. www.br.de/nachrichten/bayern/weise-will-schreibtische-bei-ba-bald-raeumen,64w3adtt6cr3ec9q6rw3cdhp64rk4 (April 4, 2020).

Stewart, Richard B. 1975. "The Reformation of American Administrative Law. *Harvard Law Review* 88(8): 1667–813.

Strauch, Christoph. 2018. "Innenminister nicht informiert: Seehofer lief beim Bamf-Skandal ins Messer." *Frankfurter Allgemeine Zeitung*. www.faz.net/aktuell/politik/inland/informationen-zum-bamf-skandal-nicht-an-seehofer-weitergegeben-15598496.html (April 4, 2020).

StudiLegali. 2015. "Come e Quando Si Può Fare Ricorso Al TAR – StudiLegali. Com." *Studilegali*. www.studilegali.com/articoli/come-e-quando-si-puo-fare-ricorso-al-tar (July 19, 2019).

Sunstein, Cass R. 1995. "Incompletely Theorized Agreements." *Harvard Law Review* 108(7): 1733–72. doi: 10.2307/1341816.

Taagepera, Rein, and Matthew Soberg Shugart. 1989. *Seats and Votes: The Effects and Determinants of Electoral Systems*. New Haven: Yale University Press.

Tadros, Victor. 2020. "Distributing Responsibility." *Philosophy & Public Affairs*. doi: https://doi.org/10.1111/papa.12163.

Tarzia, Antonello. 2008. "Public Administration" in *Introduction to Italian Public Law*, ed. Giuseppe F. Ferrari, 97–126.. Milan: Giuffrè Editore.

Bibliography

Thiel, Sandra van, and Christopher Pollitt. 2007. "The Management and Control of Executive Agencies: An Anglo-Dutch Comparison" in *New Public Management in Europe Adaptation and Alternatives*, eds. Sandra van Thiel, Vincent Homburg, and Christopher Pollitt, 52–70. New York: Palgrave Macmillian.

Ting, M. M. 2002. "A Theory of Jurisdictional Assignments in Bureaucracies." *American Journal of Political Science* 46(2): 364–78. doi: 10.2307/3088382.

2003. "A Strategic Theory of Bureaucratic Redundancy." *American Journal of Political Science* 47(2): 274–92. doi: 10.2307/3186138.

Tonkiss, Katherine, and Amy Noonan. 2013. "Debate: Arm's-Length Bodies and Alternative Models of Service Delivery." *Public Money and Management* 33 (6): 362–78. doi: 10.1080/09540962.2013.835993.

Toplak, Jurij. 2006. "The Parliamentary Election in Slovenia, October 2004." *Electoral Studies* 25(4): 825–31. doi: 10.1016/j.electstud.2005.12.006.

Truman, David Bicknell. 1951. *The Governmental Process: Political Interest and Public Opinion*. ed. Alfred A. Knopf. New York: Alfred A. Knopf, Inc.

Tsebelis, George. 1995. "Decision Making in Political Systems: Veto Players in Presidentialism, Parliamentarism, Multicameralism and Multipartyism." *British Journal of Political Science* 25(3): 289–325. doi: 10.1017/S0007123400007225.

Turpin, Colin, and Adam Tomkins. 2007. "Parliament and the Responsibility of Government" in *British Government and the Constitution*, 565–648. Cambridge, UK: Cambridge University Press.

UK Cabinet Office. 2006. Public Bodies: A Guide for Departments, Chapter 2: *Policy and Characteristics of a Public Body*. London: Cabinet Office UK. https://assets.publishing.service.gov.uk/government/uploads/system/uploads/attachment_data/file/690946/Public_Bodies_-_a_guide_for_departments_-_chapter_2.pdf (April 4, 2020).

2011. *Public Handbook – Part 1 Classification of Public Bodies: Guidance for Departments*. London: Cabinet Office UK. https://assets.publishing.service .gov.uk/government/uploads/system/uploads/attachment_data/file/519571/ Classification-of-Public_Bodies-Guidance-for-Departments.pdf. (April 4, 2020).

2018. *Public Bodies Handbook – Part 3 Executive Agencies: A Guide for Departments*. London: Cabinet Office UK. https://assets.publishing.service .gov.uk/government/uploads/system/uploads/attachment_data/file/690636/ Executive_Agencies_Guidance.PDF (April 4, 2020).

UK Government. 2019. "How Government Works." *How Government Works – GOV.UK*. www.gov.uk/government/how-government-works (April 4, 2020).

UK Ministry of Justice. 2019. *Ministry of Justice Annual Report and Accounts 2018–19*. London: Ministry of Justice & The House of Commons. https:// assets.publishing.service.gov.uk/government/uploads/system/uploads/attach ment_data/file/818854/moj-annual-report-2018-2019.pdf (April 4, 2020).

UK Parliament. 2014. "Who's Accountable? Relationships between Government and Arm's-Length Bodies – Public Administration Committee Annex: Extract from Cabinet Office Written Evidence." https://publications.parliament.uk/ pa/cm201415/cmselect/cmpubadm/110/11013.htm (March 21, 2020).

Bibliography

United Nations. 1948. "Universal Declaration of Human Rights." www.un.org/en/universal-declaration-human-rights/ (October 13, 2019).

Urbinati, Nadia. 2010. "Unpolitical Democracy." *Political Theory* 38(1): 65–92. doi: 10.1177/0090591709348188.

Vercellotti, Timothy, and David Andersen. 2009. "Voter-Identification Requirements and the Learning Curve." *PS: Political Science & Politics* 42(1): 117–120.

Volden, C. 2002. "A Formal Model of the Politics of Delegation in a Separation of Powers System." *American Journal of Political Science* 46(1): 111–33. doi: 10.2307/3088417.

Volkens, Andrea, Tobias Burst, Werner Krause, Pola Lehmann, Theres Matthieß, Nicolasa Merz, Sven Regel, Bernard Weßels, and Lisa Zehnter. 2020. The Manifesto Data Collection. Manifesto Project (MRG/CMP/MARPOR)." doi .org/10.25522/manifesto.mpds.2020b.

Waldo, Dwight. 1952. "Development of Theory of Democratic Administration." *American Political Science Review* 46(1): 81–103. doi: 10.2307/1950764.

Waldron, Jeremy. 2014. "Accountability: Fundamental to Democracy." Public Law & Legal Theory Research Paper Series Working Paper No. 14-13. New York University.

  1988. "Locke: Toleration and the Rationality of Persecution" in *Justifying Toleration*, ed. Susan Mendus, 61–86. New York: Cambridge University Press.

Walzer, Michael. 2008. *Spheres of Justice: A Defense of Pluralism and Equality.* New York: Basic Books.

Wampler, Brian. 2008. "When Does Participatory Democracy Deepen the Quality of Democracy? Lessons from Brazil." *Comparative Politics* 41(1): 61–81. doi: 10.5129/001041508x12911362383679.

  2007a. "A Guide to Participatory Budgeting" in *Public Sector Governance and Accountability Series: Participatory Budgeting*, eds. Anwar Shah. Washington, DC: World Bank, 21–53. https://elibrary.worldbank.org/doi/abs/10.1596/978-0-8213-6923-4 (April 4, 2020).

  2007b. *Participatory Budgeting in Brazil: Contestation, Cooperation, and Accountability.* University Park: Pennsylvania State University Press.

  2004. "Expanding Accountability through Participatory Institutions: Mayors, Citizens, and Budgeting in Three Brazilian Municipalities." *Latin American Politics and Society* 46(2): 73–99. doi: 10.1111/j.1548-2456.2004.tb00276.x.

Wamsley, Gary L., and James F. Wolf, eds. 1996. *Refounding Democratic Public Administration.* Thousand Oaks, CA: Sage.

Warren, Mark E. 2009. "Governance-Driven Democratization." *Critical Policy Studies* 3 (1): 3–13. doi: 10.1080/19460170903158040.

Weaver, R. Kent. 1986. "The Politics of Blame Avoidance." *Journal of Public Policy* 6 (4): 371–98. doi: 10.1017/S0143814X00004219.

Weber, Max. 1970 [1918] "Politics as a Vocation" in *From Max Weber: Essays in Sociology*, eds. H. Gerth and C. Wright Mills, London: Routledge.

  1964. *The Theory of Social and Economic Organization.* eds. A. M. Henderson and Talcott Parsons. New York: Free Press.

Bibliography

Weiss, Carol H. 1977. "Research for Policy's Sake: The Enlightenment Function of Social Research." *Policy Analysis* 3(4): 531–45.

West, William F. 2005. "Neutral Competence and Political Responsiveness: An Uneasy Relationship." *Policy Studies Journal* 33(2): 147–60.

White, Leonard D. 1933. *Trends in Public Administration.* New York: McGraw Hill.

Zacka, Bernardo. 2017. *When the State Meets the Street: Public Service and Moral Agency.* Cambridge, MA: Belknap Press of Harvard University Press.

Ziniti, Alessandra. 2019. "Migranti e Ong, Il Tar Respinge Il Ricorso Della Nave Sea Watch: 'Legittimo Il Divieto Di Sbarco'. Inchiesta Dei Pm Di Agrigento." www.repubblica.it/cronaca/2019/06/18/news/migranti_il_consiglio_d_europa_stop_alla_collaborazione_con_la_libia_-229053403/ (April 12, 2020).

Zirulia, Stefano. 2019a. "L'ordinanza Del Gip Di Agrigento Sul Caso Sea Watch (Carola Rackete)." *Diritto Penale Contemporaneo.* https://archiviodpc .dirittopenaleuomo.org/d/6767-l-ordinanza-del-gip-di-agrigento-sul-caso-sea-watch-carola-rackete (April 12, 2020).

2019b. "Soccorsi in Mare e Porti Sicuri: Pubblicate Le Raccomandazioni Del Commissario per i Diritti Umani Del Consiglio d'Europa." *Diritto Penale Contemporaneo.* www.penalecontemporaneo.it/d/6745-soccorsi-in-mare-e-porti-sicuri-pubblicate-le-raccomandazioni-del-commissario-per-i-diritti-umani-d (April 12, 2020).

Zirulia, Stefano, and Francesca Cancellaro. 2019. "Caso Sea Watch: Cosa Ha Detto e Cosa Non Ha Detto La Corte Di Strasburgo Nella Decisione Sulle Misure Provvisorie." *Diritto Penale Contemporaneo.* www.penalecontemporaneo.it/d/6760-caso-sea-watch-cosa-ha-detto-e-cosa-non-ha-detto-la-corte-di-strasburgo-nella-decisione-sulle-misur (April 12, 2020).

Index

accountability errors, 38–39, 87
  evaluability, 42–44
  identifiability, 37–42, 108–10
accountability identity, 31–32, 137
Accountability Index (ACI), 137, 166–69, 173
  in behavioral reinforcement study, 153–58
  by country, 84–138
  of Germany, 84–138, 166
  identifiability, structural reliance, and, 170–72
  of Netherlands, 148–49, 166
  of UK, 84–138, 146–49, 166
accountability values, 17–18, 23–24, 28, 30, 136. *See also* evaluability; identifiability; sanction, probability of
  as actor-relative, 9–11, 17, 52–53
  BAMF and, 100
  in controlled agency, 95
  Finer privileging, 86–87
  governance structures and, 9–11, 93–94, 135–36
  in managed agency, 103–5, 108–10, 158–59, 183–84
  in NPM, 144–47, 152
  in parliamentary government, 31–32
  positive theories on, 87–90
  with process values, tradeoffs of, 53, 76, 83, 93–94, 157–59, 164–65
  process values and, 9–11, 58, 60, 75, 87, 95, 135–36, 144–47
  representative agency and, 110–11, 113, 116–18, 122–24, 155, 158–59

sanction, probability of, 12, 38–39, 52–53, 75, 104–5, 153
Sea-Watch 3 case and, 18–22, 28–29, 31, 37–42, 44
state, legitimating, and, 183–84
in U. S., 179–81
in UK, 84–138, 146–47
accountability-enhancing structures, 10, 93–94, 204–5
accountability-obviating structures, 10, 93–94, 204–5
  independent agency as, 105–30
  NPM as, 144–45
  participatory budgeting as, 122–23
  representative agency as, 110–11, 113, 116–18, 122–24, 155
Achen, Christopher, 22–23, 47–48
ACI. *See* Accountability Index
actor-relative values, 9–11, 17, 52–53
The Administrative State (Waldo), 183
Alternative for Germany party, 29
American Political Science Association, 62
Anastasopoulos, L. Jason, 162
Ansell, Christopher, 116–18, 198–201
Arkush, David J., 207–8
Arrow, Kenneth, 59
Arts Council England, 133–35

BAMF. *See* Federal Agency of Migration and Refugees
Barnard, Chester, 4–5
Bartels, Larry, 22–23, 47–48

Index

behavioral reinforcement, 13, 161–65, 204–5
 of European managers, 143, 152–59
 informal and formal, 141–42
 value reinforcement hypothesis, testing, and, 152–54
Bertelli, Anthony Michael
 on accountability heuristics, xvi
 on ACI, Kam, Held, and, 137, 146–47, 173
 on NDPBs, Sinclair and, 145
 Public Policy Investment, xvi–xvii
 Sartori and, 33
 on UK, conditional representation and, 38
bipolarity, 32–33, 39, 62
Bipolarity Index, 148–49
Blair, Tony, 148
blame avoidance strategies, 49–50, 157–58
 effective independence, 50, 52
 obfuscating information, 50–52, 144–45
 source relocation, 50–51
blind retrospection, 22–23, 47
Bloomberg, Laura, 118
Blumenau, Brazil, 121–23
Bohman, J., 64–65
Borda count, 58–59, 67–68, 72
Bouckaert, Geert, 85–86
Bovens, Mark, 17–18
Brazil, 118–24
Bryson, John M., 118
Buckland, Robert James, 107
Bulgaria, 197
bureaucracies, 186–87
 as controlled agency structures, 95–99
 neutrality of, 97–99
 political control of, 87–90
 reputation in, 200–1
Burke, Edmund, 36–37
Busuioc, Madalina, 200–1

capability, control and, 8, 10, 141, 188–89, 202–3
champions, 7, 9, 16–17, 174–75
 complementarity principle and, 11, 13, 175, 203–5, 207–8
 governance structures designed by, 11, 75–76, 83–85, 93–94
 value tradeoffs made by, 12–13, 76, 83–85, 174, 183, 204, 206
champion's dilemma, 9–10, 12, 85–86, 209–10

complementarity principle and, 175, 204–5, 207–8
 epistemic claims and, 84
 Finerian response to, 86–88, 94
 Friedrichian response to, 86, 94
 independent agency and, 129
 structural responses to, 93–94
 value tradeoffs in, 12–13, 83–85, 174, 204, 206
characters, 5
 champions, 7
 managers, 6–7
 policy workers, 6
 representatives, 5–6
Charlottesville, Virginia, rally in, 1–2, 6–7
Christiano, Thomas, 35–36, 42, 61, 63–64, 73, 87
citizens, xv
 complementarity principle and, 203
 conditional representation of, 36–38
 on democratic values, 71–76
 European, on democracy, 12, 73–82
 expectations of, gaps in, 73–75, 77–82
 heuristics of, 45–49, 53, 88–89
 Italian, on immigration, refugees, 44, 54–56
 policy workers and representation of, 11
 on process values, 71–76
 in representative agency, bringing back, 111–18
 from state, separation of, 13, 175–77
 third-parties and representation of, 35–36
 in U. S., on democracy, 72–73
 value reinforcement and, 209–10
 value tradeoffs and representation of, 12
city management movement, U. S., 180
COCOPS survey. *See* Coordinating for Cohesion in the Public Sector of the Future survey
collaborative governance, 115–18, 198–99, 207–8
collective decision mechanisms, 58–60, 66, 73, 75
 Borda count, 58–59, 67–68, 72
 for collective rationality, 68–71
 majoritarianism relaxed by, 67–68, 72
collective rationality, 12, 69, 71–72
 completeness and, 68–72
 consistency and, 68–69, 71–72
 in managed agency, 104–5

Index

in representative agency, 114–15, 123–24
U. S. citizens on, 73
complementarity principle, 196–99, 201–2
anti-democratic sentiment and, 208–9
champions and, 11, 13, 175, 203–5, 207–8
critiques of, 198
ultra vires action and, 202–3, 205
in value reinforcement, 175, 197–98, 200–7, 209–10
conditional representation, 36–38, 42, 53, 61, 187–89
Condorcet Jury Theorem, 59
consociationalism, 149–52
control
capability and, 8, 10, 141, 188–89, 202–3
literature on, 87–90
controlled agency, 10–13, 95, 116–18, 183–84
BAMF as, 99–103
bureaucracies as structures of, 95–99
costs of, 128
in NPM, 143–44
responsible value reinforcement and, 191–94
retrospective answerability in, 101, 103
in U. S., 179–83
Coordinating for Cohesion in the Public Sector of the Future survey (COCOPS survey)
ACI and, 154, 166–73
behavioral reinforcement tested by, 152–55
coordination, 154–55
Cordelli, Chiara, 184–87
Cordt, Jutta, 101–2
coronavirus, government responses to, xviii, 125–26
costs, of governance structures, 127–30
credibility, 126–27
imperative, 125–26
motivational, 125–26, 130
Crosby, Barbara C., 118

Dahl, Robert, 24, 63–64, 66, 174–75
Datla, Kirti, 130
delegation
in collective rationality, 69–71
studies on, 162
values conveyed by, 85–86
deliberative democracy, 64–66, 72, 75

democracy, 1, 4–5, 23–24, 71–72
anti-democratic sentiment, 208–9
European citizens on, 12, 73–82
U. S. citizens on, 72–73
Denhardt, Janet, 185–86, 203
Denhardt, Robert, 185–86, 203
Denmark, 197
Dimock, Marshall, 181–82
disaggregated aims, 104–5, 107–10
discretion, 6
of managers, 6–8, 10, 85–86, 104, 189–96, 204–5
responsible value reinforcement and, 189–90
ultra vires use of, 189–96, 198–99, 202–3, 205
Dixon, Ruth, 145–46
Dublin Regulation (2013) (EU), 19, 28–29, 41, 43–44
Dubnick, Melvin, 17
Duverger, Maurice, 33

ECHR. *See* European Court of Human Rights
Eckstein, Harry, 142–43
effective independence, 50, 52
electoral accountability, 12–13, 23–24
electoral rules in, 30–32
retrospective, 22–30, 34, 37, 45–49
sanctioning view of, 22–31, 33, 37–38, 44, 53
Sea-Watch 3 case and, 28–29, 31, 44
selection view of, 24–25, 34–35, 38–39, 44
electoral rules, 30–32
epistemic democracy, 63–65, 72, 84
epistemic metaconsensus, 91–92
ESS. *See* European Social Survey
Estlund, David, 63–64, 84
EU. *See* European Union
Europe
on democracy, citizens of, 12, 73–82
managers in, behavioral reinforcement of, 143, 152–59
under NPM, managers of, 145–46
European Commission. *See* European Union
European Convention on Human Rights (1950), 20–21
European Court of Human Rights (ECHR), 20–22, 28–29

Index

European Social Survey (ESS)
  2012, 77–82
  2016, 73–75
European Union (EU)
  COCOPS survey of, 152–55, 166–73
  Sea-Watch 3 case and, 19–22, 28–29,
    37–44
  ultra vires action prohibited by, 189–90
evaluability, 52–53, 75, 86–87, 91
  behavioral reinforcement and, 153–54
  blame avoidance strategies and, 49–50, 52
  errors in, 42–44
  heuristic of, 45–49, 53
  of managers, 38–39, 104–5
  in NPM, problems of, 145–46
  in representative agency, 122–23
  sanctioning view and, 28–29
  strong, 50
  in U. S., 180–81
  weak, 50
executive agencies, in UK, 106–10

Federal Agency of Migration and Refugees
  (BAMF) (Germany), 99–103
Federal Reserve System (U. S.), 126–28
Federalists (U. S.), 179
Fernandez, Raquel, 36
Finer, Herman, 178
  champion's dilemma and, 86–88, 94
  controlled agency and, 95
  on value tradeoffs, 87–88, 90–94
Fishkin, James, 65
Follett, Mary Parker, 198–99
forward-looking representation, 179–80,
  183–84, 187–88
Fox, Justin, 90
Fraenkel, Jon, 67–68
Frederickson, H. George, 202–3
Friedrich, Carl, 86, 90–94, 178, 184–87
Frug, Gerald, 207–8
fundamental problem, of public
  administration, 85–93, 103–4, 135–36,
  203, 205
  complementarity principle and, 206–7
  international organizations and, 206–7
  representative agency and, 116, 118
  value reinforcement and, 175
Fung, Archon, 112–15

Gaebler, Ted, 7
Gailmard, Sean, 91–92

Gamson's Law, 32
Gaus, John, 181–82
Germany, 84–138, 166
  BAMF, 99–103
  general election in, September 2017, 29
Gibbard-Satterthwaite theorem, 59
Gigerenzer, Gerd, 45
Gombrich, E. H., 133
Goodnow, Frank, 181–82
governance structures, 8–12, 15–17, 209.
  See also controlled agency; independent
  agency; managed agency;
  representative agency
  accountability, process values and, 9–11,
    93–94, 135–36
  champions designing, 11, 75–76, 83–85,
    93–94
  complementarity principle for, 11, 13
  control, capability, and, 8
  costs of, 127–30
  democratically evaluating, 93–94
  managers and, 8, 10–11
  representation and, 183–86
  types of, agency in, 10–11
  value reinforcement and, 8–9, 11, 13–14,
    24, 136, 155, 197–98
  value tradeoffs and, 8–13, 93–94, 135–36
governance values, political values and, 85,
  139–40, 152, 197–98, 205
Grofman, Bernard, 67–68

Hammerschmid, Gerhard, 145–46, 152–53
Hammond, Thomas, 97–100
Hatch Act (1939) (U. S.), 29–30
Held, Alexander, 30–31, 33, 137, 146–47,
  173
Her Majesty's Prison and Probation Service
  (HMPPS) (UK), 107–10, 135, 142,
  144–45
Herring, E. Pendleton, 181–82
heuristics, citizen, 47–48
  blame avoidance strategies and, 49
  evaluability, 45–49, 53
  identifiability, 45–49, 53
  for retrospection, 45–49
  sanctioning and, 45–47, 88–89
  Sea-Watch 3 case and, 46–47
Hibbing, John, 72–73
HMPPS. *See* Her Majesty's Prison and
  Probation Service
Hobbes, Thomas, 175–82, 187

Index

Honig, Dan, 206–7
Hood, Christopher, 49–50, 104–5, 145–46
Horn, Murray, 127–28
House of Representatives Committee on
   Science, Space and Technology (U.S.),
   69–70
Howard, Michael, 110
hybrid organizations, 206

ICCP. *See* Issue Competition Comparative
   Project
identifiability, 75
   as accountability value, 17–18, 28–30,
      38–39, 52–53, 90
   ACI, structural reliance, and, 170–72
   behavioral reinforcement and, 154–58
   blame avoidance strategies and, 49–50,
      52
   in Brazil, reduced, 118–19
   in bureaucracies, 96–97
   coordination and, 154–55
   errors in, 37–42, 108–10
   Finer on, 86–87
   heuristic of, 45–49, 53
   in managed agency, 104–5, 108–10
   in NPM, 144–45, 152
   Pennock on, 87
   in representative agency, 113, 122–23
   sanctioning view and, 28–29
   in *Sea-Watch 3* case, 28–29, 37–42
   strong, 50
   structural reliance and, 170–72
   in U. S., 180–81
   weak, 50
immigration
   asylum and migration, EU on, 19, 28–29,
      41, 43–44
   Italian citizens on, 44, 54–56
impossibility theorems, 58–60
incompletely theorized agreement, 71–72
independent agency, 10–13, 124–25, 155
   as accountability-obviating structure,
      105–30
   champion's dilemma and, 129
   complementarity principle and, 200–1
   costs of, 128–30
   credibility and independence in, 125–27,
      130
   in NPM, managed agency and, 143–48,
      164–65
   representation and, 184–88

in U. S., 130
in UK, 131–35, 144–45
value reinforcement and, 193–96, 200
institutional reinforcement mechanism,
   139–40
   in empirical study, 162, 164–65
   formal and informal, 140–42, 152
   in NPM, 141–43, 147–52
   in value reinforcement hypothesis,
      139–43
international organizations, 206–7
Issue Competition Comparative Project
   (ICCP), 54–57
Italy
   bipolarity in, 39
   elections, 2018, in, 44, 54–57
   ICCP on, 54–57
   on immigration, refugees, citizens in, 44,
      54–56
   questore in, 2–3, 6–9, 95, 209
   Sea-Watch 3 case in, 18–22, 28–29, 31,
      39, 41–44, 46–47, 66–67

Javits, Jacob, xv
Jefferson, Thomas, 4–5
John, Peter, xvi–xvii, 36, 38
Jordan, Stuart V., 90

Kam, Christopher, 30–31, 33, 137, 146–47,
   173
Kessler, Jason, 1–2, 6–7
Kingdon, John, 7
Krause, George, xvi–xvii
Krehbiel, Keith, 69, 71

Lægreid, Per, 143–44
Lafont, Cristina, 65, 114–15
Lampedusa, Italy, port of. *See Sea-Watch 3*
   case
Lega party (Italy), 37–42
legitimation, 176–77, 179–82
   accountability values in, 183–84
   process values in, 184
   by representation, 175, 178–79, 183, 187
   by toleration, 177–78
León, Sandra, 40–41
A Letter on Toleration (Locke), 177–78
Lewin, Kurt, 174
Lewis, Derek, 110, 142
Liberalism Against Populism (Riker), 59–60
linear probability models (LPM), 56–57

List, Christian, 63, 71
on majoritarianism, 66, 68
on metaconsensus, 61–62
on process values, trilemma of, 60, 83, 111
Locke, John, 177–79, 181
LPM. *See* linear probability models
Lynn, Laurence, 23–24, 85–86, 179–80, 188–89

Mackie, Gerry, 59–60
Madisonian view, of state, 117, 179–80
majoritarianism, 12, 30–32, 66–67, 75, 89–90
collective decision mechanisms relaxing, 67–68, 72
impossibility theorems and, 59
mandate in electoral, 34
NPM and, 146–47, 151–52
pluralism and, 8–9, 12, 75, 90–91
reflective equilibrium relaxing, 68, 72
in representative agency, 113–15, 117–18, 123, 128
U. S. citizens on, 73
of UK, 106, 108
managed agency, 10–13, 116, 124–25
accountability values in, 103–5, 108–10, 158–59, 183–84
costs in, minimizing, 128
ingredients of managerialism, 104–5
metaconsensus and, 105–7, 128
in NPM, independent agency and, 143–48, 164–65
process values in, 103–5
responsible value reinforcement in, 193–94
in UK, 106–10, 142
managers
behavioral reinforcement among European, 143, 152–59
control literature on, 87–90
discretion of, 6–8, 10, 85–86, 104, 189–96, 204–5
electoral accountability and policy work of, 13, 22–23
evaluability of, 38–39, 104–5
governance structures and, 8, 10–11
ingredients of managerialism, 104–5
non-neutral inaction of, 192–93
under NPM, survey of European, 145–46
political neutrality of, 29–30

from representative government, autonomy of, 90–93
to representative government, accountability of, 86–90
reputations of, 200–1
value reinforcement and, 11, 189–96
value tradeoffs and, 6–7, 22–23
mandate, 25–26
conditional representation and, 36–38
deviation from, 30, 34–38
in majoritarian system, 34
in proportional representation system, 35
Manin, Bernard, 26–27, 34, 37, 52–53
Mansbridge, Jane, 24–26
markets, 5
Mathews, John Mabry, 180–81
McCubbins, Matthew D., 88–89
mediated deduction, 16
Merkel, Angela, 29
metaconsensus
deliberative democracy and, 65–66
epistemic, 91–92
List on, 61–62
managed agency and, 105–7, 128
pluralism and, 61–63, 65–66, 72
technical, 91
migrants. *See* immigration; refugees
Millett, John, 87
mini-publics, 65–66, 121–23, 184, 194–95
Ministry of Justice (UK), 107–8
Mitchell, Gregory, 163–64
Moore, Mark, 200
Mosher, Frederick, 92–93, 184
Movimento Cinque Stelle party (Italy), 28–29, 37–42
Moynihan, Donald, 124

Nabatchi, Tina, 116–18
NDPBs. *See* Non-Departmental Public Bodies
Netherlands, 158–59, 166
consociationalism in, 149–52
institutional reinforcement mechanism in, 141–43, 148–52
NPM in, 141–43, 147–52
ZBOs in, 150–52
neutrality, 186
of bureaucracies, 97–99
for controlled agency, impossibility of, 97–99

of managers and policy workers, political, 29–30

New Public Management (NPM), 104
controlled agency in, 143–44
evaluability problems in, 145–46
identifiability in, 144–45, 152
independent agency in, 143–48, 164–65
institutional reinforcement mechanism in, 141–43, 147–52
managed agency in, 143–48, 164–65
in Netherlands, 141–43, 147–52
performance indicators in, 147–48, 151–52
process values and, 146–47, 151–52
success of, scholarship on, 145–47
in UK, 141–52
value reinforcement and, 11, 13, 141–52, 164–65

New Public Service, 203
The New State (Follett), 198
Non-Departmental Public Bodies (NDPBs) (UK), 131–35, 143–45, 155
non-fiscal partnerships, in U. S., 140–42
non-neutral inaction, of managers, 192–93
North, Douglass, 124–25, 186–87
Notes on the State of Virginia (Jefferson), 4–5
NPM. *See* New Public Management

obfuscating information strategies, 50–52, 144–45
Organ Procurement and Transplantation Network (U. S.), 130
Osborne, David, 7

Papadopoulos, Ioannis, 17–18
parliamentary government, 30–32
accountability identity in, 31–32
bipolarity in, 32–33
as indirect government, 31
participatory budgeting, 119–24
Partito Democratico (Italy), 44, 54–57
party system, 31
accountability identity in, 31–32
bipolarity in, 32–33, 39, 62
in electoral accountability, role of, 30–31
ICCP survey of, 54–57
path independence, 98–99, 108–10
Patty, John, 59–60, 91–92
Penn, Elizabeth Maggie, 59–60
Pennock, J. Roland, 87

performance indicators, 147–48, 151–52
Perlman, Mark, xvii–xviii
Pettit, Philip, 36–37
Pitkin, Hannah, 36–37
pluralism, 12, 61
bipolarity and, 62
conditional representation and, 61
deliberative democracy and, 64–66, 72
epistemic democracy and, 63–65, 72
majoritarianism and, 8–9, 12, 75, 90–91
metaconsensus and, 61–63, 65–66, 72, 75–76, 89–90
in representative agency, 113–17
U.S. citizens on, 73
value reinforcement of, 190–97
policy entrepreneurs, 7
policy work, responsible, 186–96
policy workers, 38–39
discretionary authority of, 6–8
electoral accountability and, 13, 22–23
laws implemented by, 6
political neutrality of, 29–30
representation and, 11, 187
value reinforcement by, 196–97
political control, of bureaucracy, 87–90
political values, governance values and, 85, 139–40, 152, 197–98, 205
Pollitt, Christopher, 85–86, 146–47
populism, 208–9
Porto Alegre, Brazil, 119–23
positive theories, 87–90, 186–87
Powell, G. Bingham, 159
Powell, Jay, 126–27
practice-based approach, to representative government, 15–16
principal-agent conception, of representative government, 35
prisons, in UK, 107–10, 135, 142, 144–45
privatization, 129–30, 146–48, 184–86, 200
process values, 58. *See also* collective rationality; majoritarianism; pluralism
with accountability values, tradeoffs of, 53, 76, 83, 93–94, 157–59, 164–65
accountability values and, 9–11, 58, 60, 75, 87, 95, 135–36, 144–47
citizens on, 71–76
collective decision mechanisms and, 58–60, 66–72
collective rationality as, 12, 68–72, 75
in control literature, 89–90

Index

process values (cont.)
  in controlled agency, 95, 99
  impossibility theorems and, 58–60
  in legitimation, state, 184
  majoritarianism as, 12, 66–68, 72, 75, 89–90
  in managed agency, 103–5
  NPM and, 146–47, 151–52
  pluralism as, 12, 61–66, 72, 75–76, 89–91
  in representative agency, 110–11, 113–18, 123–24, 128
  trilemma of, 60, 83, 111
  value tradeoffs of, 8–10, 12, 53, 58–60, 71–72, 76, 83, 87, 90, 93–94, 103–4, 157–59, 164–65
process-enhancing structures, 10, 93–94
process-obviating structures, 10, 93–94, 144–45
proportional electoral rules, 32
proportional representation system, mandate in, 35
Przeworski, Adam, 25–26, 52–53
public administration. *See specific topics*
Public Policy Investment (Bertelli and John), xvi–xvii

questore (Italian official), 2–3, 6–9, 95, 209

Rackete, Carola, 21, 28–29, 41, 43–44, 46–47
Rawls, John, 68, 202–3
Redford, Emmette, 184–87
reflective equilibrium, 68, 72
refugees
  EU on, 19, 28–29, 41, 43–44
  in Germany, BAMF regulating, 99–103
  Italian citizens on, 44, 54–56
  Universal Declaration on Human Rights, Italian Constitution on, 66–67
Regional Administrative Court, Italian (*Tribunale Amministrativo Regionale*) (*TAR*), 20–22, 28–29
reinforcement mechanisms, 11
Reinventing Government (Gaebler and Osborne), 7
representation
  conditional, 36–38, 42, 53, 61, 187–89
  forward-looking, 179–80, 183–84, 187–88
  governance structures and, 183–86
  independent agency and, 184–88

policy workers and, 11, 187
proportional, mandate in, 35
state legitimated by, 175, 178–79, 183, 187
third-parties and, 35–36
value tradeoffs and, 12
representative agency, 10–13, 116, 198–99
  accountability values and, 110–11, 113, 116–18, 122–24, 155, 158–59
  as accountability-obviating, 110–11, 113, 116–18, 122–24, 155
  citizens in, bringing back, 111–18
  collaborative governance in, 115–18, 207–8
  collective rationality in, 114–15, 123–24
  costs in, 128
  participatory budgeting, Brazilian, 119–24
  process values in, 110–11, 113–18, 123–24, 128
  public administration, fundamental problem of, and, 116, 118
  responsible value reinforcement in, 193–94
  value tradeoffs in, 110–11, 113–15, 118
representative government, 1, 3–5, 11, 85–86, 202–3
  accountability to, positive theories on, 87–90
  champions and values of, 16–17
  governance structures and values of, 15–17
  managerial accountability to, 86–90
  managerial autonomy from, 90–93
  principal-agent conception of, 35
  values of, Europeans on, 12
representatives, 5–6
  managers, policy workers, and incumbent, 29–30
  value tradeoffs and, 12
reputation, 200–1
responsible policy work, 186, 189–96
responsible value reinforcement, 190–91, 197
  controlled agency and, 191–94
  discretionary authority and, 189–90
  in independent agency, 193–96
  in managed agency, 193–94
  pluralism in, 190–96
  in representative agency, 193–94
retrospection, heuristics for, 45–49

Index

retrospective answerability, 49–50, 87, 101, 103

retrospective electoral accountability. *See* electoral accountability

retrospective sanctioning. *See* sanctioning view, of electoral accountability

Revesz, Richard L., 130

Riker, William, 59–60

Rodrik, Dani, 36

Romzek, Barbara, 17

Rosanvallon, Pierre, 200–1

Salvini, Matteo
  identifiability of, 28–29, 39, 41
  in *Sea-Watch 3* case, 18–21, 28–29, 31, 39, 41

sanction, probability of, 12, 38–39, 52–53, 75
  behavioral reinforcement and, 153
  in managed agency, 104–5

sanctioning, heuristics and, 45–47, 88–89

sanctioning view, of electoral accountability, 22–31, 44, 53
  bipolarity and, 33
  conditional representation and, 37–38
  evaluability, identifiability and, 28–29

Sandel, Michael, 5

Sangiovanni, Andrea, 16

Sartori, Giovanni, 33

Schmidt, Manfred, 100–1

Schultz, Martin, 29

Schwartz, T., 88–89

Schwartzberg, Melissa, 63–64

Sea-Watch 3 case, 66–67
  accountability values and, 18–22, 28–29, 31, 37–42, 44
  EU and, 19–22, 28–29, 37–44
  evaluability errors on, 42–44
  heuristics for, 46–47
  identifiability in, 28–29, 37–42

Seehofer, Horst, 99–100, 102

Selznick, Philip, 200

Shepsle, Kenneth, 69, 125–26

Silberman, Bernard, xvii–xviii

Simon, Herbert, 174–75

Sinclair, J. Andrew, 127, 145

single-peakedness, 61–62

Skinner, Quentin, 176

Slovenia, 67–68

social choice theory, 58–60

source relocation, 50–51

Spain, 40–41

state
  accountability values and legitimating, 183–84
  Hobbesian, 175–82
  legitimating, 175–84, 187
  Locke on, 177–79, 181
  Madisonian view of, 117, 179–80
  not neutral, 186
  process values and legitimating, 184
  representation legitimating, 175, 178–79, 183, 187
  self-restraint of, 186–87
  separation of, 13, 175–77
  toleration legitimating, 177–78
  in U. S., public administration and, 179–83
  in value reinforcement, 175
  value tradeoffs and, 186

Steinberger, Peter, 178

Stokes, Susan C., 52–53

structural reliance, 170–72

Sunstein, Cass, 71

TAR. See Tribunale Amministrativo Regionale

technical metaconsensus, 91

Tetlock, Philip, 163–64

Thatcher, Margaret, 106–7, 147–48

Theiss-Morse, Elizabeth, 72–73

Thomas, Paul, 97–100

toleration, 177–78

Tribunale Amministrativo Regionale (TAR) (Italian Regional Administrative Court), 20–22, 28–29

Trump, Donald, 126–28

turflessness, 98–99, 108–10

U. S. *See* United States

UK. *See* United Kingdom

ultra vires action, 190–96, 198–99
  complementarity principle and, 202–3, 205
  prohibition of, 189–90

"Unite the Right" rally, 1–2, 6–7

United Kingdom (UK)
  accountability in, 84–138, 146–47
  ACI of, 84–138, 146–49, 166
  conditional representation and, 38
  executive agencies in, 106–10
  HMPPS, 107–10, 135, 142, 144–45

United Kingdom (UK) (cont.)
  independent agency in, 131–35, 144–45
  institutional reinforcement mechanism in, 141–43, 147–52
  majoritarianism in, 106, 108
  managed agency in, 106–10, 142
  NDPBs in, 131–35, 143–45, 155
  NPM in, 141–52
United States (U. S.)
  accountability values in, 179–80
  city management movement in, 180
  on collective rationality, citizens in, 73
  congress in, 69–70
  controlled agency in, 179–83
  on democracy, citizens in, 72–73
  evaluability, identifiability in, 180–81
  Federal Reserve System in, 126–28
  Federalists and constitutional debate in, 179
  Hatch Act, 29–30
  independent agency in, 130
  on majoritarianism, citizens in, 73
  non-fiscal partnerships in, 140–42
  Organ Procurement and Transplantation Network, 130
  on pluralism, citizens in, 73
  state in, public administration and, 179–83
  Trump in, 126–28
  "Unite the Right" rally in, 1–2, 6–7
United States Postal Service, 91–92
Universal Declaration on Human Rights, Article 14 of (1948), 66–67

value reinforcement, xvi, xviii, 204–6. *See also* behavioral reinforcement
  behavioral reinforcement and testing, 152–54
  COCOPS survey testing, 152–54
  complementarity principle in, 175, 197–98, 200–7, 209–10
  controlled agency and responsible, 191–94
  discretion and responsible, 189–90
  empirical study for, 160–64
  formal, 140–42, 152, 160–61
  fundamental problem, of public administration, and, 175
  governance, political values and, 139–40, 152, 197–98, 205

  governance structures and, 8–9, 11, 13–14, 24, 136, 155, 197–98
  hypothesis of, 11, 13, 24, 139–43, 152–54, 205
  independent agency and, 193–96, 200
  informal, 141–42, 152, 160–62
  institutional, 139–43, 147–52, 162, 164–65
  in managed agency, responsible, 193–94
  of managers, 11, 189–96
  normative basis for, 13, 17, 143, 159, 165, 175, 186, 204–5, 209
  NPM and, 11, 13, 141–52, 164–65
  pluralism and, 190–97
  in representative agency, responsible, 193–94
  research agenda for, 159–65, 205
  responsible, 189–97
  in responsible policy work, 186, 189–96
  state in, 175
  theoretical development for, 159–60, 165
value tradeoffs, xvi, 1–3, 5, 12, 85–86
  accountability and process, 53, 76, 83, 93–94, 157–59, 164–65
  actor-relative and process-relative, 9–10
  champions making, 12–13, 76, 83–85, 174, 183, 204, 206
  collective decision mechanisms and, 58–60
  in empirical study, 162–63
  Finerian, 87–88, 90–94
  Friedrichian, 90–94
  governance structures and, 8–13, 93–94, 135–36
  majoritarianism and pluralism, 8–9, 90
  in managed agency, 103–4, 108–10
  managers and, 6–7, 22–23
  of process values, 8–10, 12, 53, 58–60, 71–72, 76, 83, 87, 90, 93–94, 103–4, 157–59, 164–65
  in representative agency, 110–11, 113–15, 118
  state and, 186
Van Ryzin, Gregg, xvi, 48–49
voters. *See* citizens
voting, administering, 189–96

Waldo, Dwight, 183, 198
Waldron, Jeremy, 23–24, 177–78
Walker, Harvey, 182

Index

Wampler, Brian, 124
Warren, Mark, 111
Weber, Max, 95–97, 177–78, 187–89
Weingast, Barry, 186–87
Weise, Frank-Jürgen, 100–1
What Money Can't Buy (Sandel), 5
White, Leonard, 180–81

"Who Are the Policy Workers and What are They Doing?" (Bertelli), xvi
Workers' Party, Brazilian, 121

Zacka, Bernardo, 142
Zelfstandige Bestuursorganen, Netherlands (ZBOs), 150–52

Printed in the United States
by Baker & Taylor Publisher Services